MAN AND WOMAN, WAR AND PEACE

THE STRATEGIST'S COMPANION

BY
ANTHONY WILDEN

FRONTISPIECE 'He's Watching You': In the *Home Front* volume of the Time-Life history of World War Two, from which this picture is taken, the caption reads' 'A cat-eyed German soldier glares from a 1942 American factory poster that was criticized by workers who took the figure to be an American'.

MAN AND WOMAN, WAR AND PEACE

THE STRATEGIST'S COMPANION

BY
ANTHONY WILDEN

ROUTLEDGE AND KEGAN PAUL
LONDON AND NEW YORK

First published in 1987 by
Routledge & Kegan Paul plc
11 New Fetter Lane, London EC4P 4EE

Published in the USA by
Routledge & Kegan Paul Inc.
in association with Methuen Inc.
29 West 35th Street, New York, NY 10001

Set in 10/12pt Sabon
by Columns of Reading
and printed in Great Britain
by TJ Press (Padstow) Ltd, Padstow, Cornwall

Library of Congress Cataloging in Publication Data
Wilden, Anthony.
  Man and women, war and peace.
  Companion vol. to: The rules are no game.
  Bibliography: p.
  Includes indexes.
  1. Communication. 2. Sociology. I. Title.
P91.W456 1986   001.51   86-10094

British Library CIP Data also available
ISBN 0–7100–9867–7

For my mother
Lilian Elizabeth Ballard

If you wish for peace, prepare for peace.
Traditional

If war is innate or if war is written in the genes, why
is there so much propaganda designed to make men fight?
Irenäus Eibl-Eibesfeldt in 1976

Contents

To the reader (xi)

Illustrations

Figures

Tables

Maps

To the reader

Murphy's rule

In his account of dogfighting with North Vietnamese Migs in the 1960s, in *Phantom over Vietnam*, John Trotti, a US Marine Corps pilot, tells you always to assume that your opponent will make a mistake. Then if he does, you are already ahead of him by the milliseconds you need to break away or shoot him down.

Trotti's Rule might be phrased: 'Expect the other to be unexpecting'.

There is nothing particularly military about Trotti's Rule, nor is it confined to tactics. (We all use strategies (what we want to do) and tactics (how we do it) at every minute of our lives, just as we do theories and practices.) And in any case, any such strategical and mainly mental preparation for a sudden tactical and mainly bodily event is an ordinary rule of life.

Trotti's Rule is in fact one of a large family of principles all of which are versions of the Rule of Rules, Murphy's Rule:

If anything can go wrong it will.

Murphy's relevance to practically anything you can think of means that the entire working world is informed by thousands of anti-Murphy rules, like 'Don't force it', for example, or 'If it's working don't touch it', or the old showbusiness maxim: 'Do everything, and something will work out', or the artisan's injunction: 'Know something about everything and everything about something', or the flier's warning: 'There are old pilots, and bold pilots – but no old, bold pilots'. Trade by trade and day by day, these maxims are designed to outflank Murphy's Rule strategically, or at least to dodge it before it reproduces, because it really can be catching.

I call these anti-Murphy rules 'Riley's Reservations'.

And that was how I first met Murphy, in a Riley's Reservation.

It happened at Three Cups Corner in East Sussex in England in the early 1950s: I was about fifteen. My father, my brother, and I had been out hunting rabbit. We'd had no luck and hadn't fired a shot.

The shotgun we were sharing belonged to Mr English French. This was an ancient 12-bore with 32-inch barrels and external hammers, the stock bound up with copper wire. If you had the hammers cocked and hadn't fired the gun, the only way to make the weapon safe was to stick your thumb on the hammer, pull the trigger, and then let the hammer down.

My father was very strict about guns – one of the legacies of his experience in the Jersey Militia in the Channel Islands in the 1920s. His basic maxim was 'Never point a gun in any shape or form at anyone unless you intend to shoot them if they make it necessary'.

Naturally he had a Riley's Reservation about guns like Mr French's: First point the weapon at the ground, with the muzzle a couple or three inches from the soil, and only then uncock the monster.

It was getting dark. My father had the gun, with my brother and I on each side of him, forming a triangle.

'That's it for today then', said Dad, as he set about uncocking the gun. 'Lemme do it, Dad!' spouted one of us, grabbing at the stock . . .

Baboomm! It echoed round and round for ages.

I looked at my father. I remember thinking 'He's as white as a sheet, just like they say in books.' We all looked down. Between our feet was a hole, a definite hole, in the county of Sussex. But that was all. Nobody'd had their foot blown off. And all because my father had been following his own rules, and had kept the muzzle down.

I can't remember ever being so truly and tremendously impressed by any other single event in my life.

That is why I called the companion to this book *The Rules Are No Game*. That is why I have never been a metaphysical idealist. That is why I define reality as what trips you up when you don't pay attention to it.

On the defensive side, Murphy's Rule says: 'Expect the unexpected'.

In the counterattack, guided by the principle 'Take advantage of adversity', Murphy also says: 'Use the unexpected'.

But Murphy exists in another offensive version too, as I was reminded by Randolph Scott the other day, in his opening speech to the killers-in-training in the 1943 epic *Gung Ho!*, which is said to be the story of Carlson's Makin Island Raiders (2nd Marine Battalion) in the Gilberts in the Pacific in 1942.

The film – a quick lesson in collective tactical suicide – recalls that the real unit was bound by Carlson's egalitarian rule that while rank, once earned, was respected, every Makin Island Raider was the equal of every other; and that all aspects of operations would be shared as widely as possible. ('Everyone a strategist', says the Democratic Rule.)

The script of *Gung Ho!* was based on a story by Lt W.S. LeFrançois, USMC. The highly respected Colonel Carlson (1896–1947) is represented as having learned guerrilla warfare by joining Mao and General Chu Teh on the 6000-mile Long March of 1934-35, the strategic retreat of 80,000 people from Kiangsi to Shensi, of whom only 8000 survived. From this tiny base sprang the truly popular Eighth Route Army, victorious over both Japan and Chiang Kai-Shek and the other warlords in 1945 and 1949.

'Gung-Ho', adopted as a slogan by the Marines in China in World War II, originally meant 'working in harmony'. The phrase was hijacked by Jim Shults in the 1970s for one of the first of the mercenary magazines – a field presently dominated by Special Forces Colonel Robert K. Brown's *Soldier of Fortune*, ten years old in 1985.

Among their subscribers one might expect to find ex-Vietnam platoon leader Marine Lt. Col. Oliver North – no reservations here – the efficient cause of the stunning strategic envelopment of the Reagan Administration in 1986 in the Iran-Contra affair – the arms-for-hostages, guns-for-cocaine-dealers swaps – the grand strategic error by which Ollie's Rule became known to history as the seventh blunder of the world.

But back to Murphy's Rule: What Randolph Scott told his Makin Island raiders in *Gung-Ho!* that day in 1942 was the key to offensive guerrilla strategy:

Always do the unexpected.

This is it.

IMPACT

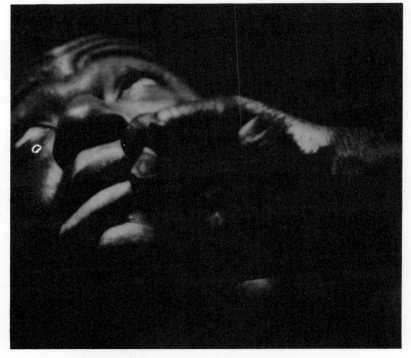

ACCORDING TO WEBSTER: The single instantaneous striking of a body in motion against another body.

ACCORDING TO YOUNG & RUBICAM: That quality in an advertisement which strikes suddenly against the reader's indifference and enlivens his mind to receive a sales message.

YOUNG & RUBICAM, INCORPORATED · ADVERTISING

NEW YORK · CHICAGO · DETROIT · SAN FRANCISCO · HOLLYWOOD · MONTREAL · TORONTO · MEXICO CITY · LONDON

FRONTISPIECE: The deeply structured and no doubt unintentional racism of this advertising icon is practically palpable. Raymond Rubicam wrote in 1949 that in each of the ads for the Young & Rubicam series

I attempted to do two things: (1) to leave the reader with a valuable thought with regard to the effective use of advertising; (2) to make our own ad a forceful demonstration of our skill in presentation.

The series began in 1930; this version dates from 1946. It was 'the greatest single hit' and was repeated periodicaly over many years. Reprinted from: Julian Lewis Watkins: *The One Hundred Greatest Advertisements: Who Wrote Them and What They Did* [1852-1958] (1959).

CHAPTER 1

Oscillation, opposition, and illusion East and West: the ideology of error

What you are going to do here is saunter along, keeping in the shade and out of the hot sun, moseying on down to the salt lick where at sunset, in chapter five, you're going to shoot the reader through the goddamned head.

Bruce Lee, editor, to Loren Baritz, author, in *Backfire* (1985)

1.1 Images and icons

The word 'icon', meaning 'likeness', 'representation', 'illustration', 'picture' (sacred or profane), 'simile', or 'image' (in a mirror, in a mind, on a page, in words), usually implies a visual relation. For human beings, vision is the dominant non-verbal sense and medium of communication, and in Greek, as in Sanskrit, one of the expressions for 'I know' (*oida*) means literally 'I have seen' (I hope you can see what I mean). The same Greek verb (*eido*), from which Plato takes the word for 'shape' or 'form', also gives us 'idea', 'idol', and 'ideal'.

In this chapter, as elsewhere in this book, the visual icon is an integral part of the argument. But there is no reason to restrict the term 'icon' to visual images, gestalts, figures, or forms. It can just as usefully be employed to refer to gestalts of any of the senses and sensations. These will include: taste, touch, sound, smell, and sight: heat, hunger, pressure, pain, and pleasure: balance, duration, depth, and direction; similarity, identity, difference, distinction, opposition, and contradiction; proportion and propriety; vitality, movement, and desire; humor, meaning, recognition, and accomplishment; the sense of self, self-esteem, and the relationship to others.

An icon is not a thing but a relationship between perceiver and perceived. Consider an icon of taste or odor. Within the field of an odor, such as a perfume, the sensation is continuous but varies in intensity. As we pass into or out of it, or as it passes over us, there is at some point a definite boundary between perceiving it and not perceiving it. It is thus a continuity bounded by a discontinuity. At the same time it may echo other odors like the overtones of a musical note, it may trigger memories and associations like a dream, it may communicate meanings like an idea, and it may touch us with other sensations such as sorrow, happiness, regret, or desire.

An icon is a *Gestalt* (a 'structured whole') in the original sense of the term in the Gestalt psychology of Wertheimer, Köhler, and Koffka. It is an emergent quality of the process of perception, and cannot be understood by any analysis of its parts, requiring instead an analysis of its relationships.

Words themselves are icons. This was the argument of the poet, essayist, and teacher of English in Japanese schools, Lafcadio Hearn (1850–1904). Born in Greece, the son of a British surgeon, he later worked in America, lived in Martinique, and eventually became a Japanese citizen. In 1893 in his *Japanese Letters*, edited by Elizabeth Bisland in 1910, and quoted by Eisenstein in *The Film Sense* (1947, pp. 92–3), Hearn said that for him

> words have colour, form, character; they have faces, parts, manners, gesticulations; they have moods, humours, eccentricities; – they have tints, tones, personalities . . .

In another letter he argued:

> Because people cannot see the colour of words, the tints of words, the secret ghostly motions of words:–
>
> Because they cannot hear the whispering of words, the rustling of the procession of letters, the dream-flutes and dream-drums which are thinly and weirdly played by words:–
>
> Because they cannot perceive the pouting of words, the frowning of words and fuming of words, the weeping, the raging and racketing and rioting of words:–
>
> Because they are insensible to the phosphorescing of words, the fragrance of words, the noisomeness of words, the tenderness or hardness, the dryness or juiciness of words – the interchange of values in the gold, the silver, the brass and the copper of words:–
>
> Is that any reason why we should not try to make them hear, to make them see, to make them feel?

Let us take this as a working definition of an icon in the abstract:

An *icon* is a combination of (continuously coded) analog information and (discontinuously coded) digital information. Icons are patterns, or patterns of patterns, fixed or moving, made up of an infinity (or several infinities) of information in one or more dimensions, framed and punctuated by one or more digital boundaries in one or more dimensions.

The icon for infinity ∞ is itself a combination of analog continuity and digital discontinuity.

An iconic infinity can be defined as the number of accounts, at all levels (including the molecular, the mathematical, the poetic, the political, the personal, and so on), that satisfactorily interpret the combined analog and digital information framed in the icon.

Thinking is more interesting than knowing, but less interesting than looking.

Johann Wolfgang von Goethe (1749–1832)

1.2 Yin and yang, day and night, figure and ground

Distinct media of communication can be better understood and compared by looking at the role played in human communication by the basic relations of difference, distinction, opposition, contradiction, and paradox.

We can begin by considering the role of the binary opposition in our way of knowing (our epistemology) and our value system (our ideology). As I argued in *System and Structure* in 1972, and again in the revised edition of 1980, and in further detail in the expanded French edition of 1983, the root metaphor of the binary opposition – a mutually exclusive conflict between two supposed opposites at a single level – is in most cases an imaginary projection of a logical or ideological value on to nature, or society, or the individual, or the relationships between them.

We find a similar doctrine at work in a non-atomistic, but no less improper, way in the Chinese symbolism of the two cosmic principles of yin and yang. The yin-yang relationship is often referred to as a 'complementary interpenetration of opposites' (forming a 'unity' or 'identity' of opposites). Here the root metaphor of an 'oscillating opposition between equals' denies the reality of Chinese society, where yang ('male, light, active') always dominates yin ('female, dark, passive').

In comparing the patterns of binary oppositions independently invented in both East and West, Joseph Needham points out in his *Science and Civilisation in China* that the followers of Pythagoras in the fifth century BCE – the members of the elitist Pythagorean Brotherhood – embodied their dualism in a table of ten pairs of 'opposites' (Needham, 1956, pp. 276–8; see also pp. 95, 460–7):

the limited	the unlimited
the one	the many
odd	even
right	left
male	female
good	bad
motion	rest
light	darkness
square	oblong
straight	curved

In his *Dictionario de Simbolos Tradicionales*, translated into English in 1962, the Spanish poet, J.E. Cirlot (b. 1916), gives the following reading of the root metaphor of yin and yang:

A Chinese symbol of the dual distribution of forces, comprising the active or masculine principle (*Yang*) and the passive or feminine principle (*Yin*). It takes the form of a circle bisected by [an S-shaped] line, and the two parts so formed are invested with a dynamic tendency which would be missing if the division were by diameter. . . . Each half includes an arc cut out of the middle of the opposing half, to symbolize that every mode must contain within it the germ of its antithesis.

In the *Dictionnaire des symboles* edited by Jean Chevalier and his colleagues (1969), Pierre Grison notes that the length of the S-shaped dividing line is equal to half the circumference of the whole circle. The perimeter of each half of the symbol is the same length as that of the circle that frames it.

Grison correctly goes back to the origins of the terms in the image of two sides of a valley, the one in sunshine and the other in shade. (As the sun passes overhead, the boundary between light and dark passes from one valley side to the other. Both sides are dark at night; both are light at noon.) By extension, he says:

They designate the dark and light aspects of all things; the earthly aspect and the celestial aspect; the negative aspect and the positive aspect; the feminine aspect and the masculine aspect; in sum they are the expression of a universal dualism and complementarity. . . . They are inseparable, and the rhythm of the world is the rhythm of their alternation. . . .

Drawing on René Guenon's *Le Symbolisme de la croix* (1931), Cirlot suggests that yin and yang may be viewed as a symbol of a helix, rather than a simple circle. The icon of the helix or spiral (commonly modeled on a classical machine, the rotating wedge of a

FIGURE 1.1(a) The yin-yang icon with the eight basic trigrams (Fu Hsi's arrangement by pairs of opposites). The binary system of the yin-yang icon utilizes both analog (continuously coded) information and digital (discretely coded) information. The lines in the trigrams (the *kua*) utilize binary-digital information. As explained in the text, the closed inner circle of the icon frames a paradoxical figure-ground relation. The paradoxical image itself is punctuated by an S-shaped digital boundary. In the visual oscillation (which appears as a rotation) the two small circles (symbolizing 'interpenetration') appear to travel with the half they are in (they are themselves digitally bounded and enclosed icons within the larger icon). As the Danish psychologist Edgar Ruben recognized in 1915 – he designed the classic paradoxical image, the vase and the two faces – it is not possible to see both parts of a binary paradoxical image as figures at the same time (Teuber 1974; on the combinations of the trigrams, see Gardner 1974). Unlike life, history, and society, the yin-yang system is a closed system. It is a cyclic, completely conservative system, closed to novelty, innovation, evolution, and revolution. In cybernetic terms its closed oscillations are analog-digital oscillations around a central mean (the boundary between them).

screw thread) is also a common metaphor used to portray Hegel's imaginary 'dialectic of ideas through history' – with or without a waving of the hands.

Cirlot explains the reference to the helix:

> Guenon considers [the yin-yang symbol] as a section of a universal whirlwind which brings opposites together and engenders perpetual motion, metamorphosis and continuity in situations characterized by contradiction.

Perpetual motion is, of course, as imaginary as it is impossible. Guenon also equates 'contradiction' and 'opposition', a common epistemological mistake (a mistake in perspective) to which I'll return later in this chapter. The yin-yang icon really involves no more than a distinction between two shapes (calling this relation an opposition or a contradiction is a social rather than a scientific interpretation). But the distinction between the two shapes in the yin-yang icon is a distinction of a special kind: it creates paradox.

Cirlot almost sees this. He makes a crucial point, which reveals that yin and yang, whatever else they symbolize, also form a visual icon of

FIGURE 1.1(b)   In this representation of the anti-clockwise yin/yang symbol that forms the emblem of Korea, the artist has prevented the paradoxical oscillation by introducing contour (and thus the third dimension) at the boundary between yin and yang (blue and red in the original). The example is No 24 in the series of fifty cigarette cards issued by the John Player Company of Nottingham in 1928, *Flags of the League of Nations*.

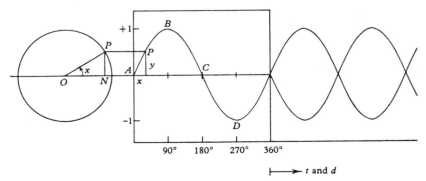

FIGURE 1.1(c)   Joseph Needham's diagram to illustrate the relationship between cyclical and wave conceptions. The system in question is the closed system sine wave oscillation of yin and yang through time – and not, one must add, through history, because in all of the many 'theories of the eternal return' (e.g. Mircea Eliade's work), the passage of time has no influence on the action. As in the matter-energy world of physics time in these myths is mere background, and symmetrical fore and aft. Time in history is an active and irreversible participant. Reprinted from *Science and Civilisation in China*, vol. 4, Physics, Part 1 (1962), p.9.

a three-way relationship in two dimensions: yin, yang, and the boundary between them:

> The vertical axis through the centre of the Yang-Yin constitutes the 'unvarying mean' or, in other words, the mystic 'Centre' where there is no rotation, no restlessness, no impulse, no suffering of any kind.

This is for the most part a statement about perception. The circular frame of the yin-yang icon (Figure 1.1a) encloses a two-dimensional, discretely bounded, figure-ground relation in its simplest form. Because of the way the eye-brain system processes information, the yin-yang icon requires an either/or decision as to which half of the image is to be dominant, forming the figure, and which is to be subordinate, forming the ground. If you rest your eyes on the image, you will see that the result is an oscillation between the two alternatives.

The Gestalt psychologists Max Wertheimer, Wolfgang Köhler, and Kurt Koffka showed in the early years of the century that we see relationships, rather than objects, in the world around us, and that the perception of an object is the result of an interpretation of what we see. We make thousands of shifting but stable figure-ground distinctions as we focus our attention on one aspect or another of the visual field projected on the retina of the eye. The information of the two-dimensional retinal image is transformed into three dimensions by the eye-brain system.

When we make a figure-ground distinction, we insert by projection a perceptual boundary between figure and ground. The boundary frames a definite depth of field (whatever is in focus from 'front' to 'back') and a definite center of attention. In a simple image like the yin-yang icon, the boundary is the locus of 'depth' or the third dimension. The figure thus appears to stand out from the ground: the oscillation is not a (single-level) 'figure-ground reversal', but as M.C. Escher insisted, a figure-ground inversion (cf. Figures 1.2, 1.3, 1.4).

The figure-ground boundary is a contribution to perception by the viewer. Like all such boundaries − as distinct from barriers − the boundary between figure and ground is neither part of the figure, nor part of the ground. Similarly, as Cirlot indicates by his reference to the 'mystic center' of the visual symbol, the boundary between yin and yang is neither yin nor yang.

This may be translated into the Three-Way Rule:

The Three-Way Rule: The minimum number of connections required to establish a relation is three: system, environment, and the boundary mediating between them.

FIGURE 1.2   *Eight Heads*, a 1922 woodcut by the Dutch artist and theorist of perception and self-reference, Maurits C. Escher (1902–72). All the heads oscillate between figure and ground. Teuber (1974) comments that this was Escher's first attempt at an infinitely repeating subdivision of a plane surface. Note that Escher consistently referred to figure-ground oscillations as inversions (between levels), not as 'reversals' (implying a single level), as most perceptual theorists do, including Fred Attneave, Marianne L. Teuber, R.L. Gregory, and J.B. Deregowski.

Psychologically, however, we see the figure-ground boundary as a property of the figure, unconsciously reducing it to the same level of perception as the figure. In this way we interpret a three-way relation, where the boundary mediates between figure and ground, as a binary one – and a host of ideological fictions ensue.

The yin-yang symbol is a paradoxical image, with just three levels, figure, ground, and boundary. In this kind of two-term, either/or paradoxical image, no sooner is one figure decided upon than it changes into the other (compare Figure 1.4). The paradoxical switch between levels in the figure-ground inversion is independent of our

FIGURE 1.3   *Day and Night*, a 1938 print by Maurits C. Escher. Here Escher uses the visual idiom of the figure-ground boundary to communicate about its own function, merging analog continuity with digital discontinuity, and transforming figure into ground in two directions. (Note that each half of the print is the conceptual mirror-image of the other.) The increasingly abstract images in the central zone oscillate between figure and ground in a series of inversions. As Marianne L. Teuber explains (1974), Escher was familiar with the work on this subject by Edgar Rubin before 1920; by Kurt Koffka (1886–1941) (with Wolfgang Köhler (1887–1967), one of the developers of the Gestalt psychology originated by Max Wertheimer (1880–1943) in Prague between 1910 and 1912); and by Molly R. Harrower. If Escher's image were a motion picture, the central zone of transformation would require a processed fade-over edit to cross the either/or boundary between Day and Night.

consciousness; it takes place at the organic level of eye and brain, not at the social level of mind.

In 'Approaches to Infinity' (1968), Escher wrote:

> No one can draw a line that is not a boundary line; every line splits
> a singularity into a plurality. Every closed contour, no matter
> what its shape, whether a perfect circle or an irregular random
> form, evokes in addition the notions of 'inside' and 'outside' and the
> suggestion of 'near' and 'far away', of 'object' [figure] and
> 'background' [ground].

One can easily test the two aspects of this proposition: Draw an enclosed shape, then divide it in two with a random squiggle. A paradoxical figure almost always results, and (because of our inborn propensity to pay closer attention to faces than to other visual patterns), it will usually appear as two alternating human profiles.

> That infinity that things do not attain in progression, they attain in rotation.
>
> Ferdinando Galiani: *Della moneta* (1750)

1.3 Neither obey nor disobey

The term 'paradox' is not used here in its weaker sense of 'strange', 'against common sense', or 'contradictory'. (As will be clear later, a paradox is a tangled, and therefore an oscillating, contradiction.) It is used in the strong sense of a paradoxical command which produces an oscillation between either/or alternatives when we try to obey it.

An everyday example: 'Be spontaneous!'. If we obey, we disobey (we are not spontaneous); if we disobey, we obey (we are spontaneous).

A command need not be communicated by the imperative mood in language or by its equivalent in other modes of communication. In the 1950s Warren McCulloch pointed out that any message in any communication system (including both mind and brain) is both a *report* – about some situation or other – and a *command* or demand – to respond in some way (including refusal to respond). Gregory Bateson later noted that a message is also a *question* – about the response. Report, command, and question: each aspect or level frames the interpretation of the message in a different way – as for instance when a parent says 'I love you' sarcastically, and the child oscillates between report and command (Croner et al., 1982).

It is impossible to deal consciously with all three of these aspects at one time. Miscommunication or pathological communication may result when one party frames a message one way, and others frame it differently.

As popular wisdom tells us – 'Actions speak louder than words' – all behavior, whatever else it may also be, is communication. Communication – the sending and receiving of information (whether understood or not) – may be verbal or non-verbal, conscious or unconscious, intended or not. Mutually intelligible messages are created by selecting and combining information according to the rules of the codes the communicators share (e.g. the code of English, the highway code). Communication is characteristic of all goal-seeking and goal-directed systems, including thermostats, organisms, persons,

FIGURE 1.4 A three-way paradoxical figure: Silver inlay on a brass pencil case from Ancient Egypt. As J.B. Deregowski explains in *Distortion in Art: The Eye and the Mind* (1984, pp. 101-2), that part of a figure-ground inversion which becomes the background is seen as continuous and as extending 'behind' the figure. Both figure and ground are seen as occupying distinct parallel planes. The Egyptian pencil case offers three geometrically identical perceptual units, any one of which may become the ground, and thus be seen as the pattern lying 'behind' the other two. Escher did the same with amazing grace in his color print, *Sun and Moon*, in which the sun and moon alternate as figure and ground, while birds of the day and birds of the night provide the other plane of oscillation.

families, corporations, and so on. Goal-seeking need not be conscious or purposive; it varies in its diversity and flexibility according to the complexity of the system that displays it.

Communication is invariably transitive: monologues are imaginary. Reports, commands, and questions are messages with symbolic, imaginary, or real referents (what they are about) and symbolic, imaginary, or real addressees (who they are for). (When we talk to ourselves, the Other is imaginary. The addressee of general messages is 'to whom it may concern'.) Every message thus displays both *content* and *relationship*. Relationship (ultimately that between the communicators) usually contextualizes content, and meaning is of course contextual.

It is impossible for an organism or a person *not* to communicate.

Silence is a message. Or as Ray Birdwhistell put it in the 1960s: 'In a communications system, nothing never happens'.

Double binds

A logical example of a paradoxical command is the 'Cretan Paradox': 'I am lying.' In analytic logic – where time and change play no significant role – 'I am lying' reports on a situation, demands an either/or response, and asks a question about its truth or falsity. But if true, it is false, if false, it is true – a digital oscillation *ad infinitum*. The command can neither be obeyed nor disobeyed.

(The paradox can however be outflanked by treating it as a joke or by metacommunication: communicating about what makes it paradoxical.)

In ordinary communication, however, which takes place in irreversible and infinitely variable human time, and where future goals direct – but do not determine – present actions, 'I am lying' is rarely paradoxical. The admission, 'Okay, I'm lying', is not a self-referential statement outside time, judging its own validity, as it is in analytic logic. It is a communication, after the fact, about one or more actual instances of lying.

(Note that the present tense in the idiom 'Depuis trois heures je mens' – 'I've been lying for three hours' – is not paradoxical.)

In *The Pragmatics of Human Communication* (1967), a useful if not always critical introduction to the modern theory of communication, Paul Watzlawick, Janet Beavin, and Don J. Jackson give the following examples of 'Be spontaneous!' paradoxes (p. 200):

> 'You ought to love me';
> 'I want you to dominate me' (wife to passive husband);
> 'You should enjoy playing with the children, just like other fathers';
> 'Don't be so obedient' (parents to child);
> 'You know that you are free to go dear; don't mind if I start crying' (from *Lie Down in Darkness*, 1951, by William Styron).

FIGURE 1.5   Do not read this. Question authority.

Taking a 'phenomenological' and therefore relational approach to human reality, as the Gestalt psychologists had taught them, Gregory Bateson and his colleagues discovered the 'paradoxical injunction' in the 1950s in pathological communication in the family, where some family members, usually the parents, unconsciously collaborate in driving another family member crazy – and come to depend for their own relationship on the presence of their 'mad or bad' victim-cum-scapegoat.

('Phenomenology' is a long word for studying reality 'as it appears', which requires a holistic, hierarchic, contextual, and eventually 'transcontextual' strategy of inquiry (as Bateson put it in 1969), a strategy that deals not only with contexts but also with the creation of contexts and the contexts of contexts This I call simply 'context theory'.)

The communications therapists called these paradoxes 'double binds', some of which are amusing, many of which are harmful, others of which are useful, and yet others unavoidable (Chapters 3 and 4). As Bertrand Russell and Kurt Gödel showed, for example, there are similar strategic and structural paradoxes in the foundations of mathematics that cannot be eliminated, even in such apparently simple matters as the definition of class memberhsip in the logic of classes or the consistency and completeness of the axioms of elementary arithmetic.

The following double bind is a classic and pointed but still anti-mother joke from Dan Greenberg's *How to be a Jewish Mother* (1964) – it was after all Freud and God who really specialized in loading the unwary and the impressionable with Oedipal Guilt and Original Sin:

Give your son Marvin two sports shirts as a present. The first time he wears one of them, look at him sadly and say in your Basic Tone of Voice:
'The other one you didn't like?'.

To outflank this double bind strategically watch your timing and reply: 'Like it, Ma? This *is* the other one'.

In keeping with a social ideology that so cruelly and illogically blames mothers for family ills from divorce to drugs to drinking to vandalism to rape that even suburban giveaway magazines like *Homemakers* seek to expose the lie, the double bind and other therapists, including R.D. Laing, directed their attention to the so-called 'schizophrenogenic mother' (mothers who supposedly cause schizophrenia) in pathological families. Here we see a theory in full flight from the terrors of the Freudian father – and one that ignores the role of male domination in insanity, as well as the role of insanity in male domination (Chapter 5).

According to experienced therapists, often the only way to help people help themselves out of a dangerous double bind they cannot ordinarily escape is to explain how double binds work, and then put them into a double bind they can get out of. In society, depending on their function, collective double binds may or may not be harmful (Chapters 3 and 4).

A double bind may produce apparently continuous or analog oscillations; discontinuous or digital oscillations; and combined analog-digital oscillations, such as an oscillation between thresholds in a continuum (see Figures 1.14 and 1.17).

As Yves Barel has most pertinently emphasized in *Le Paradoxe et le systéme* (1978), paradoxes and double binds are derived from tangling levels of communication and reality. Most paradoxes are tangled contradictions.

(In 'Double Bind, 1969', which reviewed errors in the original statement of the double bind theory in 1956, Bateson called these paradoxes 'tangles in the rules' for transforming reality into perceptions, images, and ideas, and tangles in the rules about 'the acquisition or cultivation of such tangles'. The former concern learning; the latter, learning how to learn. On 'tangled hierarchies' (Figure 1.14), see Hofstadter, 1979; Cronen et al., 1982.)

In an ordinary contradiction, verbal, logical, or otherwise, it is possible to make a stable decision in favor of one aspect or another. The same is true of a distinction (whether at a single level or between levels) and an opposition (a relation at a single level). But a paradox is a question that requires two simultaneous answers. A two-way double bind is an either/or message in which each alternative excludes the other (in analytic logic). But it is coded in such a way that the either/or relation of exclusion demands to be read as a both-and relation of inclusion at the same time. Hence the paradox. And so long as we accept the context of the coding and constraints that create the paradox, there is no way out of it (cf. Figures 1.6 and 1.16).

For reasons of long-range survival – matters of life and death – the eye-brain system cannot tolerate the collapsing of levels between figure and ground. When confronted by the collapsing levels of a paradoxical image, the visual system labors to put the levels back again. It seeks to insert into the image a distinction between levels of perception, and in the process it sets off an oscillation between levels.

Collapsing figure and ground is a form of what I shall call 'symmetrization'. Symmetrization means the collapsing of a hierarchic relation between levels into the equal and opposite sides of an opposition or a paradox (1.8 below).

FIGURE 1.6   Jailbound. A subjective double bind for the prisoner. One way out of this double bind – the subject is freedom – is through the wall. For another version, see Figure 1.16. Reprinted from : B. Kliban. *Tiny Foot Prints*.

> If the cultivation of the understanding consists in one thing more than in another, it is surely in learning the grounds of one's own opinions.
>
> John Stuart Mill (1806–1873)

1.4   Action and reaction

In social reality, a paradoxical representation of relations between people is usually an ideological cover for a symmetrized social contradiction. (A social contradiction is defined as a relationship of conflict between levels in a social hierarchy.) The yin-yang symbolism is an example. It collapses the real contradiction between the power of man and the power of woman in Chinese society into a paradox between imaginary opposites.

The 'perpetual motion' of the visual oscillation of the yin-yang icon is a product of code/message relations and organization, not of matter-energy relations and forces. The paradoxical oscillation of the icon – unending so long as the viewer is involved in it – does not contravene the rule of positive entropy in thermodynamics, as a real perpetual motion machine would do. The 'perpetual motion' of the visual icon is possible only because it involves information.

(Code/message systems are open systems: their use of matter and energy does not produce an increase in positive entropy in the image or the information; it produces an increase of positive entropy in their matter-energy environment: Section 1.9.)

To return to Cirlot. He concludes his explanation of the boundary between yin and yang by saying that this 'mystic and unchanging center' between the 'forces' of yin and yang corresponds to

> the central zone of the Wheel of Transformations in Hindu symbolism, and the centre or way out of the labyrinth in Egyptian and western symbolism.

When we recall the supremacy of circularity and simplicity in the metaphysics of Plato and Aristotle, we are perhaps not surprised that Cirlot takes us back to the invention of the axle. But, besides referring us to two slave-supported societies, in which oppression was justified by caste ('genetics') and fatalism, his 'Symbolist' reading also makes the icon determinist. He evokes the popular myth of the 'eternal return', said to determine history, and the Freudian labyrinth of the supposedly instinctual 'compulsion to repeat', said to determine the life of the individual.

The symbol is also an expression, says Cirlot, of 'the two counterbalancing tendencies of evolution and involution'. However, just as the 'force' of yin or yang is a matter-energy metaphor (rather than a semiotic or informational one), so also is 'counterbalancing'. 'Counterbalancing' is a metaphor of a classical machine, the lever and fulcrum. It is a metaphor applicable to Newton's 'laws of motion' in classical mechanics, the simplest model of determinism in science. In the definition given by John Harris in his *Dictionary of Arts and Sciences* in 1704 (the expression 'right line' signifies a straight line), the three 'laws' (really axioms) are as follows:

> 1. That every Body will continue in its State, either of Rest, or Motion uniformly forward in a Right Line, unless it be made to change that State by some Force impressed upon it. [Definition of mechanical inertia. Previously it had been thought that motion required the continuous application of an 'impetus' to the moving body.]
> 2. That the Change of Motion is proportional to the moving Force impressed; and is always according to the Direction of that Right Line in which the force is impressed. [Central aspect of determinist causality in general: the cause-effect relation is linear (proportional) and lineal (straight-line).]
> 3. That *Reaction* is always equal and contrary to Action; or, which is all one, the mutual Actions of two Bodies one upon another are equal, and directed towards contrary Parts: As when one Body

presses and draws another, 'tis as much pressed or drawn by that body. [Central aspect of determinist causality in mechanics: the cause-effect relation is reversible, commutative, and symmetrical.]

(Causality in open systems is distinct from the determinist (or statistical) causality applicable to closed systems. Following the Gestaltists and others, Ludwig von Bertalanffy in his *General System Theory* (1968, p. 40), defined open system causality as *equifinality*:

In a closed system, the final state is unequivocally determined by the initial conditions . . . This is not so in open systems. Here, the same final state may be reached from different initial conditions and in different ways.

We may add to this the concept of *multifinality*, where different final states may be reached in different ways from similar initial conditions.)

In Symbolist contexts, 'evolution' usually stands for the process of 'unfolding' or 'turning outwards', and 'involution', for the complementary process of 'infolding' or 'turning inwards'. In Chinese society, one of the real symbols of 'perfect involution' was the result of binding the feet of women. This mutilation, whose results could still be seen in China in 1976, was reserved for women whose social position meant that they did not have to labor in the fields or in industry (on this and other mutilations, see Daly, 1978).

The actual dominant-subordinate relationship between yin and yang is spelled out in more detail in the *I Ching* (Table 1.1), which also defines kinship, notably the authoritarian hierarchy of the traditional Chinese family. (In the Wilhelm commentary, see in particular the hexagrams Chia Jên, The Family, and K'uei, Opposition.)

Grison summarizes the overall relationships:

Yin is expressed in the *I-Ching* by the broken line — —, and yang by the continuous line ——. The combination of the two forms the trigrams and the hexagrams. Three (or six) broken lines, all yin, stand for *k'ouen*, or *perfect passivity*, the Earth; three (or six) full lines, all yang, stand for *k'ien*, or *perfect activity*, the Sky. Earth and Sky are the polarization of the primordial Unity, the polarization of *T'ai-ki* [the 'supreme pole' (*thai chi*), or *Grand Faîte*].

In the heavens yang represents the sun, the male. Yin represents the moon, the female. Woman is here defined as the reflection of man, as his imaginary mirror image, as his imaginary 'complement', a definition common to East and West. In both ideologies, the

Table 1.1 Some of the meanings of the eight basic trigrams, taken from Martin Gardner's 'Mathematical Games' in the *Scientific American* for January 1974 (pp. 108–13). The title of the article is 'The Combinatorial Basis of the *I Ching*' (*The Book of Changes*). The full lines represent yang, the broken lines represent yin (in a binary-digital form). Gardner explains that the trigrams form a binary code like that of the digital computer. When the mathematician, philosopher, and theologian Gottfried Wilhelm Leibniz (1646–1716) discovered the binary notation he thought it to be God's very own design, where One is sufficient to create Everything out of Nothing.

TRIGRAM	NAME	IMAGES	TRAITS	FAMILY RELATIONS	PARTS OF BODY	ANIMALS
‾‾‾ ‾‾‾ ‾‾‾	CHIEN	HEAVEN COLD	STRONG FIRM LIGHT	FATHER	HEAD	HORSE
‾ ‾ ‾ ‾ ‾ ‾	KUN	EARTH HEAT	WEAK YIELDING DARK	MOTHER	BELLY	OX
‾ ‾ ‾ ‾ ‾‾‾	CHEN	THUNDER SPRING	ACTIVE MOVING AROUSING	FIRST SON	FOOT	DRAGON
‾ ‾ ‾‾‾ ‾ ‾	KAN	WATER MOON WINTER	DANGEROUS DIFFICULT ENVELOPING	SECOND SON	EAR	PIG
‾‾‾ ‾ ‾ ‾ ‾	KEN	MOUNTAIN	RESTING STUBBORN	YOUNGEST SON UNMOVING	HAND	DOG
‾‾‾ ‾‾‾ ‾ ‾	SUN	WIND WOOD	GENTLE PENETRATING FLEXIBLE	FIRST DAUGHTER	THIGH	BIRD
‾‾‾ ‾ ‾ ‾‾‾	LI	FIRE SUN LIGHTNING SUMMER	BEAUTIFUL DEPENDING CLINGING	SECOND DAUGHTER	EYE	PHEASANT
‾ ‾ ‾‾‾ ‾‾‾	TUI	LAKE MARSH RAIN AUTUMN	JOYFUL SATISFIED COMPLACENT	YOUNGEST DAUGHTER	MOUTH	SHEEP

dominant-subordinate relation is collapsed into an imaginary symmetry. In the Chinese code: 'The sun shares the sky with the moon'. In the Western code: 'My woman (girl, wife) and I are equals'.

Both formulas reduce a social contradiction to an apparently single-level relationship, while still covertly maintaining the real contradiction between levels. The same 'subordinate equality' for women was still part of the dominant ideology in China in 1976, before the death of Mao.

The metaphor of reflection occurs in the following passage from the biography, published in 1806, of Colonel John Hutchinson (1615–64), by his widow Lucy Hutchinson (?1620–80), daughter of Sir Allen Apsley. Puritan soldier, sometime Governor of Nottingham, and Member of the Long Parliament, Colonel Hutchinson was one of those who signed the death warrant of Charles I in 1649. Lucy Hutchinson says of him:

> never a man had a greater passion for a woman, nor a more honourable esteem of a wife; yet he was not uxorious, nor remitted he that just rule which it was her honour to obey, but managed the reins of government with such prudence and affection that she who would not delight in such an honourable and advantageable subjection, must have wanted [lacked] a reasonable soul. He governed by persuasion, which he never employed but to things honourable and profitable for herself; he loved her soul and her honour more than her outside . . .

Moreover:

> If he esteemed her at a higher rate than she in herself could have deserved, he was the author of that virtue he doated on, while she only reflected his own glories upon him; all that she was, was *him*, while he was here, and all that she is now at best is but his pale shade.

In the Western tradition the real relation between men and women is made explicit in the violence of male pornography (distinct from human eroticism). In the Chinese tradition the same male supremacy is made explicit in the sex manuals of certain Taoist sects, sects lacking the democratic vein of Taoist thought compared with the authoritarian and elitist cast of Confucianism. These manuals laid down the rules for men to obtain long life by 'nourishing the vital spirit' – by feeding on the vital spirit of women, having intercourse with as many as possible.

Dealing with caste and class in the emperor's harem in *Science and Civilisation in China*, Joseph Needham says:

> the women of the highest rank approached the emperor at times nearest to the full moon, when the Yin influence would be at its height, and matching the powerful Yang force of the Son of Heaven, would give the highest virtues to children so conceived. The primary purpose of the lower ranks of women was rather to feed the emperor's Yang with their Yin (vol. 4, part 2, 1965, pp. 477–8).

The Rule of Rules in the Taoist manuals – the level of general strategy – was that they were never to be shown to women, so that no woman could learn the sexual techniques and thus be able to use them against men (Maspero, 1971, pp. 479–577).

All the Enginous Wheeles of the Soule are continually going.
   Thomas Dekker: *The Seven Deadly Sinnes of London* (1606)

1.5 Equal and opposite

A root metaphor like that of the binary opposition is a 'representative anecdote'. It stands for oft-told tales about crucial social relationships, such as those between individual, society, and nature; between self, others, and otherness; between woman, child, and man; and between the many different expressions of creativity, such as love and work and play.

The question is to be able to recognize when a root metaphor is appropriate to what it represents, and when it is not. Consider the usual coding of the term 'opposition' in further detail.

If one describes the relationship between the 'raw' and the 'cooked' as an opposition, as Claude Lévi-Strauss has done, the metaphor is improper. It is an imaginary representation of a real relation. The relation is not an opposition at a single level, but a distinction between levels in a hierarchy. The real hierarchy between 'raw food' and 'cooked food' is a dependent hierarchy: 'cooked' depends on 'raw' in the same way that society depends on nature (Figure 1.10).

In response to the metaphysical idealists, who will argue that 'raw' does not exist as a category without its relationship to the category of 'cooked', we need only to point out that if 'cooked' disappears, 'raw' continues to exist. It is not 'raw' that disappears when 'cooked' disappears. What disappears is the distinction between them.

The term opposition usually implies a commutative relation between opposed terms or systems. Commutation literally signifies 'changing back and forth' or 'reciprocal interchange'. In a direct current electric motor, such as the starter in a car, the 'commutator' is a revolving switch that changes the polarity of the magnetic fields from positive to negative and back again as the armature spins.

In arithmetic and algebra, commutation signifies that the order of terms can be altered without affecting the result. In the ideology of the binary opposition, commutation signifies that the terms can exchange places without affecting the nature of the relation between them. Commutative causality is Newtonian, symmetrical, reversible causality.

In a commutative relation, the serial, temporal, spatial, or

"Occupation?"
"Woman."

FIGURE 1.7   A *New Yorker* cartoon from the early 1940s by Chon Day. Reprinted from: *The New Yorker Album 1925–1950*.

apparently hierarchical ordering of the relation is not significant: $abC = aCb = bCa = baC = Cba = Cab$.

(For English speakers, *Cab* displays two levels. Read as a simple sequence, it is of the same logical type as abC or the other terms. Read as a word, however, *Cab* is distinct in logical typing from abC and the other terms.)

Information in communication is not commutative. Communication depends on order, time, and timing – and on coding, goal-seeking, and direction. A given communication is not reversible, it has a beginning, a middle, and an end.

Multiplication of numbers is commutative; multiplication of species is not. When spoken, 'Madam I'm Adam' reads the same in both directions (it is a spoken palindrome), but 'I mean what I say' is not synonymous or symmetrical with 'I say what I mean'. In physics, the principle of commutation is illustrated by the absolute identity and symmetry of all particles of the same type: if two electrons exchange places, nothing has happened.

We can now write the Commutation Rule:

The Commutation Rule: When the order or sequence in which two or more terms or systems is arrayed is such that they can exchange places without changing their actual relation, there is no hierarchy: the relation is commutative. Commutative or symmetrical relations can exist only between items of the same level of reality, or of the same level of logical type.

If we apply the Commutation Rule to the binary relation between positive and negative electricity, or to that between the north and south magnetic poles, or to the structurally similar relation between the positive and negative integers, we find no hierarchy. Provided we recognize in these three sets of relations the mediating role of the boundary between 'positive' and 'negative' (zero charge, zero polarity, and the numeral zero, which are neither positive nor negative), the term binary opposition is entirely appropriate.

'When I make a word do a lot of work like that', said Humpty Dumpty, 'I always pay it extra.'
          Lewis Carroll: *Alice Through the Looking Glass* (1871)

1.6   Difference, distinction, opposition, contradiction

The dominant discourse in English uses terms based on the concept of opposition as ordinary connecting expressions. The commonest examples are 'as opposed to', on the one hand, and 'on the one hand', on the other.

The role of these two connectives in the code of the dominant way of knowing (the dominant epistemology) of our society is to create and maintain the unfounded assumption that 'opposition' (symmetrical conflict) is the fundamental category 'lying behind' most other kinds of relationship, whether logical, grammatical, social, or natural. These expressions also imply that oppositions are binary, single-level, two-sided (bilateral), and symmetrical.

Thus we say:

nature, as opposed to society;
man, as opposed to woman;
white, as opposed to non-white;
capital, as opposed to labor.

We also say 'society on the one hand, and nature on the other' – and so on.

But the real relationship described by each of these phrases is in fact hierarchical. In reality the first term constrains the second. In the case of nature and society, the hierarchy of constraint is a necessary one: it is a product of evolution. In all the others, the hierarchy of constraint is a hierarchy of social and economic power, and such hierarchies are contingent; they are products of history.

The constraints of nature can be changed by nature. The constraints of history can be changed by people.

Most assumptions about opposition fail to recognize that 'difference' and 'distinction' are more basic relations than opposition. (Following Bateson, a distinction is defined as 'a difference that makes a difference'.) Figure 1.8 uses the poverty of two dimensions to illustrate the contrasts between difference, distinction, opposition, and contradiction. It also defines the 'unity of opposites' and 'identity of opposites' so often encountered in mystical thinking and in what was called the dialectical perspective in the nineteenth century.

The four parts of Figure 1.8 stand for the following relations:

Figure 1.8(a) represents a *unity of differences* at a single level. Difference is defined as a continuous or analog relation, e.g. the rippled surface of a lake, direction in multidimensional space and time, the real number system.

Figure 1.8(b) represents a *unity of distinctions* at a single level. Distinction is defined as a discontinuous or digital relation, e.g. the squares on a checkerboard, the alphabet in writing, the points of the compass, the genetic code, the whole number system, the streets of a city, a moment of decision.

Figure 1.8(c) represents a *unity (and identity) of opposites* (a single level, by definition). Examples of real opposites: positive and negative electricity, the northern and southern hemispheres, the positive and negative integers. Examples of imaginary opposites: one dyad of the split and imaginary personality in psychosis, the imaginary symmetrization of a two-term hierarchy.

Figure 1.8(d) represents a three-way *unity of contradictions*, a three-term hierarchy with *A* dominant. Viewed as a social hierarchy, *A* might represent state and/or corporate business, *B* farmworkers, and *C* industrial workers. The dominance of *A* is maintained by the oldest imperial strategy, the strategy of divide-and-rule.

Many a so-called 'opposition' (implying conflict) is in fact a distinction (not implying conflict). Distinctions may exist between terms or persons or systems at a single level; they may also exist between levels in hierarchies (Figure 1.10).

Many other uses of the term 'opposition' do correctly identify a locus of conflict, but they also collapse a contradiction. They reduce a real conflict between levels in a hierarchy to an imaginary conflict between 'opposites' at a single level (Figure 1.11).

In the common ideology, East and West, the usual result is that a real conflict between social levels (defined as a contradiction), and notably a conflict between levels of power, is symmetrized – and thus

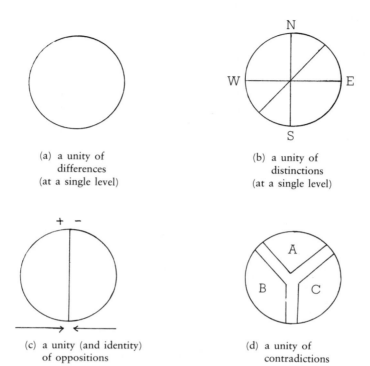

(a) a unity of
differences
(at a single level)

(b) a unity of
distinctions
(at a single level)

(c) a unity (and identity)
of oppositions

(d) a unity of
contradictions

FIGURE 1.8 Difference, distinction, opposition, contradiction. In each figure
the circle is the digital frame of the icon (a distinction between outside and
inside). Not represented is a 'unity of distinctions' between levels, as in an
adaptive, non-conflicting, dependent hierarchy between nature, society, and
culture (Fig. 1.10). Modified from: Richard M. Coe and Anthony Wilden,
'Errore', *Enciclopedia Einaudi* (1978), vol. 5, p. 702.

neutralized. When neutralization by symmetrization involves only two
levels, the levels of the contradiction are made to appear as the 'two
sides' of an imaginary equation, viz. 'business versus labor', 'upper
class versus lower class'.

There may be a better term to label hierarchical conflicts in society,
but 'contradiction' has by common usage lost it linguistic sense when
applied to social relations. In the social context, 'contradiction'
signifies social, economic, and political conflicts between levels in an
illegitimate hierarchy.

Social contradictions involve levels of relation. Logical contradictions
involve levels of communication. An affirmation is a statement about a
situation (two levels). (The situation may be symbolic, imaginary, or
real.) An affirmation is negated (or contradicted) by inserting 'not' or

a similar negative word into the affirmation. Thus the negation (or contradiction) of an affirmation is a statement about an affirmation about a situation (three levels). The negative sentence using 'not' is in fact a verbal metacommunication about an affirmation, not the 'opposite' of the affirmation. An affirmation and its contradiction by 'not' (or a similar negative word) are not of the same logical type.

When the two 'sides' of an imaginary equation between 'opposites' – 'man'/'woman', for instance – are seen in the imaginary as symmetrical, then the relation is generally viewed as an 'either/or' relation of (competitive) exclusion. When the imaginary opposites are seen as complementary – master/slave, for instance – then the relation is generally viewed as a 'both-and' relation of (collaborative) inclusion.

(On both-and relationships of co-operation, see Chapter 2.)

This critique does not imply – as it may appear to do if read as an either/or opposition – that we should do away with either/or thinking. Either/or thinking is required to make decisions between real alternatives: my central nervous system is making billions of such decisions as I insert this caveat.

Nor does the critique of symmetrization imply that all both-and thinking is derived from single-level, bilateral, either/or thinking. The both-and relationship between inorganic nature, organic nature, society, and culture is not only real, it is also a both-and relation between four distinct levels of reality (Figure 1.10).

The category of opposition was reaffirmed as a supposedly basic relationship by the structural linguists of the 1930s. In the 1950s and 1960s, it was reaffirmed again in a much more sensitive area by the structural anthropology of Lévi-Strauss. In his *Grundzüge der Phonologie* (*Principles of Phonology*) the linguist N. Troubetzkoy, who greatly influenced Lévi-Strauss, defined opposition this way (1939, p. 33):

> The idea of difference presupposes the idea of opposition
> [*Gegensatz*]. Two things can only be differentiated from each other
> in so far as they are opposed to each other, i.e. in so far as there
> exists a relation of opposition between them.

This is simply a 'deep-structure' statement of Hegel's 'surface-structure' dictum that 'Man exists only in so far as he is opposed', a definition of human relationships taken up without change in our own time by the Marxist philosopher Herbert Marcuse (d. 1981).

In complete contrast with Troubetzkoy and the Hegelian view, the linguist and philosopher C.K. Ogden (1889–1957), writing in 1932 in *Opposition* (pp. 36–7), defined the terms in the following way:

The sole source of all opposition is the possibility of a reciprocal neutralization of like actions . . .

(This is equivalent to the commutative oppositions just defined.)

In order to balance one another two terms must be equivalent, must have a common measure, which implies their similarity and equality, from the point of view in question.

(As with the electromagnetic poles, or any other similar terms of the same logical type.)

It follows that where there is no neutral point between the two extremes of a series [or spectrum] there is no opposition, only heterogeneity. Difference, however great, does not create opposition.

In other words, if difference is to be transformed into opposition, it must undergo a change of structure, not a mere change of state (1.7 below).

Against the mistaken use of expressions implying symmetrical opposition – notably 'as opposed to' and 'on the one hand, on the other' – we may invoke the Levels Rule:

The Levels Rule: A relationship between levels (or orders) in a hierarchy, whether or not it involves conflict, does not constitute an opposition. It may be a simple distinction between levels; it may be a conflict or a contradiction between levels; it may in some special circumstances be a paradox (a collapsed or tangled contradiction).

In most contexts, errors of symmetrization can be resolved as follows:

by restricting the concept of opposition to single-level relations implying conflict or exclusion or negative identity between items of the same logical type;
by using expressions carrying no covert judgments about levels, dualisms, or conflicts, e.g. 'as different from', 'as distinct from', 'as compared to', or 'in contrast with';
by using expressions, such as 'in conflict with', which identify the relation as a conflict, whether hierarchical or not;
by using terms such as 'in contradiction with' to signify conflicts between levels.

The same may be said for the expression 'on the one hand, on the other'. In referring to hierarchies, the proper connective expression will commonly be 'at one level, at another' – as when we speak of society, at one level of complexity, of living nature, at another, and of inorganic nature, at yet another. When we are not dealing with levels of relation, we can always say 'in one respect (or aspect), in another respect (or aspect)'.

The Difference Rule will clarify the point:

The Difference Rule: Two or more terms or systems may be related to each other by difference, distinction, opposition, contradiction, or paradox. The nature of such boundaries between terms, between systems, or between systems and environments, cannot be correctly ascertained without reference to their context.

The alternative '*either – or*' is never expressed in dreams, both of the alternatives being inserted in the text of the dream as though they were equally valid. . . . An 'either – or' used in *recording* a dream is to be translated by 'and'.

Sigmund Freud: *On Dreams* (1901)

1.7   The unity or identity of opposites

We may now consider the role of the notion of opposition in what was called 'dialectics' in the nineteenth century and is still called that today. In Chapter 2 of the *Dialectics of Nature*, written between 1872 and 1882, Frederick Engels states the three 'laws of dialectics', derived directly from Hegel:

the law of the transformation of quantity into quality and vice versa;
the law of the interpenetration of opposites;
the law of the negation of the negation (*Negation*).

Engels' knowledge of the physical and life sciences was far in advance of most of his contemporaries, and his *Dialectics of Nature* is an important document in the history and philosophy of science, as is the *Anti-Dühring* of 1878.

But as regards the three Hegelian 'laws' of dialectics, we must recognize that there is nothing particularly dialectical about the first, the 'transformation of quantity into quality (and vice versa)', for this is simply a statement about reversible emergent qualities in chemistry and physics (e.g. $H_2 + O = H_2O$), as explained in *The Rules Are No Game* (1987).

The third so-called 'law of dialectics', the 'negation of the negation' (which Engels professes to see even in geological change) refers to the negation of concepts by concepts and cannot be legitimately applied to the processes of change in nature or society.

The second 'law', the 'interpenetration of [binary] opposites' (*Durchdringung der Gegensätze*) requires further comment.

In Lenin's notebooks on Hegel (1961, pp. 359–60), this notion appears as the 'identity of opposites', which Lenin equates with the 'unity of opposites'.

The idea of the unity and/or identity of opposites has a long history in the Western metaphysics of the imaginary, notably in the mysticism of Meister Eckhart (1260?–1327), Cardinal Nicholas of Cusa (1401–1464), Giordano Bruno (1548–1600), Blaise Pascal (1623–1662), and William Blake (1757–1827).

(Meister Eckhart is also a probable source of Hegel's 'negation of the negation': Eckhart, 1941, p. 147.)

The symmetry or identity or unity of opposites does have real existence in mechanics, for it is synonymous with Newton's Third Axiom of Motion: 'Action and reaction are equal and opposite'.

The mechanical metaphor of the identity or equality of 'opposites' appears in classical economics in the work of Jean-Baptiste Say (1767--1832), who popularized the theories of Adam Smith in France. 'Say's Law of Markets' states that production and consumption are always equal and opposite, and thus that any crisis of overproduction (i.e. depression) in our system is impossible (4.2 below).

In his notes on Hegel, Lenin also speaks of difference and distinction. Hegel had said in 1817 in the *Science of Logic* that

Difference in general is already contradiction *an sich* [in itself, in the abstract]. . . . When one pushes difference between realities far enough, one sees diversity become opposition, and consequently contradiction. . . .

The transition from difference to contradiction thus requires a change of structure. Lenin describes motion as a 'unity of contradictions' (1961, p. 258). At one point he writes:

Ordinary imagination grasps difference and contradiction, but not the *transition* from the one to the other. . . . Thinking reason (understanding) sharpens the blunt difference of variety, the mere manifold of imagination, into *essential* difference, into *opposition*. Only when raised to the peak of contradiction do the manifold entities become active . . . and lively in relation to one another . . . (p. 143).

Lenin's point about 'transition' (process) is well taken. Also, when he says that understanding 'sharpens the blunt difference of variety', we can see this as a way of saying that understanding, like the senses, codes variety as information, and makes decisions about transforming (analog) differences into (digital) distinctions. But he is still equating difference with opposition.

Setting Hegel on his feet, Marx remarks on the concrete process by which a relation of difference may be restructured into a relation of contradiction. In the rough draft of his early critique of political economy, the *Grundrisse* (1857–8, p. 147), he discusses the relationship between the use value of a commodity (what it is for) and its economic exchange value (what is it worth in the market):

> The simple fact that the commodity exists doubly, in one aspect as a specific product whose natural form of existence [its use value] ideally contains (latently contains) its exchange value, and in the other aspect as manifest exchange value (money), in which all connection with the natural form of the product is stripped away again – this double *differentiated* [*verschieden*] existence must develop into a *distinction* [*Unterschied*], and the distinction must develop into *opposition* [*Gegensatz*] and *contradiction* [*Widerspruch*] (translation modified).

The notion of the 'unity of opposites' and that of the 'identity of opposites' can be usefully applied to non-living nature. But except in the imaginary, these concepts cannot be properly applied to non-linear and non-lineal systems, including living nature, society, and history.

In the study of non-living systems, the notion of the unity, identity, polarity, and symmetry of opposites has had and still has strategic value. Indeed physics would be lost without it (cf. Wigner, 1965; Freedman and van Nieuwenhuizen, 1978).

Historians of science tell us that the discovery of electromagnetism in 1820 by the Danish physicist, Hans Christian Oersted, was the result of an attempt to demonstrate the unity and polarity of the forces of nature, and that the early statement of the principle of the conservation of energy, by Julius Robert von Mayer in 1841, was the product of a similar strategy of inquiry. (The first and second axioms of thermodynamics – conservation and entropy – were made explicit by Rudolf von Clausius in 1850.) Both Oersted and Mayer were influenced by the German 'nature philosophers', notably Goethe and Schelling.

Mao's essay on contradiction (1937, revised 1952) draws on the yin-yang tradition as well as on Engels and Lenin. In the English translation, besides the unity and the identity of opposites, we find the following expressions: the movement of opposites, the complementarity

FIGURE 1.9　(a) Opposition (duey li), (b) opposition (hsian fan), and (c) contradiction (mao dueng). The two characters of 'duey li', translated 'opposition' in the English text of Mao's essay *On Contradiction* (1937), stand respectively for 'correct, right, a pair' and 'stand up'. The two characters of 'hsian fan', also translated 'opposition' (and the expression used in the saying from Pan Ku quoted in the text), stand respectively for 'mutual' and 'to turn over, to retreat, to rebel, to turn back'. In 'mao dueng', usually translated 'contradiction', but also translated 'opposition' in some cases, as when Mao speaks of the 'unity of contradictions', the first character represents a spear or lance; the second, a shield or buckler. (Calligraphy and translations by Victoria Chen.)

of opposites, the antagonism of opposites, the transformation of opposites, the reciprocal unity of mutually exclusive opposites, and the identity of contradiction. Mao quotes a popular saying, first written down in the first century by Pan Ku, a historian: 'Things that oppose each other also complement each other.' Or more literally, in so far as that is possible with Chinese: 'Mutually oppose, mutually perfect (each other).'

But Mao also goes beyond tradition, dialectical and otherwise, by introducing the concept of hierarchy into his epistemology. He distinguishes between principal and secondary contradictions in society, and between the dominant and subordinate aspects of a contradiction (1966, pp. 51–60):

One must not treat all the conditions in a process as being equal but must distinguish between the principal and the secondary [or non-principal] contradictions, and pay special attention to grasping the principal one. But, in any given contradiction, whether principal or secondary, should the two contradictory aspects be treated as equal?

Again, no. In any contradiction the development of the contradictory aspects is uneven. Sometimes they seem to be in equilibrium, which is however only temporary and relative, while unevenness is basic. Of the two contradictory aspects, one must be principal and the other secondary. The principal aspect is the one playing the leading role in the contradiction. The nature of a thing [one would now say a relationship] is determined [one would now say constrained] mainly by the principal aspect of a contradiction, the aspect which has gained the dominant position (p. 54).

One Law for the Lion and the Ox is Oppression.
                              William Blake (1757–1827)

1.8   Symmetrization and inversion

There are just four major orders of complexity in our universe, inorganic nature, organic nature, society, and culture. (An order of complexity is defined as including more than one level of complexity.) As indicated in Figure 1.10, each is distinguished from the others by a clearly defined boundary.

At the micro-level the (open-system) boundary between life and non-life is marked by the genetic communication system of RNA and DNA. At the macro-level the (open-system) boundary between inorganic and organic nature is marked by photosynthesis in green plants and marine organisms, the source of oxygen, fossil fuels, plant matter, and the only way the energy of sunlight can enter the biosphere. Photosynthesis is the process on which practically all kinds of life ultimately depend.

The (open-system) boundary between society and nature is marked by the historical emergence of language and the division of labor in economic production and the reproduction of society itself, largely governed by myth, ritual, and kinship based on exchanges between named kinship groups. Culture, the domain of representation, is defined as what makes societies with the same basic social and economic organization, such as Germany and France, distinct from each other.

The four orders of complexity form a dependent hierarchy: the lower orders in the diagram depend on the higher orders for their existence. To see whether a dependent hierarchy is the right way up, apply the Extinction Rule:

The Extinction Rule: To test for the orientation of a dependent

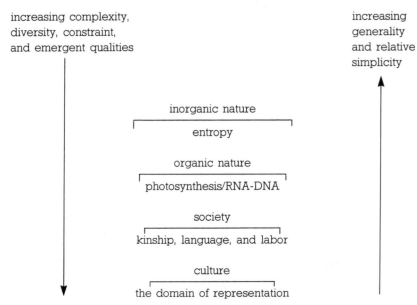

increasing complexity,
diversity, constraint,
and emergent qualities

increasing
generality
and relative
simplicity

inorganic nature

entropy

organic nature

photosynthesis/RNA-DNA

society

kinship, language, and labor

culture

the domain of representation

FIGURE 1.10   In context theory the four major orders of complexity form a dependent hierarchy coded and constrained at each level by ever more diverse kinds of information. The higher orders constrain and sustain (but neither cause nor determine) the scope and extent of the goal-seeking activities of open systems at lower levels (note that the human individual is a complex of all four orders). Open systems are goal-seeking adaptive cybernetic systems involving or simulating life or mind (cells, organisms, individuals, corporations, societies, systems of ideas, and so on), dependent on their environments for matter-energy and information (and thus for sustenance and survival), and conditioned in their behavior by hierarchies of constraints (the hierarchy of complexity is also a hierarchy of constraints). The ultimate constraint on open systems (but not their cause) is the ordinary causality (and eventually the entropy) of closed physical systems. The more levels and kinds of constraint or coding a goal-seeking open system is subject to, the more diverse and complex it becomes (Wilden, 1987, pp. 73–9, 167–76). The lower levels in the dependent hierarchy thus display emergent qualities (unpredictable novelty). (Culture is the most complex and diverse of all, for culture can be symbolic and imaginary as well as real.) A dependent hierarchy is a complex of 'both-and' distinctions between levels of reality (Wilden, 1987, pp. 250–3, 276–8); it is completely inexplicable from the perspective of the 'either/or' and one-dimensional analytic logic criticized in the study of oppositions in this chapter.

hierarchy, mentally abolish each level (or order) in turn, and note which other levels (or orders) will become extinct if it becomes extinct.

Obviously the extinction of nature entails the extinction of society, but if society self-destructs nature continues as before.

Nature thus belongs at the top of this dependent hierarchy, and its position there is the result of necessity, not of theory. In Voltaire's words, 'Men argue, nature acts.' Or as Goethe put it, 'Nature is always right.'

Symmetrization is an imaginary operation that by neutralizing a real hierarchy prepares the way to turn it upside down. Once a real hierarchy has been reduced to a single level in the imaginary – as in the phrase 'society, as opposed to nature' – then it can be inverted – as in the common belief that with modern technology society dominates nature (Figure 1.11).

The three structural components of the modern economic system are capital, land, and creativity (labor potential). The first capitalist revolution (c. 1450–1850) remade the deep structure of the economy and society by its growing capacity to turn any relationship into a commodity measured by exchange value in the market. With the commoditization of land, labor, and capital the first fully capitalist economy, itself remolded by the industrial revolution and the factory system, emerged in Britain in the early nineteenth century.

The real relationship between these three structural components is a long-term dependent hierarchy (Figure 1.12a). Land, standing for

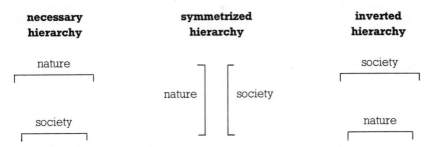

FIGURE 1.11   Two-way symmetrization and inversion in the imaginary. Other distortions of the real (in Freud *Enstellung*, or 'misplacing') will be found in the way the dominant ideology depicts the present power relations between white and non-white, man and woman, and capital and labor (cf. Wilden, 1980b, p. 80). There is of course no 'natural' or necessary hierarchy in the relations between the races or the sexes, but there is a necessary hierarchy between labor (creativity) and capital (tools). Labor is the source of capital: without labor, capital becomes extinct (Figure 1.12).

photosynthesis, is the source of labor power (creativity), and creativity is the source of capital (tools). This hierarchy is a both-and relationship of distinctions between levels, without conflict.

When spoken of in modern economics as the 'three factors of production', however, land, labor, and capital are symmetrized into antagonistic oppositions at a single level (Figure 1.12b), and made to appear interchangeable.

The present power relations between the three orders form a hierarchy of short-term, antagonistic, and either/or contradictions. The real hierarchy has been inverted: capital exploits creativity to exploit nature (Figure 1.12c).

The oppositions of heaven and earth, spirit and nature, man and woman, when reconciled, bring about the creation and reproduction of life. In the world of visible things, the principle of opposites makes possible the differentiation of categories through which order is brought into the world.
The I Ching or Book of Changes (Wilhelm translation):
                    Commentary on the Hexagram K'uei, Opposition

1.9   Paradox, perpetual motion, and entropy

When a dependent hierarchy is flattened out in the imaginary, the result is one or more 'strange loops' in a 'tangled hierarchy', as defined by Douglas Hostadter in *Gödel, Escher, Bach* (1979, pp. 10–15, 684ff; Bateson, 1972, p. 272 (1969) appears to be the first use of 'tangle' in this sense).

As a statement about hierarchies, the three-way symmetrization of land, labor, and capital in Figure 1.12b is structurally similar to the impossible and imaginary object (the Penrose triangle) depicted in Figure 1.13, where three dimensions are looped together in two. In both cases, reading the image requires us to make discrete jumps between distinct levels.

In the three-way symmetry of Figure 1.12b, three jumps between real orders of complexity are reduced to a single-level and imaginary neighborhood. In the impossible object, a single jump in dimensions is made and unmade and remade *ad infinitum* by the paradoxical command about the third dimension implicit in the image of the triangle. The coded cues about dimensions in one part of the image are switched into a conflicting code in another part. To see exactly where this happens, cover the imaginary triangle with a piece of paper, then uncover it from left to right.

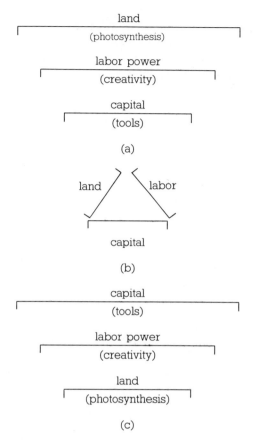

FIGURE 1.12   Land, labor, and capital, the structural components of the
economy, symmetrized and inverted. (a) The actual and long-term dependent
hierarchy between the three orders of organization. Land (standing for
photosynthesis) is the environment and the source of labor power (creativity),
and labor power is the environment and the source of capital (tools, means of
production). In (a) the three orders of complexity are both-and distinctions
between levels in a hierarchy, and this system displays long-range survival
value.

In (b) the hierarchy is symmetrized into the 'three factors of production'.
Here the three levels of reality seem to be either/or, interchangeable, and
conflicting oppositions at a single level. In (c) the real dependent hierarchy is
inverted by the present and short-term power relations of the economic
system. Here the three structural orders form either/or, antagonistic contradictions between levels. Capital directs labor to exploit land.

Unlike figure-ground oscillations, which are products of nature, the imaginary triangle with its oscillation in dimensions is a product of culture. For people and societies that have not decided (collectively) and learned (individually) to see three dimensions in two-dimensional pictures, the paradox of the imaginary triangle does not exist. For them the line-drawing of the triangle in Figure 1.13 is simply a flat pattern. For us, however, when we try to see it their way, we find we cannot. What we have learned about reading dimensions into pictures we cannot unlearn later on.

Collapsed or tangled contradictions, symmetrizations and inversions, imaginary opposites and tangled hierarchies – all such paradoxical relations depend on 'strange loops', such as the strange loop Hofstadter points to in *Waterfall*, a 1961 print by Maurits C. Escher (1902–72), where an imaginary river drives a water wheel in perpetual motion (Figure 1.14).

(a)

(b)

FIGURE 1.13   (a) An impossible object, a collapsed contradiction in dimensions: the imaginary triangle designed by L.S. Penrose and R. Penrose in 1958; (b) Swedish postage stamps, designed by Oscar Reutersvärd, issued in 1981 (from *Discover*, June 1982). (Objects can be fashioned to simulate these paradoxical objects, but the simulation fails the moment one looks at them from other angles.) The paradoxical nature of the Penrose triangle is the result of an implicit switch in the coding of two-dimensional cues about seeing three dimensions. To see the shift in coding, cover the image with a piece of paper and then uncover it from left to right.

In one respect, Escher's *Waterfall* is a tangle in dimensions, just like the imaginary triangle of Figure 1.13a. To see the switch in the coding of dimensions, follow the energy flow through the imaginary machine as it passes up the strange loop (the zig-zag channel) and down the waterfall that together translate up to down and down to up, in an oscillation without end.

In another respect, Escher's imaginary machine is a statement about reversibility and irreversibility in natural processes, that is to say, it is a statement about entropy in thermodynamics. As the philosopher Heraclitus said 2500 years ago, no one can step into the same river twice. In Escher's perpetual motion machine, however, the watercourse is always the same: we can step into the same river, made up of the same molecules of water, an infinite number of times.

The first axiom of thermodynamics states that in any closed or isolated system of matter-energy reactions, the energy of the system remains constant: whatever its transformations in quality, the quantity of energy is conserved.

(In systems ecology an isolated system exchanges no matter or energy with its environment; a closed system exchanges energy but not matter; an open system exchanges both matter and energy and – in the sense used in this book – information as well. In general I use the simpler thermodynamic terminology of closed and open systems.)

The second axiom states that when work is done in a closed system – i.e. the transfer of energy from its more ordered to its less ordered parts, e.g. from high to low temperature – its positive entropy tends irreversibly to increase towards a state of thermodynamic equilibrium (apparently random disorder, e.g. 'waste heat') where no gradient exists between order and disorder, and from which no further work can be obtained.

(Note that the *rate* at which entropy increases is not universal; it depends on the properties of the system creating the entropy.)

The third axiom, which concerns the zero entropy of a perfect crystal at absolute zero, does not concern us here.

Entropy is a relationship between order and disorder: the greater the (relative) disorder, the higher the (positive) entropy. When we light a fire, for example, the destruction of the molecular organization of the wood by combustion liberates energy in the form of heat, which is transferred to the environment of the fire as work. As near as makes no difference to the example, the fire and the atmosphere in which it burns form a closed system. What is left in this system when the fire goes out is a disordered aggregate of what had previously been system and order: a pile of ashes in the fireplace and a random scattering of smoke and gases in the atmosphere, all at similar temperatures.

Disorder is not absolute or fixed. The wood ash is disorder compared with the molecular order of wood, but it is new order for

FIGURE 1.14(a) Escher's *Waterfall*, 1961: an impossible and imaginary machine in perpetual motion: a tangled hierarchy dependent on a strange loop (the zig-zag channel). A strange loop in a tangled hierarchy occurs 'wherever, by moving upwards (or downwards) through the levels of some hierarchical system, we unexpectedly find ourselves right back where we started' (Hofstadter, 1979, p. 10). The strange or reflexive loop supplies the information or negative entropy of new order (pp. 40, 42 below) that permits the energy gradient in the illusion to oscillate between up and down, past and future, order and disorder (positive entropy), as if in a double bind. (The boundary between these states lies in the vertical fall, which is neither up nor down). The oscillation could be represented by a cusp catastrophe in the topology of René Thom (see Zeeman, 1976; Woodcock and Davis, 1978; Paulos, 1980). Reprinted from *The Graphic Work of M.C. Escher* (1961).

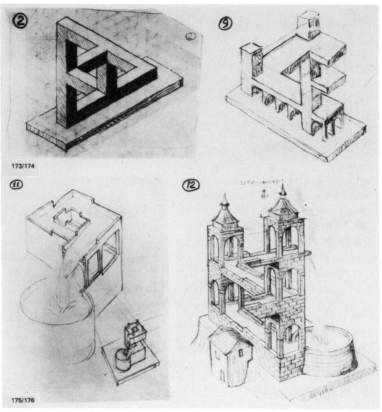

173. Study for the lithograph
     "Waterfall." 1961
     Pencil, 135×170 (5⅜×6¾")
     (version of an "impossible
     triangle," such as published by L.S.
     and R. Penrose in The British
     Journal of Psychology, February,
     1958)

174. Study for the lithograph
     "Waterfall," 1961
     Pencil 140×140 (5½×5½")

175. Study for the lithograph
     "Waterfall." 1961
     Pencil, 265×185 (10⅜×7⅜")

176. Study for the lithograph
     "Waterfall," 1961
     Pencil, 208×191 (8½×7½")

FIGURE 1.14(b)   Long after writing this analysis of paradoxical figures, I was astonished to come across Escher's preparatory drawings for *Waterfall*, in *The Infinite World of M.C. Escher* by M.C. Escher and J.L. Locher (New York: Abradale Press, 1984), which speak for themselves.

plants: the potash it contains can be used as fertilizer.

Besides the closed system axioms of thermodynamics, there is an open system principle, called in the early 1970s the 'fourth law': 'Left to itself matter-energy tends to become organized; wherever energy flows through an open system, organization results'. Drawing on H.J. Morowitz's *Energy Flow in Biology* (1968) and *Entropy for Biologists* (1970), Lewis Thomas (1974) explains this principle of negative entropy (increasing organization) in open systems far from equilibrium (in this case, sun, earth, and outer space):

> Morowitz has presented the case, in thermodynamic terms, for the hypothesis that a steady flow of energy from the [effectively] inexhaustible source of the sun to the unfillable sink of outer space, by way of the earth, is mathematically destined to cause the organization of matter into an increasingly ordered state. The resulting balancing act involves a ceaseless clustering of bonded atoms into molecules of higher and higher complexity, and the emergence of cycles for the storage and release of energy. In a non-equilibrium steady state, which is postulated, the solar energy would not just flow to the earth and radiate away; it is thermodynamically inevitable that it must rearrange matter into symmetry, away from probability, against entropy, lifting it, so to speak, into a constantly changing condition of rearrangement and molecular ornamentation.

Another interpretation of entropy relations as they apply to living systems, first put forward in the 1930s, is that information is order capable of creating new order (viz. the genetic code). Information is thus a form of negative entropy.

During the scientific revolution of the 1960s, new interpretations of the second axiom were independently recognized by a number of people involved in the study of cybernetics, open systems, communication, social organization, and ecology. The new views were given a rigorous base by Ilya Prigogine and the Brussels school of irreversible and non-equilibrium thermodynamics by the theory of 'dissipative structures' and 'order through fluctuation' (Prigogine and Stengers, 1979; Jantsch, 1980). As with organisms, societies, and other open systems, dissipative structures permit the systems in which they occur to export the entropy they create. Entropy does not increase in the open system; it increases in the system's environment.

(For an account of matter-energy oscillation in a chemical system far from equilibrium, see Epstein et al., 1983. This is a system of 'order through oscillation'.)

In open systems, organization may be maintained (as in the metabolism of organisms or in the economic subsistence of societies), or it may increase over time (as in the programmed development of the organism from embryo to adult, the non-programmed evolution of more complex species in nature, or the evolution of more complex societies in history).

In their ordinary activities, open systems depend on the principle of 'order from order': they import order from their environments (matter-energy and/or information), reorder it to maintain their own organization and their distinction from their environments, and export the resulting disorder as entropy.

Economic systems also depend on the principle of 'order through oscillation' (in the semiotic sense of information organizing matter-energy) (Chapters 3 and 4). In the evolution of a new species, or in a social and economic revolution (e.g. the capitalist revolution), the principle at work is 'order from disorder' (Wilden, 1987).

Return now to Escher's waterfall. To make legitimate statements about entropy, we have to define the closed boundaries of the system to which the statements apply. Let us assume for the moment that a waterfall is a closed system bounded by the top and bottom of the fall.

The waterfall exists because the water level above the fall contains 'potential energy', simply by virtue of its position in a gravity system. This potential energy can be made to do work by inserting suitable devices into the water flow. As the water falls, the 'free energy' (or relative order) available at the top is converted into 'bound energy' (or relative disorder) at the bottom.

(In reality, of course, the 'bound' energy at the bottom of the fall will be 'free' potential energy, capable of work, at any point farther downstream, until the river meets the sea.)

The quantity of energy in the closed waterfall system remains the same, but in this system as defined, it undergoes a change in quality: it changes from 'free' energy to 'bound' energy, from relative order to relative disorder, from a more organized state to a less organized state.

A waterfall is an example of a thermodynamic gradient, similar to the electrochemical gradient between the negative and positive poles of an electric battery. When this energy gradient is depleted, we say that the battery is 'dead'.

In a given system, disorder cannot be converted into new order without some new input of matter-energy or information (negative entropy). In the case of the battery, the relative disorder of a 'dead' battery can be converted into the relative order of a 'live' battery by recharging the cells. The charging unit, which uses electricity to rearrange the chemicals in the battery, is a source of negative entropy.

Note that 'disorder' is not equivalent to chaos. In keeping with the principle of order from order, we import into our bodies by eating the new order of matter-energy (principally carbohydrates) and information (principally proteins). We reorganize this new order as needed and excrete the disorder left over. But what is disorder for us is new order for other creatures, such as the micro-organisms that aid in the decomposition of organic materials.

The real river that supplies a real waterfall is an open system. The river continues to flow because of the input of new matter-energy via the weather, through the water cycle of the atmosphere, powered mainly by the sun and the rotation of the earth. The water in the river is constantly replenished by precipitation. For the river system, precipitation is an input of negative entropy.

The river system may well be open to new order, but the environment it depends on, the total system (sun, air, earth, and water), is effectively closed to new order. (The input of new matter-energy and/or information into the sun-earth system is not necessary to the system's survival.) Within the sun-earth system, in keeping with the second axiom of thermodynamics, positive entropy increases, principally in the sun.

The increase of entropy in the sun is irreversible. This is the same as saying that the increase of disorder in the sun is linked to the one-way flow of time for observers moving at velocities below the speed of light in this part of the cosmos. As Arthur Eddington put it in 1928, entropy is the arrow of time.

In Escher's *Waterfall*, however, time is paradoxical: it flows in opposite directions at the same time. When we follow the flow of water from top to bottom (from order to disorder), we are moving forward in time. When we follow the flow from bottom to top (from disorder to order), we are moving backwards in time. This we can do because of Escher's paradoxical organization of space in the strange loop. In Escher's machine, the water flows from the present through the future into the past and back into the present again.

Alternatively, we are moving back and forth between order and disorder, without introducing negative entropy into the system, which is impossible in reality. It is possible in the imaginary in *Waterfall* because negative entropy is supplied to the system by means of information, by the semiotic organization of the strange loop.

Isaac Asimov has recently drawn attention to one of the paradoxes inherent in going back in time (*It's About Time*, Nova, British Broadcasting Corporation/Public Broadcasting System, 1979). Assume that I can go back in time, he says, to before my own birth, and that once arrived in the past I shoot my father. The moment my father dies in the past, I of course disappear from both the past and the present. But the moment I disappear from the present, my father is restored to life in the past. The moment my father is brought back from the dead in the past, I arrive from the present and shoot him again . . . and so on, in a digital oscillation *ad infinitum*.

This oscillation is of course outside time. The father paradox makes an irreversible relation of 'before' and 'after' go round in a circle, which is impossible – so long as perpetual motion is impossible. Perpetual motion is impossible for several reasons, the most important of which are that it would contravene the first and second axioms of thermodynamics – which is why Escher's waterfall, like the perpetual motion of yin and yang, is possible in the imaginary but impossible in the real.

Escher's machine creates an imaginary symmetry between 'order' and 'disorder'. But – like 'free' and 'bound' energy, like 'organization' and 'disorganization', and like 'information' and 'noise' – order and disorder in any given system are not of the same logical type, or level of reality. By symmetrizing these two levels, Escher makes an irreversible entropy relation into a commutative, or reversible, relation.

The strange loop of Escher's watercourse is only circular if it remains outside time. If we introduce time into the system, and ignore turbulence in the water flow, the energy circuit becomes an analog oscillation, shaped like a sine curve, based on a collapsing of the distinction between order and disorder. This makes order and disorder into symmetrical and reversible opposites, producing a pattern of 'before' and 'after' like this:

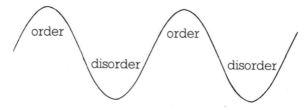

and so on, *ad infinitum*. This imaginary pattern is the same as that described by the analog oscillation between yin and yang over time.

Escher's explicit view of the order/disorder relation is however a very narrow one (Figure 1.15). In *Order and Chaos* (1950), order and disorder are presented as absolute, static, physical states, devoid of life, not as dynamic states relative to the system they are in. The broken social artefacts surrounding the crystal are not examples of chaos (a state not easily found in the cosmos); they are examples of disorder that can be recycled into new order. In equating order with the frozen and inanimate simplicity of a perfect crystal enclosed in a translucent sphere, Escher is more Greek than modern. (For Plato, as for Aristotle, perfection meant simplicity and lack of change.) The print tells us that Escher was unacquainted with the twentieth century 'revolt against simplicity' (the discovery of complexity).

In his *Universal Dictionary of Arts and Sciences* (second volume, 1710), John Harris explains the impossibility of one kind of perpetual

FIGURE 1.15 *Order and Chaos* by M.C. Escher, 1950. Other renderings of
the Dutch title, *Tegenstellung* ('placed in opposition'), are: in German,
Ordnung und Chaos and in French, *Contraste*. Beside the fact that neither
chaos in fact nor the supposed chaos in the print are absolute disorder, as
Escher makes them, order and disorder are not of the same logical type: they
cannot form an opposition or antithesis (at a single level), only a distinction or
a contradiction (between levels). Escher calls the crystal 'a symbol of order
and beauty'. A crystal is an example of organized simplicity or *organized
variety* (its constituent molecules are all of one kind of variety), which is a
basic state of matter often contrasted with the *unorganized variety* of the
molecules moving about in a gas. The order/disorder relationship we are most
concerned with, however, is the *organized diversity* of living systems, which is
utterly unlike the other two. (Two kinds of variety create one kind of
diversity; diversity is the basis of organized complexity (on complexity and
context theory, see Wilden, 1987, pp. 172–6, 309–13).

motion by the fact that frictionless motion is impossible. By perpetual motion is meant

> an uninterrupted Communication of the same degree of Motion from one part of Matter to another, in a Circle (or such like Curve returning unto it self) so that the same Quantity of Matter shall return perpetually undiminished upon the first mover . . . .

The proposers of perpetual motion machines, says Harris, could have saved time and reputation had they understood the implications of Newton's discoveries in mechanics:

> For, since by [Newton's] second Law of Nature or, Motion . . . the changes made in the Motions of Bodies are always proportional to the impress'd moving force, and are produced in the same direction with it, no Motion can be communicated to any Engine or Machine greater than that of the first force impressed . . .

On our earth, Harris continues, since

> all Motions are performed in a Fluid which resists them, it must of necessity retard them; and consequently a considerable quantity of the Motion must be spent upon the resisting *Medium*; so that it is impossible that the same Quantity of it can return undiminished on the first mover . . .

Another kind of perpetual motion and double bind is dealt with in the Celtic custom noted below. This is taken from *Credulities Past and Present*, by William Jones, F.S.A., a chronicler of popular lore, published by Chatto & Windus of London in 1880.

> The miners of Devon and Cornwall place great faith in the virtues of a horseshoe affixed to some of the erections of the mine to prevent witchcraft. It is supposed that the devil travels in circles, and is consequently interrupted when he arrives at either of the heels of the shoe, and is obliged to take a retrograde course.

The devil is in a perpetual double bind. The interruption of the circle produces an analog-digital oscillation. Later interpretation of this tradition say that it is 'bad luck', rather than the devil, that travels in circles.

Readers of a certain age will recall Joseph Heller's display of paradoxical injunctions in *Catch-22* (1955), before the publication of Bateson, Jackson, Haley, and Weakland's article on the double bind in 1956.

There is a paradoxical injunction about getting out of flying combat missions. You have to be crazy to keep flying into danger, says Doc Daneeka, but if you want to be grounded, first you have to ask. But asking to be relieved of combat is the act of a rational person.

Orr would be crazy to fly more missions and sane if he didn't, but if he was sane he had to fly them. If he flew them he was crazy and didn't have to; but if he didn't want to he was sane and had to. Yossarian was moved very deeply by the absolute simplicity of this clause of Catch-22 and let out a respectful whistle.

'That's some catch, that Catch-22' he observed.

'It's the best there is', Doc Daneeka agreed. Yosarian saw it clearly in all its spinning reasonableness. There was an elliptical precision about its perfect pairs of parts that was graceful and shocking, like good modern art, and at times Yossarian wasn't quite sure that he saw it at all. . . .

Looking again at the imaginary and elliptical precision of Escher's waterfall, we see that the background is distinct in texture and

FIGURE 1.16 Sign on sign, the classic double bind, based on a collapsing of levels of communication (a tangle in logical typing). If we accept that we must obey all signs, the act of obeying the sign makes us disobey it, which makes us obey it, an oscillation without end. The paradox results from the fact that the word 'this' refers to two levels of communication at the same time. It refers both to the sign and to the message carried by the sign. The way out of this double bind, like others, is to communicate about it. The simplest metacommunication would be to rip the sign off the wall — but this is implicitly forbidden by the authority behind the sign. If that authority is not contested, no escape is possible. Reprinted from: B. Kliban, *Tiny Foot Prints*.

intensity from that of the machine. This provides a clue to the puzzle Escher has set us. We have only to retrace the energy flow through the machine to see that the water flow does not pass through the machine's environment, the natural environment that permits us to design real water wheels to do real physical work. Escher's picture puzzle imposes an imaginary closed system, isolated from its environment (the figure), on a real open system in a real natural environment (the ground).

WAIVE, is a Woman that is Outlaw'd; and she is called *Waive*, as forsaken of the Law, and not an *Outlaw*, as a Man is; for Women are not sworn in Leets to the King, nor to the Law, as men are, who are therefore within the law; whereas Women are not, and for that cause they cannot be *Outlawed*, since they never were within it.
John Harris: *Lexicon Technicum: An Universal English Dictionary of Arts and Sciences* (1704).

1.10   Cruel and not so unusual punishment

We may return now to the role of symmetrization, inversion, oscillation, and paradox in human relations. Figure 1.17 is an example of pathological communication between the sexes, taken from *The Pragmatics of Human Communication* by Paul Watzlawick, Janet Beavin, and Don Jackson (1967, p. 57).

The explanation of the diagram is that the husband perceives only the triads 2-3-4, 4-5-6, 6-7-8, and so forth, so that he punctuates his behavior as 'merely' a response to the wife's behavior. With the wife, on the other hand, 'it is exactly the other way around'. She punctuates the sequence of events into the triads 1-2-3, 3-4-5, 5-6-7, and so on, so that she perceives her behavior as 'merely' a response to his.

The authors explain that the two conflicting punctuations of the relationship by husband and wife result in pathological communication. However, nothing is said about the framing of the relationship by the authors of the analysis. The framing of a relation constrains all the possible punctuations within the frame. Real frames permit real punctuations; imaginary frames produce imaginary punctuations.

The diagram and the explanation impose an imaginary frame on a real relation. The symmetrical oscillation depicted in Figure 1.17 is the result of collapsing a social contradiction between real levels of power into a paradox between imaginary opposites. This would not of course be the case if men and women really occupied positions of equality in the present social structure. But as long as they do not, then the 'equal

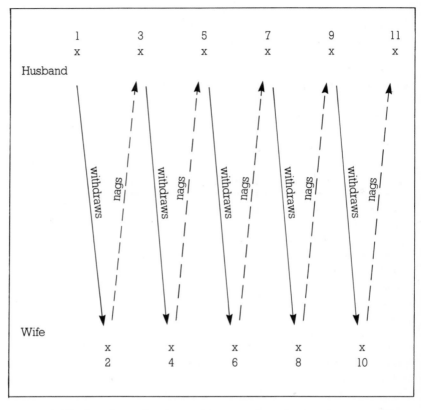

FIGURE 1.17   Imaginary framing and punctuation. An imaginary equality is drawn between 'withdraws' and 'nags', symmetrization becomes inversion. Failure to recognize the realities of the present power relation between the two sexes results in a double-bound oscillation, analog between thresholds, digital at each threshold. Without reframing in the real, the oscillation is unending. It could be represented in another topology by a Thomian cusp catastrophe. Reprinted from: Watzlawick, Beavin, and Jackson, *The Pragmatics of Human Communication* (1967).

and opposite interaction' of husband and wife, as depicted here, is not a scientific analysis, but a repetition of the imaginary status men and women occupy in the dominant ideology.

As long as the two communicants are depicted as social equals, and as long as 'nags' is made to equal 'withdraws', then the real contradiction and conflict between two levels of power is reduced to an imaginary and paradoxical opposition in which no valid judgments about responsibility can be made. Each participant will feel double bound by the other. The resulting oscillation between thresholds of irritation or worse, an oscillation requiring the participation of both, will remain insoluble until the relationship is correctly framed and perceived as such by both wife and husband.

In a society based on illegitimate hierarchies, responsibility for framings and punctuations is not equal and opposite in individuals. Responsibility in any given context is a function of the power to be responsible. The more power, the more responsibility.

This is not to deny responsibility to the woman, but rather to note the male responsibility for framing this pathological communication between marriage 'partners' in such a way that no matter how she tries, and whether in any circumstance she is right or wrong, the woman cannot reach the truth of the relation. For the woman, contesting the male punctuation gets her nowhere. What she must contest is the framing of the relation. It is the frame, not the punctuation, that collapses the real power relation into the two 'equal and opposite sides' of a paradoxical relation. This paradox cannot be resolved as long as the frame that creates and maintains it is accepted as unalterable and real.

This collapsing of a social contradiction into the two 'sides' of a paradox is of course another example of a strange loop or tangled hierarchy. But the tangled hierarchy in the zigzags of Figure 1.17 is in fact more tangled than it at first appears to be. The first tangle is a matter of outward structure (the framing of the relation); the error is symmetrization. The second tangle is a matter of inward structure (the framing of the content); the error is inversion. The result is oscillation between symmetrization and inversion.

The verb 'nags' provides the clue. This is a derogatory term for a mainly male activity that, like 'promiscuity', is (still) applied almost exclusively to women. Nagging and withdrawing are not symmetrical. A nagger is an aggressor, a withdrawer is a defender. The inversion projects the 'real' responsibility for the insanity on to the 'nagging' woman, identified as the active attacker, while the man's real role is hidden behind the passive action of 'withdrawing'.

Whereas in fact most men are highly accomplished naggers, they are almost never identified as such. Women, however, are commonly called 'nags' or 'shrews', and men long ago invented a technology to punish them for this supposedly female activity. One device, invented many hundreds of years ago, along with the equally barbaric pillory, is the 'ducking stool' for 'scolds' and 'witches', an instrument of torture based on 'half-drowning', a technique still used by fascist armies, police forces, and governments today (Figure 1.18).

Another device is the brank, the 'Scold's Bridle', or 'Gossip's Bridle'. According to an article of 1894 in the liberal journal, *The Strand Magazine*, these devices were in very general use in England and

FIGURE 1.18   The ducking stool, from R. Chambers' *Book of Days* (London and Edinburgh, 1876). Benjamin Vincent notes in the 19th edition of *Haydn's Dictionary of Dates and Universal Information* (London, New York, and Melbourne, 1889) that on September 4, 1863 'a poor old paralysed Frenchman died in consequence of having been ducked as a wizard at Castle Hedingham, Essex, and similar cases have since occurred'.

Scotland from the sixteenth to the eighteenth centuries. Figure 1.19 reproduces some examples. The brank

> was armed in front with a gag, plate, point or knife [of iron], which was fitted in such a manner as to be inserted in the scold's mouth so as to prevent her moving her tongue; or, more cruel still, it was so placed that if she did move it, or attempt to speak, her tongue was cruelly lacerated, and her sufferings intensified. With this cage upon her head, and with the gag pressed and locked upon the tongue, the poor creature was paraded through the streets, led by the beadle or constable, or else she was chained to the pillory or market cross to be the object of scorn and derision, and to be subjected to all the insults and degradations that local loungers could invent.

Although frequently mentioned in literature, it appears that the bridle, which might be used against any woman speaking out of place, was never a legalized means of punishment. Nevertheless, the brank was highly popular with local magnates,

> and was one of the means upon which arch-tyrants of provincial towns relied to sustain their power and hold the humbler folk in subjection. By it authority was preserved and vindicated at the expense of all that was noble, seemly, and just.

The democratic radicalism of that last paragraph is refreshing and remarkable. Not many Victorians understood that oppression by sex is intimately bound up with oppression by class.

A clash of doctrines is not a disaster – it is an opportunity.
                          Alfred North Whitehead (1861–1947)

1.11 Equality and identity: The riddle of the sexes

The relations between the sexes are both personal and collective, both social and sexual, both political and economic. But since the invention of the modern concept of equality by the rising bourgeoisie in the seventeenth century, the idea of equality between the sexes has been a paradox tangled in symmetrizations and inversions. The evidence is that most men and women consciously or unconsciously confuse equality between the sexes with identity between the sexes.

When 'equality = identity', then 'being equal' comes to mean 'being the same'. This imaginary starting point gives rise to arguments based on strange loops:

> Women are not the same as men.
> Women demand equal rights with men.
> This means women 'really' want to be the same as men.
> For men, being the same as men means being dominant over the other sex.
> Therefore women want to replace male tyranny by female tyranny.
> Therefore we must continue to keep women in their place.

Replace 'women' by 'non-white' or 'working class', and replace 'men' by 'white' or 'upper class' – the argument against equality remains the same.

One final example of symmetrization and paradox between the

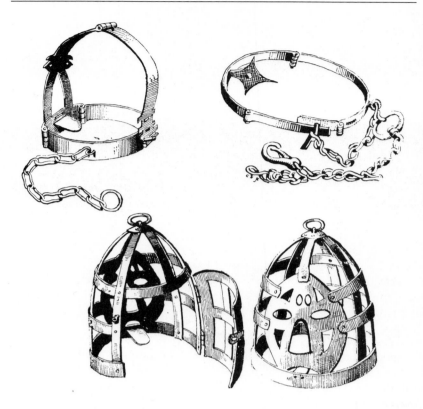

FIGURE 1.19   The Brank, or Scold's Bridle, or Gossip's Bridle, in general use in England and Scotland from the sixteenth to the eighteenth centuries. The top left example dates from 1688. The top right example (with the three-pointed knife), called the 'Witches' Brank', works on the principle of the choke chain. Throughout Europe between the fourteenth and seventeenth centuries, many thousands of 'witches', usually peasants but also the wealthy, were tortured to death by burning or strangled by hanging. It is estimated that 85 per cent of the victims were women (often midwives and nurses). The woodcut on p. 53, labeled 'a scold gagged', is taken from *Columbus and Columbia* (Richmond, Virginia, 1892), where it is used to illustrate an account of the struggle between the liberal theologian, feminist, and preacher Anne Hutchinson (1591–1643) and the Puritans of Boston, who expelled her and her allies from the Colony in 1638. She founded a 'woman's republic' in what later became Rhode Island, but in 1643 she and most of her household were killed by Indians.

sexes. Figure 1.20 is taken from R.D. Laing's *Knots* (1970, p. 52). Laing reduces the real hierarchy of power presently existing between

'Jack' and 'Jill' to a single level. As in the imaginary framing and punctuation of 'nags/withdraws' in Figure 1.17, this operation confuses the logical typing of power. The result is yet another eternal circle, and yet another kind of fatalism and determinism. Here the symmetrization and 'subordinate equality' implied by the diagram depends on at least one common paradox: 'My woman (girl, wife) and I are equals' (Figure 1.21).

Laing's circle is another isolated system, and another perpetual motion machine. If we follow the strange loop of the circuit of information in this tangled hierarchy, just as we followed the circular path of energy in Escher's machine, we see that the circuit of communication between Jack and Jill does not pass through the environment of information in which they really live, the environment of social relations. Like the zigzag diagram from the *Pragmatics*, this diagram is an imaginary system used to frame, and then to mystify, a real relation.

The logical structure of Laing's circular argument between the 'two sides of the question' can be compared to the topological structure of a Moebius strip (Figure 1.22). You can pick up a Moebius strip between your fingers, you can see and feel the two sides you are grasping, but when you follow the strip around its strange loop, you find that it has only one edge and only one side.

All successful men have agreed on one thing – they were *causationists* . . . The biggest thing in the world is the law of action and reaction, namely that for every action there is an equal and opposite reaction.

Ralph Waldo Emerson: *What is Success?* (1870)

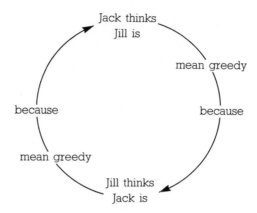

FIGURE 1.20   A tangled contradiction, both collective and individual, depicted as a wheel. As the relationship between Jack and Jill moves through time, the path of the collapsed contradiction becomes an oscillation. Like others of its kind, the strange loop concealed in this circular argument can be illustrated by a Moebius strip (Figure 1.22). Reprinted from: R.D. Laing: *Knots* (1970).

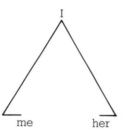

FIGURE 1.21   'My wife and I are equals': 'I' mediates between 'me' and 'her'.

1.12   The myth of Sisyphus

In *Le mythe de Sisyphe*, published in 1942, the writer Albert Camus (1913–60) asserted that there is only one really important philosophical problem: suicide.

> Beginning to think is beginning to undermine one's existence. Society has little to do with these beginnings. The worm is in the heart of man, and that is where we must look. This deadly game that leads from lucidity in the face of existence to escape from light has to be traced and understood.
>   . . . Dying voluntarily supposes that a person has recognized, even instinctively, the ridiculous character of daily habit, the absence of any deep reason for living, the insane and ridiculous character of our daily activities, and the uselessness of suffering (pp. 17, 18).

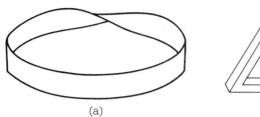
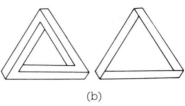

(a)   (b)

FIGURE 1.22 (a) The Moebius strip, a topological figure invented by Augustus Moebius (1790–1868). To construct it, take a length of paper, give it a 180° twist, and join the ends together. The strip is seen and felt to have two sides and two edges. In fact it has one continuous side and one continuous edge. If you cut around the middle of the strip, it becomes a large two-sided strip. If you cut along a line one third of the way in from the edge, your scissors make two complete trips in a single continuous cut. The result is two strips intertwined: one two-sided strip and a new Moebius strip.

(b) The Penrose triangle (Figure 1.13) viewed as a flattened Moebius strip with three half twists, as suggested by Patrick Hughes and George Brecht in *Vicious Circles and Infinity* (1975).

Camus went on to use the Greek myth of Sisyphus – an oscillation between absurdities – to justify a fatalist and defeatist philosophy, the 'philosophy of the absurd'.

To be able to view life as absurd is an unusual privilege. The real problem is not suicide and absurdity, but torture. Every kind of torture imagined in every kind of hell has been used and is being used on human beings by those with the power to decide who shall be the victims. The people being tortured are men, women, and children; the leading torturers and their rank and file are men. Under torture you can be put to death, but you cannot commit suicide.

Sisyphus, said to have been a king of Corinth and the father of Odysseus, was punished by the gods for playing tricks on Death. Once they had him in their power in Hades, he was forced repeatedly to roll a huge rock up a hill only to have it always roll down again as soon as he reached the summit.

Sisyphus is one of the 'tricksters' of popular mythology, a heroic rascal and radical like Prometheus. Sisyphus beat the gods at their own game until he was crushed by Ares, the god of war. The gods then condemned him to the one torture they considered most suitable for an upstart strategist of lively mind. They subjected him to an unending oscillation between the useless travail of bending to the rock and the absurdity of walking back down the hill to roll it up again. The hill is presumably just the right height to ensure that when

Sisyphus reaches the bottom, he is well enough recovered to start the next session. Had he been enlisted in the British Army, they would have made him run.

The torture sessions in George Orwell's equally defeatist *Nineteen-Eighty-Four* were the last word on the subject when the book was published in 1949. The torturer O'Brien threatens the rebel Winston with the one torture he is most afraid of, having a trapped and hungry rat burrow into his body. (According to Frank Terpil, the well-known mercenary, this is still the ultimate method.) O'Brian tells Winston that when he does submit to the Party, his conversion must be of his own free will (a double bind). Faced with the rat, Winston is converted: he betrays his friend. O'Brien stops the torture. Today the victims willingly submit, but the torture goes on and on.

The ancient and modern technology of torture, as depicted in the stereoscope cards from the 1890s in Figure 1.24, reminds us that the Greek Hades inhabited by Sisyphus is nothing compared to the Christian Hell. The idea of perpetual torment for sinners, heretics, and

EXCELSIOR!

SUFFRAGIST. "It's no good talking to me about Sisyphus; he was only a man!"

(*July 13, 1910*)

FIGURE 1.23 'He was only a man!': A modern reading of the myth of Sisyphus. This cartoon was published in *Punch* on July 13, 1910. Women were granted partial suffrage in Britain in 1918, full suffrage ten years later.

unbelievers in Hell is in fact a religious justification of the use of torture here on earth.

We see that information is *created* when a choice is made, but to be able to choose, one must be free to be a revolutionary. Therefore, an epistemology [a way of knowing] is a political issue.

Heinz von Foerster: 'Epistemology of Communication' (1980)

FIGURE 1.24 *The Last Judgment* and *Torture in Hell*. French stereoscope cards from the 1890s. The stereoscope was an immensely popular medium of amusement and general knowledge between the 1860s and the 1930s.

Postscript

We are far from having exhausted the topic of icons and oscillations – for the topic also includes the long- and short-term business cycles, as well as ecological, cybernetic, social, individual and other oscillations (for earlier outlines, see Wilden and Wilson, 1976; Wilden, 1980a, pp. 159–60, 174–8, 507–8). The topic is taken up again in Chapters 3 and 4.

We must make a distinction between *mass-energy oscillations* – such as pendulums, electric flip-flop circuits, buzzers, AC current, electromagnetic waves, the electrochemical propagation of signals in the central nervous system, and so on – and oscillations generated and sustained by information – such as cybernetic oscillations (governors, thermostats, autopilots, the self-steering wind vane), ecological oscillations (prey-predator cycles), psychological oscillations (manic-depressive cycles), logical paradoxes, psychological paradoxes and double binds, economic boom- and bust cycles, and so on – which I shall call *semiotic oscillations*.

One major conclusion follows from the study and analysis of contradiction and paradox to this point. Conflicts of race, class, and sex occur in many societies. But in social systems adapted to long-range survival, there is no contradiction, no conflict between society and nature. In contrast, under state and private capitalism, East and West, besides the other conflicts, now more acute than ever, there is also a contradiction and conflict between society and nature.

By way of confusion and concealment, it would appear, and using the technique of Edgar Allen Poe's detective story *The Purloined Letter* (the letter is hidden in plain sight), the dominant ideas and images of our system collapse all these real contradictions into either/or, imaginary, and paradoxical oppositions:

> 'society, as opposed to nature'
> 'business, as opposed to labor'
> 'white, as opposed to non-white'
> 'man, as opposed to woman'.

The present and basic crisis at the heart of capitalism appears to be a complex set of paradoxes between overproduction and war, unemployment and inflation, and production and pollution. Ever more clearly, the basic problem seems to be that state and private capitalism has created for itself a global double bind. This is a double bind between the unconstrained and quantitative growth it needs to maintain its precarious stability, and the entropic constraints on growth and pollution to which it is inevitably subjected by the requirements of long-range survival in a limited environment.

FIGURE 1.25   No oscillation here. The poster is from 1969. Reprinted from: Gary Yanker. *Prop Art* (1972).

APPENDIX A: HORRIBLE EFFECTS OF UNNATURAL CUSTOMS

> How quaint the ways of paradox –
> At common sense she gaily mocks.
>   W.S. Gilbert (1836–1911)

On the inversion of the relations between the sexes, and the question of equality and identity (Section 1.11 above), the following is the earliest modern illustration I have found. It is taken from a story by Nicholas Klimius, *A Journey to the World Under Ground*, published in about 1720. Klimius was Louis, Baron de Holbert, born in Bergen, Norway, in 1684, died 1754. The English text is from a Latin translation of the Danish original. Printed together with Jonathan Swift's *Gulliver's Travels* (1726) and Daniel Defoe's *Robinson Crusoe* (1719), the story was republished in Edinburgh in 1812, in a book called *Popular Romances: Imaginary Voyages and Travels* (pp. 115–200).

The hero travels between different countries and provinces of the world under ground. All the inhabitants are trees.

In the province of Cokclecu there is a very perverse custom. . . . The order of things is indeed inverted, but the fault is not owing to nature, but solely to the laws. . . . The males alone perform the drudgery of the kitchen, and every such ignoble labour. In time of war, indeed, they serve their country, but rarely rise above the rank of common soldier. . . . The females, on the other hand, are in possession of all honours and employments, sacred, civil, or military. I had lately derided the Potuans [in their province] for observing no difference of sex in the distribution of public offices, but that was nothing to the frenzy of this people. I could not conceive the meaning of so much indolence in the males, who, though of a far superior strength of body, could yet so tamely submit to such a yoke, and for ages together digest such an ignominy. . . . But long and ancient custom had so blinded them, that none ever thought of attempting to remove such a disgrace, but quietly believed it was nature's appointment that the government should be lodged in female hands, and that it was the business of the other sex to spin, to weave, to clean the house, and, upon occasion, to take a beating from their wives. The arguments by which the ladies justified this custom were these, that as nature had furnished the males with greater strength of body, her intention in that could only be to destine them to the more laborious and servile duties of life. . . .

Horrible were the effects of this unnatural custom: For as in other countries there are abandoned women, who prostitute themselves for hire, so here the young men sell their favours. . . . When the men drive this wicked trade with too great effrontery, and in too barefaced a manner, they are had to prison, and whipped like our street-walkers. On the other hand, the matrons and virgins here, without the least reproach, can prowl up and down, gaze at the young fellows, nod, whistle, tip the wink, pluck them by the sleeve, importune them, write love-verses upon their doors, boast of their conquests, and reckon up their gallantries with as much satisfaction as the fine gentlemen of our world entertain you with their amours. . . . There was, at the time I was there, a mighty disturbance about a noble youth, the son of a senator, who had been ravished by a young woman. . . . Upon my leaving the city, I told several that these [people] acted in downright contradiction to nature, since, from the universal voice and consent of nations, it was evident that males alone were formed for all the arduous and important affairs of life. To this they replied, that I confounded custom with nature, since the weakness we impute to the female sex is derived solely from education. This is clear from the form of government established at Cocklecu, where in that sex you find all the virtues and large endowments of mind, which the masculine sex in other places arrogate to themselves. For the Cocklecuanian women are grave, prudent, constant, and secret. The men, on the contrary, are light, empty, frothy creatures.

The stereoscope cards in Figure 1.26 are crude examples of role inversion between male and female, popular images from the Age of the New Woman at the close of the nineteenth century, during the economic boom following the depression of 1873–96. The boom led into World War I and to greater rights for women after the war, as a result of their skilled and patient contributions to the war effort.

APPENDIX B: TWO BY TWO

What we call Man's power over nature turns out to be a power exercised by some men over other men with Nature as its instrument.

C.S. Lewis: *The Abolition of Man* (1946)

In *Opposition* (1932, 1967), the writer, linguist, and inventor of Basic English, C.K. Ogden (1889–1957), who was with I.A. Richards the author of *The Meaning of Meaning* (1923), gives the following list of 'the sort of words' that can be said to have opposites 'in the ordinary sense of the term'. He calls them 'common pairs' (p. 53):

1 black and white	14 possible and impossible
2 hot and cold	15 kind and unkind
3 open and shut	16 good and bad
4 ruler and ruled	17 work and play
5 hard and soft	18 ill and well
6 right and left	19 easy and difficult
7 man and brute	20 before and after
8 up and down	21 male and female
9 acid and alkali	22 love and hate
10 pleasure and pain	23 British and alien
11 visible and invisible	24 red and green
12 town and country	25 normal and abnormal
13 learned and ignorant	

Ogden recognizes some of the difficulties, noting that the 'opposites' man and brute, town and country, and male and female 'raise questions of a verbal nature', and that red and green are seen by some as the most fundamental of oppositions, and by others summarily rejected as not an opposition at all (the latter are right). He adds:

At all points the nature of Negation proves hardly less puzzling to the practical mind than the vagaries of linguistic usage. Why is 'not-

11923. Have lunch ready at one, Charley.

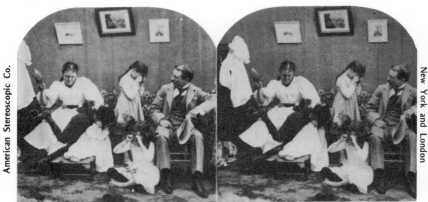

Home, Sweet Home Copyright 1896 by R.Y. Young

(18) SUBJUGATION — There's no place like home!
Copyright 1901, by Underwood & Underwood.

FIGURE 1.26 The New Woman, 1900: Three crude examples of role inversion and the male confusion of equality with identity, from turn-of-the-century stereoscope cards. The card labeled, 'Subjugation', carries its message in French, German, Spanish, Dutch, and Russian (on the back).

white' so unsatisfactory to deal with, while 'not-visible' or invisible readily recommends itself as the opposite of 'visible'?

From the arguments already advanced, it can be seen that most of these 'oppositions' are in fact distinctions which *may* under some circumstances be classed as opposites: right and left, red and green (traffic lights), open and shut, black and white. Others cannot be opposites at all because their two parts are not of the same logical type or level of reality: ruler and ruled, man and brute, town and country, and (at present) work and play. Certain of them are natural hierarchies in which the second is the environment of the first: man and brute (i.e. man and nature), ill and well, and before and after. A number of them are illegitimate power hierarchies: ruler and ruled, and (in present circumstances) town and country, learned and ignorant, male and female. 'British and alien' is of course too good to be true.

The binary and imaginary opposites listed below – they are equally imaginary unities or identities of opposites also, if you like – have strategic ideological value in modern society as presently structured.

organism	environment
society	nature
individual	society
self	others
mind	body
reason	emotion
conscious	unconscious
government	people
'civilized'	'primitive'
white	non-white
capital	labor
man	woman
colonizer	colonized
system	environment

The two 'sides' of these imaginary opposites are not of the same level of reality or logical type: the second is the environment of the first: they form a dependent hierarchy (cf. Wilden, 1980b, pp. 221–2).

It might be correctly objected that 'woman' is not truly or necessarily the environment of 'man', for each sex is ultimately the reciprocal environment of the other. That would be true in a human society, but in our present system, whoever has the power to be defined as 'organism' or 'system' exploits whatever he defines as 'environment', just as white exploits non-white, owner or manager exploits worker, and colonizer exploits colonized. In this sense woman is at present the environment of man and not the other way around.

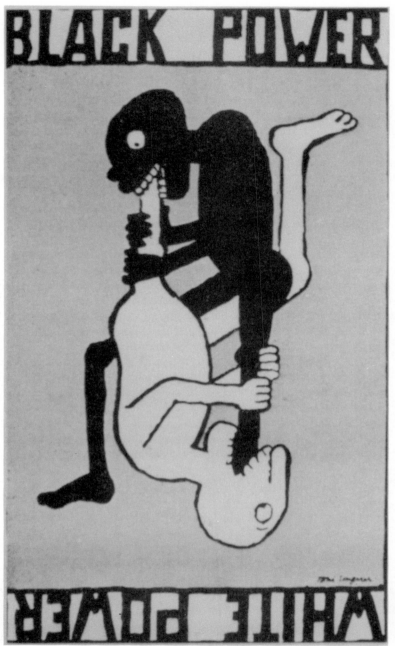

FIGURE 1.27 Black and white: An imaginary symmetrization of the real hierarchy of power between white (racism) and black (survival), followed by inversion of the imaginary opposites (black over white). The poster is by Tomi Ungerer (late 1960s). Reprinted from: Edward Booth-Clibborn and Daniel Baroni: *The Language of Graphics* (1979).

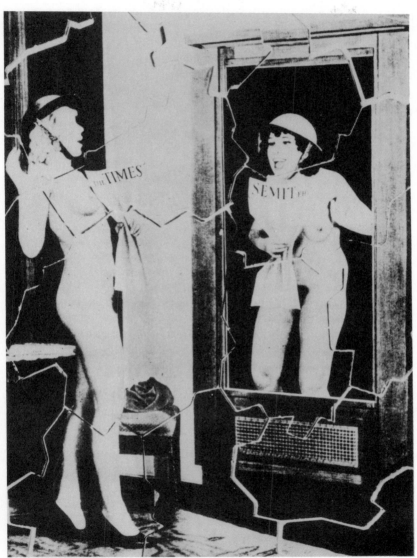

FIGURE 1.28 An imaginary identity of opposites: Anti-Semitic German jigsaw puzzle from World War II. Reprinted from: Ken Baynes: *Art and Society One: War* (1970).

In Western ideology Nature is traditionally feminine. The novel seventeenth-century ideal of 'man's conquest of nature' (a goal both imaginary and impossible) is often expressed in images of bondage, sexual servitude, and assault. In 1603, in *The Masculine Birth of Time, Or the Great Instauration of the Dominion of Man over the Universe*, Sir Francis Bacon, champion of modern science and inventor of the research grant, put it in these words:

> I am come in truth leading to you Nature with all her children to
> bind her to your service and make her your slave.

Bacon described modern science as 'putting Nature to the question' – as using torture to obtain the truth. The social Darwinist William Graham Sumner put it in another way in 1883, in *What the Social Classes Owe to Each Other*, as quoted by Richard Hofstadter in *Social Darwinism in American Thought* (1947):

> Nature is entirely neutral; she submits to him that most
> energetically and resolutely assails her. She grants her rewards to the
> fittest.

In this sense, woman – as 'body' – is the environment that man – as 'mind' – depends on for his daily comfort, emotional support, sexual needs, and above all for his existence as a supposedly 'manly' man. And just as 'body' is viewed as the property of 'mind', so too is woman viewed as the property of man.

CHAPTER 2

Competition and co-operation in logic and in life

The conditions of life are neither in the organism nor in the outer environment, but in both at once. Indeed, if we absolutely isolate a body in our thought, we annihilate it in so doing; and if, on the contrary, we multiply its relations with the outer world, we multiply its properties.

Claude Bernard: *Introduction à la médecine expérimentale* (1865)

2.1 The mother of gardens

When the Montagnais-Laskapi of the Labrador plateau north of Quebec need an answer to an important question, they employ divination by burnt animal bones, a custom found in many parts of the world, and for them the center of their religion and way of life.

When it is a matter of finding game, especially in times of scarcity, these semi-nomadic hunters use the bones of animals on the ancient principle of correspondence or 'like knows like': beaver bones for beaver, fish jaws for fish, and so on. The caribou shoulder blade is said to be particularly 'truthful'. The bone is boiled, cleaned, and dried, then held over hot coals until cracks and burns appear. It is then given a specific orientation in relation to the topography of the local environment – like a symbolic chart of the territory they share with nature – and the burns and cracks are consulted for the best direction to take on the next day's hunt.

(In Chinese divination the picture signs scratched on burnt 'oracle bones' – questions asked by aristocrats of their ancestors – led to the invention of ideographic writing (Chou 1979). By about 4000 BCE some 40 characters existed, mostly numerals or clan names, selected and combined in groups of no more than three. By 1000 BCE, under the Shang dynasty, when China first became a world power, some 4000 characters existed – there are 50,000 now – these being selected and combined in inscriptions of ten to fifteen characters, or at most fifty characters, in two or three sentences.)

Quoting the work of F.G. Speck in the 1930s, Omar Khayyam Moore (1965) explains that Montagnais-Laskapi divination begins with dreaming, induced by a sweat bath, and by drumming or shaking a rattle, followed by chanting. When the dream of game makes itself visible the dreamer uses the signs of the burnt blade, according to a traditional code of map-reading, to 'clear up' the indistinct nature of the dream and to take note of the indicated landmarks and directions.

This rite has a precise ecological and economic function, as Moore's analysis reveals. It is difficult for human beings to avoid following regular patterns of behavior, and regular patterns are not the best strategy for hunting. The rite of divination introduces a (relatively) random search strategy into the relationship between the hunters and their game. As a result the hunters avoid visiting the same areas again and again, which makes game too sensitive to humans, and especially in hard times, may result in the 'success-induced failure' of overhunting and the depletion of a vital resource. Thus the apparently magical nature of this system of making decisions is in fact a rational way — unconsciously co-evolved over hundreds of years and proven 'true' by nature — of maintaining a literally 'co-operative' and both-and relationship between predator and prey, the necessary condition for the long-range survival of both.

During the dry season the men of the Hadza tribe living in the desert-like savannah of what is now Tanzania in East Africa spend more time gambling with their metal-tipped arrowheads, the kind they use against big game, than they do in hunting (Woodburn, 1968). (Arrowheads suitable for small game are not so used.) The result is that losers of metal-tipped arrowheads are effectively removed from economic production, which tends to conserve big game.

Significantly enough, the Eastern Hadza, unwilling to give up the leisure and freedom of the hunter-gatherer's life, even in desert areas, have until recently refused to take up agriculture. The results, they say, are not worth the extra work.

(The 'neolithic or new stone age revolution' about 10,000 years ago, led to the invention of agriculture, probably by women, as well as to the domestication of animals. This entailed a massive intensification of economic production. Between 8000 and 4000 BCE in the Middle East, the population increased forty times — why we do not know (Harris, 1977, p. 43). In the fertile crescent of the Tigris-Euphrates valley of Mesopotamia, the large economic surpluses produced by more people doing more work more of the time with more technology (including the plough and irrigation) led to the emergence of the state: a class-based society of kings, lords, and peasants (often serfs), managed by priests and other specialists (who also controlled the media), along with slaves, laborers, artisans, and merchants.)

Even in the Kalahari desert in southern Africa, one of the least inviting environments in the world, Bushmen hunter-gatherers not corrupted by white colonialism live not in poverty, but in 'affluence without abundance', as Marshall Sahlins put it in his *Stone Age Economics* (p. 11) in 1972. Sahlins argued persuasively that stone age societies and the stone age itself represent leisure and affluence, not the popular ideological view of abject poverty, a so-called 'subsistence economy', and an eternal 'struggle for existence'.

Excluding the women's labor expended in cooking and rearing children, the Hadza work on the average about two hours a day gathering food; the Hawaiians, the Kuikuru of Brazil, and the Bemba (a centralized African chiefdom in Zambia, Zaire, and Zimbabwe), about four hours (in season); and the !Kung Bushmen and the Kapauku of the eastern New Guinea Highlands, perhaps six hours a day (Sahlins, 1972, p. 56).

(It is estimated that the medieval year in Europe included only about 240 actual working days. In the Bavarian mines there were in the sixteenth century between 99 and 190 holidays every year. Taking holidays into account, it is estimated that European miners in the fifteenth century worked about 35 hours a week. In the early nineteenth century, in contrast, men, women, and children worked 13 or 14 hours a day or between 75 and 80 hours a week for subsistence and often starvation wages in British and European sweatshops, factories, and coalpits, and the worker's prayer was the 10-hour day (Mandel, 1962). A century later, the plight of the nineteenth-century laboring poor, where it has not been exported via the world market into Third World countries, is generally reserved for non-whites, farm workers, women in domestic service, and foreigners.)

Hunter-gatherer societies are among the most egalitarian of all societies. Among long-settled agricultural village dwellers, in contrast, the social structure may depend on the labor of slaves, or serfs, or a class of working commoners, not to mention women, for its continuing existence.

And hunter-gatherers are egalitarian only between men. Here too, and in spite of their considerable social power, women are considered to be physically and mentally inferior to men – and by long experience of that status, they come to believe it too – and by being raised to act inferior they seem to prove it true. Men (the men say) are better or worse than other men because of what they do. Women, however (say the men), are inferior because of what they are – guilty of being women, guilty of not being men – and for that they have only themselves to blame.

Blaming the victims justifies the original male coercion and the continuance of male control. In almost all societies, including our own, the most effective medium of this coercion and control is work, woman's work, the hardest work of all: physical, emotional, and mental labor supporting society by supporting the social superiority of men.

Not much has changed over the centuries; in fact matters seem to be getting worse. The *New Internationalist* reported in November 1983 that according to the United Nations, women do 66 per cent of all the work in the world but receive only 10 per cent of the income.

Most band and village societies not disintegrated by colonialism, wage labor, or cash cropping, work far less than they might if they chose to. Estimates of the number of people that a given society's labor and technology (and the carrying capacity of its environment) could potentially support, as compared with the population they actually do support, show that many 'slash-and-burn' cultivators deliberately underuse their productive capacity (Table 2.1).

The underuse of available resources in these societies – and the consequent protection of the habitat from exploitation – is intimately connected with the role of kinship and the family. Loosely understood to include large and small nuclear and extended families, the household and its members are to the tribal economy what the manor and its serfs were to the feudal economy or the corporation and its employees are to the capitalist economy. Each is the dominant institution in its particular mode of production (Sahlins, 1972, p. 76).

The role of the family as the unit of production in most band and village societies means that young people do not become fully part of

Society	Actual production as a percentage of potential production
Naregu Chimbu (New Guinea)	64 per cent
Tsembaga (Maring) (New Guinea)	55–65
Yagaw Hanunoo (Philippines)	63
Lamet (Laos)	20–25
Iban (Borneo)	50–66
Kuikuru (Brazil)	7
Ndembu (Zambia)	8–19
W. Lala (Zambia)	>75
Swaka (Zambia)	>40
Dogomba (Ghana)	42–100

Table 2.1   The underuse of productive capacity by slash-and-burn cultivators (data assembled by Sahlins, 1972, pp. 44–5). (The last three figures are more approximate than the others. Information on several African populations confined to reserves or otherwise disturbed by colonialism shows them to be over the capacity of the traditional system. These have been excluded.)

the economic system until they marry, and marriage is often delayed. The result is that underproduction, protection of the environment, and considerable leisure time become structural features of the economic organization of these societies.

Among the cattle-raising Maasai of East Africa, for instance, the young men train as athletes, warriors, lion hunters, dandies, and local stars, living in 'brotherhoods', and not marrying before the age of 25. !Kung women marry between 15 and 20: !Kung men about five years later. Among the Lele of the Congo region, a class and caste society of nobles and commoners, with rainforest Pygmies in semi-servile dependency as well, polygyny permits the older men to monopolize the young women, with the result that the young men have to wait. The associated result is that a Lele man begins work late in life and retires early, working in all little more than twenty years (Sahlins, 1972, p. 52).

(The Lele also practice a form of polyandry, but this follows from the elders' monopoly of women; it is not an equalization of sexual roles. A girl becomes the 'wife of the village' for several months, during which any man of the village has the right to have sex with her. After this she becomes the common wife for unmarried men and finally, as these men marry, she becomes the sole wife of the last unmarried man of that group.)

In the other societies, people work with tools; in our society, tools – machines – work with people. And as Sahlins points out (p. 81), a stone age society with the same proportion of poorly educated and unskilled labor as our society produces would soon become extinct.

Notably since the two complementary revolutions in anthropology in the 1960s – the French-speaking revolution being largely 'structural', formalist, abstract, and context-free, and its English-speaking equivalent being largely 'systemic', ecological, concrete, and context-dependent – alert ethnographers have realized that many and probably most societies of hunter-gatherers lack any concept of ownership comparable to our own. Acting as stewards of their territory, and thus using it rather than 'exploiting' it, they lack the concepts of dominion over nature and the private property of the means of production (this Marvin Harris noted in 1971 (p. 300) was a 'most startling discovery'). In many such societies even personal property (a tool, weapon, ornament) is constantly loaned, borrowed, handed round, or given away, and the concept of individualistic possession itself – with the probable exception of control over women – rarely exists.

With the exception of peoples living in highly provident environments, such as the Indians of the Pacific Northwest, the real wealth – the way of life – and the long-range survival of hunter-gatherers, the most egalitarian of societies, is based on mobility: possessions one has to care for and carry about can be dangerous. Accumulation of goods or storage of food might lead to staying too long in one place, possibly depleting or overloading the local habitat. Ecological conditions for hunter-gatherers thus favor cheerful, carefree, temperate, and (we would think) improvident (and even lazy) peoples, prepared if necessary to go hungry for days at a time, but whose supreme confidence that 'nature will provide', even in times of drought, is the product of many years of real experience.

(This does not apply to populations whose economic structure has been destroyed by wage labor, cash-cropping, or the drilling of wells, as in the case of the many thousands of pastoralists and others who died in the recent and recurring droughts in Africa.)

It is not that these diverse hunters have suppressed or given up some 'natural' desire 'imprinted' in so-called 'human nature', some biological 'urge' to obtain and accumulate personal possessions or private property, for this 'natural' desire simply does not exist. As the philosopher Helvétius said in *De l'Esprit* in 1759:

> Men are born neither good nor bad but ready to be one or the other according to the way they are united or divided by common interest.

The modern desire to possess property is not a product of the genes or heredity or human nature or biology or sociobiology or territoriality; it is a product of modern education, indoctrination, alienation, and insecurity.

(The European doctrine that human desires are inherently infinite and insatiable was the result of the invention of the uniquely modern idea of progress – infinite progress in space, time, perfection, and complexity – which we inherited from the capitalist revolution in the deep structure of European society as it passed through the eighteenth century.)

In band and village societies behavior co-evolved with nature and expressed, remembered, and handed on in myth, custom, religion, and ritual (societies inherit acquired characters), may not be science as we conceive it, but when long-range survival in a human context is in question, the fact of being right, whether you know why or not, is the ultimate test of a society's social structure, technology, values, and dominant ideology.

The 'slash-and-burn' (or 'swidden') cultivation referred to in the representative list of societies practicing underproduction (Table 2.1) is a system of shifting cultivation used in medieval and earlier times in the temperate forests of Europe and used by many tropical forest peoples raising root crops in various parts of the world, as well as by dry-rice farmers in Southeast Asia.

In the late 1950s the Food and Agriculture Organization of the

United Nations estimated that some 14 million square miles, occupied by 200 million people, were being cultivated by this method.

Areas of primary or secondary forest are cleared for planting, the trees and litter being burned, which provides some fertilization. The plot is cultivated for a season or more, eventually being left fallow. The method is practically the only way of 'farming the forest' in the tropics. But as late as the 1950s many anthropologists regarded slash-and-burn cultivation as wasteful, inefficient, destructive, and typical of the 'genetic inferiority' of . . . the 'savage mind'.

(Others have accused North American Indians of destroying the environment by setting fire to prairie grass while hunting game. But like Douglas fir forest and the evergreen chaparral vegetation of southwestern North America and elsewhere, the grasslands were adapted to the ecology of fire – which gets rid of accumulated detritus, assists the germination of certain seeds, and fertilizes the soil – long before the Indians came. Frequent small fires also prevent fierce and truly destructive fires: cf. Cooper, 1961.)

The Tsembaga, a group of about 200 slash-and-burn cultivators, egalitarian between males, living in the central highlands of eastern New Guinea, were studied by Roy A. Rappaport in the early 1960s. Rappaport analyzed the Tsembaga ritual cycle and made detailed energy studies of their gardening practices. In 1968 he demonstrated in *Pigs for the Ancestors*, a classic text in ecological and cultural anthropology, that Tsembaga ideology, ritual, wars and pigs are all part of a ecologically self-regulated political, social, and economic system.

The tropical rainforest is probably the most intricate, productive, efficient, and stable of all ecosystems, comparable only to the coral reef: it is certainly the most diverse (Rappaport, 1972). It is stable, however, only so long as its structure is respected – as it is not in the continuing invasion of the Amazon (after the ocean, the Amazon rainforest is the largest single source of oxygen on earth), along with the destruction of its Indian inhabitants, especially in Brazil, by money, construction workers, traders, settlers, disease, commodity relations, and even bombs.

Alone the rainforest of New Guinea can support perhaps a single person per square mile. With swidden agriculture (slash and burn gardening) it can support between 60 and 200 people per square mile, without significant reduction of its diversity, complexity, or stability.

Before the 1950s, when steel machetes were introduced, the Tsembaga cleared the forest with stone axes. The garden is cleared of brush and between 150 and 200 trees are felled (the largest are left standing). The litter is burned, the area fenced to keep pigs out, and rows of logs to retain the soil are laid in place. After this – from one to four months after clearing starts – the plot is weeded and the litter burned again before planting begins.

The Tsembaga cultivate a great diversity of crops. They distinguish between at least 264 named varieties of edible plants from 36 species. The staples are taro and sweet potatoes. They also grow yams, cassavas, bananas, beans, peas, maize, sugar cane, leafy greens, and other items.

Plants are not laid out in rows, nor are all plants of the same kind grown in the same spot. The result of this practice, as Clifford Geertz has pointed out, is that the swidden garden is structurally similar to the rainforest it temporarily replaces. Like the rainforest its inter-mingled plants become stratified horizontally and vertically, fitting together and making maximum effective use of the available space. The diversity and intermingling of plants and root structures serves to protect the soil from rain-caused erosion or 'laterization' (hardening like cement), and discourages species-specific pests.

(In modern monoculture, such as a field of cotton, a species-specific pest, such as the boll weevil, starts at the beginning of one neat row and eats or otherwise makes its way to the end of the row, then starts over with the next neat row. . . .)

The stability and 'co-ordination' of the rainforest is the result of diversity produced by competition between species in natural evolution; the stability of the Tsembaga garden, and its correspondence with its environment (its *convenientia* or 'fitting in'), is the result of imitating that diversity by co-operation between species.

A month or two after planting the Tsembaga begin the most laborious task of all, weeding, which soon becomes virtually continuous. They remove all plants and grasses that compete for matter and energy with their own crop, but they leave tree seedlings alone. A Tsembaga gardener is likely to be more irritated by a visitor trampling on a tree seedling than by the same person squashing an edible plant.

Allowing tree seedlings to grow unhindered in the garden has several important ecological consequences. The seedlings provide a web of deep roots that bind the thin and fragile topsoil now exposed to the elements – it is typically a mere two inches thick – and recover nutrients that might otherwise be lost from the system by rainwater leaching. Their developing leaves also protect the soil from erosion by tropical downpours.

But the presence of the seedlings greatly increases the amount of labor spent on weeding and harvesting the crop. The result is that after a year or two the gardeners are induced to abandon the garden – long before they might have seriously depleted the soil, which then lies fallow for ten or twenty years.

Rappaport goes on to point out that Ramon Margalef of the University of Barcelona and Howard T. Odum of the University of Florida have argued that in complex ecosystems the most successful species are not those that merely capture energy more efficiently than their competitors, but rather those that sustain in some way the species supporting them – by the detritus they leave, for instance, or the shade they provide, or the nutrients they retain in the material cycles of the local ecosystem.

The Tsembaga fit this condition. They support not only the domesticated plants, they depend on for food – outside the pig festivals, the gardens provide 99 per cent of their usual diet, besides much of the food for their precious pigs – but they also support by their sophisticated practices the tropical forest itself, obtaining the greatest return in plant matter for the least disturbance of the system as a whole.

By allowing the tree seedlings to grow undisturbed in their gardens, in spite of all the extra toil it entails, the Tsembaga help to avoid a grassy stage in the ecological succession back to secondary growth forest after the plot is abandoned. This not only tends to protect the plot from invasion by *Imperata* grass, which once established is there to stay, but it also speeds up the process of succession, ensuring the more rapid development of the root structure and canopy of the secondary forest, which protects the soil from rain, conserves its nutrients in the biological cycle, and ensures the regeneration of the forest itself. That is why the Tsembaga call tree seedlings *duk mi*, 'the mother of gardens'.

Cybernetics refers to systems. . . . A cybernetic system influences the future, or bridges time, in the sense that the present state sets limits on patterns for future states. Thus the present state is a bearer of information. . . . The ecosystem may be considered as a channel which projects information into the future.

Ramon Margalef: *Perspectives in Ecological Theory* (1968)

2.2 Ecosystems

'Economy' in ancient Greek means 'the control or management of a household' (*oikos*). 'Ecology', a word coined by the German biologist Ernst Haeckel in 1873, has the same literal meaning; it is used to signify the science of organisms in their habitats.

An ecosystem (the word was invented in the 1930s) consists of an organic system or systems and the environment or environments necessary for its survival. It may vary in size and complexity from a drop of water to a cornfield to a tidal zone to a coral reef to a forest to the entire biosphere. As Margalef points out in his *Perspectives in*

Ecological Theory (1968, p. 20), an ecosystem is a self-regulating, adaptive, cybernetic system: it tends to remain in the most stable of all the possible states permitted by its dynamic structure.

In ecosystems, says Margalef, the structures that endure with stability through time are those most able to influence the future with the least expense of energy (p. 29) – including the energy required to possess and store information. Information is 'anything that can influence and shape the future' (p. 81).

Living systems, he argues,

> have always been energetic systems competing for materials. The distinction is important because transmission of information is more closely linked to the possibility of organizing huge amounts of matter than to the possibility of letting through high amounts of energy (p. 101).

In any ecosystem the total amount of organic matter and the number of species tend to increase over time towards a limit defined by the system's carrying capacity. This process involves an increase in diversity and complexity, the requisite diversity of the system being an index of its stability.

Diversity of species is the long-range result of 'divergent evolution' between competing species. This is the result of the principle of 'competitive exclusion', meaning that no two species using the same limited resource in the same way can both survive. Like Darwin's finches in the Galapagos Islands – where fourteen species with divergent feeding habits evolved from a single common ancestor – the diverging evolution of competing species results in the division of the available resources of the ecosystem into many dimensions, or ecological niches, in space and time.

Unlike competition under capitalism, which leads to monopoly, competition in nature leads to increased diversity and thus to greater complexity and stability – and finally to the dominance of (unintended) co-operation over competition.

Natural evolution is the result of the interaction of four principles. Accidental *variation* in the gene pool of a species produces individuals differing from the majority of other individuals; *heredity* produces offspring resembling their parents more than other individuals; *natural selection* results in different variants leaving different numbers of offspring either immediately or in remote generations; and *adaptation* in competition with other organisms and in the face of environmental factors favors the survival and reproduction of certain variants rather than others. This is the essence of the 'struggle for existence'.

Natural evolution takes place within the context of existing ecosystems, whose structures constrain the opportunities available to organic novelty produced by genetic variation. Margalef believes that these ecological constraints may account for the apparent direction of evolution. (Changes in the constraints and flexibility of the 'grammar' of DNA, as occurred with the advent of the vertebrates, which greatly accelerated the pace of evolution, are also part of this story, as Campbell notes in *Grammatical Man*, 1982.)

Natural evolution is neither teleonomic (goal-directed) nor teleological (the result of a master plan), but it has resulted in increasingly complex organisms. Evolutionary novelty has its origin in accidental or random errors in the replication, translation, transcription, editing, or expression of the instructions of DNA, which form the genetic memory of the species and the individual. Natural selection is an 'anti-chance agent' capable of making those errors make a new and unexpected kind of sense. A surviving mutation translates the noise (or disorder) of the original error into information (or new order) in its own genetic instructions (an example of the principle of 'order from disorder', which also occurs in social evolution and revolution, as well as in the evolution of science and in individual learning).

The 'central dogma' of molecular biology asserts that the genetic information moves in only one direction, from the DNA molecule to the individual organism, and never in the other direction, so that the Lamarckian 'inheritance of acquired characters', which is the basis of social and personal evolution, is impossible in natural evolution.

But populations of organisms do not exist passively in the environment, and the genetic instructions of the organism cannot themselves survive without passing through it. When the activities of organisms change their local environment – what Jacob von Uexküll called their *Umwelt*, or milieu – in such a way that the changes accidentally favor some genetic types more than others, then they are passing on a memory of 'acquired characters' via the environment.

Co-operation and competition in nature

An immature or relatively simple ecosystem differs from a mature or relatively complex one largely by changes in the relationship between competition and co-operation.

An immature ecosystem contains short-lived 'pioneer' species that are able to maintain high rates of reproduction, to disperse themselves widely, to compete strongly for dominance, and to survive under unstable and perhaps wildly oscillating conditions.

A mature ecosystem contains a greater number and diversity of longer-lived species. These species do not maintain high rates of reproduction; they are unable to disperse themselves widely; they are not dependent on competition for survival; and they are unable to survive under unstable conditions. The result is that their increasing specialization militates against overt competition among them; instead the relations among species are often characterized by an increased mutual reliance (Rappaport, 1972, p. 125).

V.C. Wynne-Edwards has argued that among and between many species, competition evolves away from real competition for real resources towards symbolic or displaced competition in which real resources are never at stake. The substitution of a piece of ground, or territory, as the object of competition in place of the actual food it contains is the simplest and most direct kind of limiting convention (or regulator) it is possible to have (1962, p. 12).

He goes on to say that 'free contest for food – the ultimate limiting resource – must in the long run end in over-exploitation and diminishing returns' (p. 132). The reason is that such outright competition tends to overshoot and deplete carrying capacity before the populations involved can adjust to the changed circumstances.

Sexual selection through the 'pecking order' or rank hierarchy among gregarious animals is one of the commonest examples of displaced or symbolic competition. Competition for mates depends on 'symbolic display' and on the threat of fighting, rather than on fighting itself. Its effect is to select against the reproduction of the genes of the lower-ranking animals in the hierarchy.

But not all competition is of this type: 'Indirect competition that never involves rivalry is apparently a common phenomenon in nature' (p. 226). When symbiosis is taken into account, especially at the level of cells, bacteria, parasites, and other micro-organisms, it is probably true that most associations between living creatures in nature are co-operative, rather than competitive (Margulis 1971, 1982).

The immature ecosystem is characterized by high yields, low efficiency, short food chains, low diversity, small sized organisms, more open nutrient cycles, and low stability.

The mature ecosystem is characterized by low yields, high efficiency, complex food webs, high diversity, larger organisms, closed nutrient cycles, and high stability.

Young ecosystems display production, growth, and quantity, while mature ecosystems display protection (of production), stability, and quality (E. Odum, 1974, p. 284).

When ecosystems differing in complexity are in contact, the less organized (or less mature) ecosystem feeds the more organized (or more mature) ecosystem.

Rappaport points out that self-sufficient farming ecosystems like that of the Tsembaga, which neither export nor import matter, energy, or information, are rapidly disappearing. The modern farm is increasingly dependent on a relatively simple chain of relationships that are international in scope and open to every kind of commercial and political manipulation – as in the case of the price of oil, or the use of food as a weapon. The more any agricultural system is susceptible to change or disruption by distant events, the less control people have over their food production, and thus over their lives.

Over the past two centuries the Western industrial societies have 'de-developed' or destroyed the once independent economies of their colonies and neocolonies. They have degraded and simplified the once great diversity of Third World ecological and economic systems, most of which did not depend on growth for survival or stability and did not seriously deplete their environments.

In the modern system, based as it ultimately is on the single-level yardstick of economic exchange values, rather than on the many levels of ecological, economic, and social use values, short-range adaptivity has come to replace long-range adaptivity. Wage labor, cash crops, tenant farming, monoculture, hybrids, petrochemical fertilizers and pesticides, and the domination of exchange values over use values have homogenized, not diversified, the world system. In the process quantitative variety has destroyed or replaced qualitative diversity.

It is [exchange] value that converts every product of labor into a social hieroglyphic . . . for to stamp an object of utility as a value is as much a social product as is language. . . . [A commodity] is a 'marker of value' [*Träger von Wert*]. . . . As soon as it comes into communication [*Umgang*] with another commodity . . . it betrays its thoughts in that language with which it alone is familiar, the language of commodities.

Karl Marx: Capital I (1867)

2.3 Use value, exchange value, and survival value

Use value (what a product can do) and exchange value (what a product can be traded for) are relationships rather than things. They are values in process, rather than static values. In a given set of historical and ecological circumstances, labor power creates use values out of energy, information, and raw materials. The useful qualities of the product – symbolic, social, or economic – and the time it takes to make it become the basis of its exchange value – again symbolic, social, or economic, although it is economic exchange value that most concerns us here.

Exchange values have uses – one of which is the links they establish between people by being exchanged (this is especially true of symbolic exchange, as in the Kula ring of Malinowski's *Argonauts of the Western Pacific*). As for use values, it is only by being exchanged that they can express their social, rather than individual, utility. Phosphorus, carbon, the information of DNA, and so on all have use value in organic nature. Economic exchange value, however, is strictly a product of society.

Every product of labor displays both use value and exchange value, the one or the other being the dominant value depending on the system of production (the dominant mode of production). Where a division of labor exists, a system of exchanges (but not necessarily a market economy in the modern sense) also exists. In non-capitalist societies based on long-range both-and adaptations to their natural environments, use values dominate exchange values. Co-operation constrains competition and both use value and exchange value contribute to long-range survival value.

Under capitalism, however, exchange values dominate use values, competition dominates co-operation, and short-range survival takes precedence over long-range survival. The relationship to nature – as well as to human beings – is (temporarily) either/or (Figure 2.1, Figure 2.2).

As already noted, what distinguishes capitalism from all other economic systems is its capacity to convert any and all relationships or values into commodities for sale in the market. The system retains aspects of feudalism and slavery, but these are subordinate to the novel mode of production founded on the so-called exchange of value (work for wages) between labor and capital.

Wage labor is the decisive commodity. It first became the dominant form of labor – regulated by a 'labor market' capable of depressing its

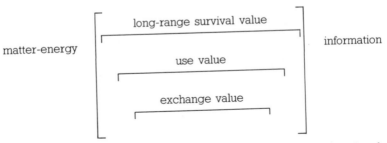

FIGURE 2.1 Exchange value, use value, and long-range survival value, a dependent hierarchy. (Long-range survival value is the ultimate use value.) As the vehicles or media of value, matter-energy and information do not form part of the hierarchy. As its logistical supports, they are required at every level of organization; hence their position in the diagram.

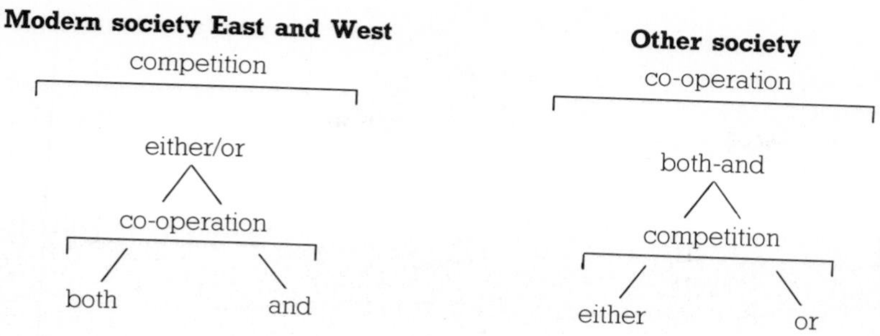

Modern society East and West

competition

either/or

co-operation

both   and

Other society

co-operation

both-and

competition

either   or

FIGURE 2.2   Competition and co-operation: two hierarchies of mediation and constraint (compare Figure 2.3: the triangle of mediation). The diagram indicates the relative dominance of (either/or) competition or (both-and) co-operation in two kinds of society. The both-and capacities of systems dominated by either/or relations are relations at a single level. In contrast, systems dominated by both-and relations not only recognize (horizontal) relationships at a single level, but more importantly (vertical) relationships between levels. In Western society most co-operative relationships are responses to the mediation of competition (compare Figure 2.5). In other societies competition is subordinate to co-operation, constrained competition being necessary for production, reproduction, and survival. Under competition, relationships are *either* either/or *or* both-and. When co-operation rules they are *both* both-and *and* either/or.

price below the level of subsistence – in the 1830s in England. Here the medieval principle of the laborer's 'right to live' was lost and forgotten; while the revolutionary combination of artisans outproduced by factories, family (or cottage) industrials ruined by automation (notably in textiles), and landless laborers displaced by new enclosures of tenanted and common land, came to form the modern industrial working class.

Wage labor makes human creativity into a commodity; a relationship is converted into a thing. What employees sell to employers under state and private capitalism is not simply their labor time, but control over the expression of their creativity, control over the use value of their labor power (the only commodity capable of creating value).

Wage labour

The radical empiricist and conservative philosopher Thomas Hobbes (1588–1679), one of the prophets of early English capitalism in the century of the English Revolution (1642–88), said of wage labor in his *Leviathan, Or the Matter, Form, and Power of a Commonwealth* (1651):

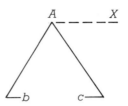

A: level of the code (and rules), constraints of the deep structure, locus of mediation, and (under state or private capitalism, East or West) the level of the general equivalent of exchange (in our system the measure of exchange value is money or labor time)

b, c: goal-seeking sender-receivers whose relationships are mediated by the constraints of the code(s) in use

b–c: level of the messages, constraints of the surface structure, message channels

A–b, A–c: coding channels

X: relationship to an environment

FIGURE 2.3   Code and message: the triangle of mediation (compare Figure 2.2: mediation and constraint). The level of the code, or deep structure, is not of the same logical type, not of the same level of communication or reality, as that of the messages, or surface structure. The diagram also defines the minimum requirements for a system of communication

> The value, or worth of a man, is, as of all other things, his price; that is to say, so much as would be given for the use of his power. . . . A man's labour also, is a commodity exchangeable for benefit, as well as any other thing.

In *Wage Labor and Capital*, based on discussions with the German Workers Club in Brussels in 1847, modified for publication in 1891 by Frederick Engels (1820–1895), Karl Marx (1818–1833) explained the historical novelty of the commoditization of labor:

> Labor [power] was not always a *commodity*. Labor was not always wage labor, that is [so-called] *free labor*. The *slave* did not sell his labor [power] to the slave-owner . . . [*someone else* sold *him*]. The slave, together with his labor [power], is sold once and for all to his owner . . . He is *himself* a commodity, but the labor [power] is not *his* commodity. The *serf* sells only a part of his labor [power]. He

axis of the code
selection and substitution
similarity
langue (language)
simultaneity and synchrony
paradigmatic
metaphor
condensation
harmony

axis of the message
combination and contexture
contiguity
parole (speech)
succession and diachrony
syntagmatic
metonymy
displacement
melody

FIGURE 2.4   Metaphor and metonymy, or selection from the code (similarity) and combination in the message (contiguity): the two basic principles of language and communication as identified by Roman Jakobson in 1956. Each sign communicated is interpreted by a reference both to the code (the dictionary meanings of 'rules', for example) and to the message (the meaning of 'rules' in the context of a given sentence in a given situation). The two lists of terms do not form lists of synonyms. They form one list of the basic structures of communication and exchange in a many-valued and many-leveled system of production and reproduction. The two axes of this diagram are the same as those of the code/message triangle of mediation in Figure 2.3, but here the environment and the communicators mediated by the code are left out. 'Condensation' (*Verdichtung*) and 'displacement' (*Verschiebung*) are the two basic processes of dream and joke formation according to Freud. This and the preceding figure are reproduced from 'Metaphor and Metonymy' in *The Rules Are No Game* (1987).

does not receive a wage from the owner of the land; rather the owner of the land receives a tribute from him.

The serf belongs to the land and turns over to the owner the fruits thereof. The *free laborer* . . . sells himself and, indeed, sells himself piecemeal.

Use values vary qualitatively, and cannot easily be digitalized or measured against each other. Economic exchange values vary quantitatively, and depend on digitalization to be expressed in terms of price. Use values are relative to long-range survival value. Monetary exchange values have no such necessary relationship to any real environment, except the environment of short-range survival.

One kind of economic exchange value dominates all kinds of use value under capitalism: commodities measured in units against a 'general equivalent of exchange' – money in the surface structure of wages, price, and profit; quantified creativity (abstract labor) in the deep structure of use value, exchange value, and surplus value. An exchange value is a digitalized value, and the scale of exchange value under capitalism is expressed in a single dimension.

In contrast, in many non-capitalist societies, including those using forms of money, there is no single general equivalent of exchange. As noted among the Trobrianders by Bronislaw Malinowski in his classic *Argonauts of the Western Pacific* (1922), there are distinct domains of exchange, e.g. food, kinship obligations, symbolic valuables, whose values cannot be reduced the one to the other.

Since use values are real, they cannot be multiplied beyond the carrying capacity of their environment(s). In contrast, since capitalist exchange values are mainly imaginary, the pursuit of exchange value appears unlimited. This infinite expansion seems possible because the dominant ideology ignores the fact that the production of capitalist exchange values ultimately depends on industrial and agricultural processes that result in the irreversible destruction of use values.

In a limited environment, the diversity of use values is necessarily constrained in ways that exchange values are not, and it is their diverse qualities that make the most significant use values non-interchangeable with each other. If oxygen and stable water flows are the significant values, for instance, you cannot trade a factory or a coalfield for a forest.

The annals of all nations bear witness that an enslaved people always suffers more deeply from those of its own blood who take service under the conquerors than it suffers from the conquerors themselves.

Edward Augustus Freeman (1823–92)

2.4   Competition and co-operation in society and the family

'Another scene I observe now and then', wrote Laura Carper, director of the Mayflower Nursery Playcenter in Detroit, in *Harpers* in April 1978, speaking of 4-year old children, 'goes like this':

Three or four little boys seat themselves around the play table in the play kitchen. The boys start issuing orders such as 'I'd like a cup of coffee!' or 'Bacon and eggs!' or 'Some more toast!' and the girl runs back and forth between stove and table, cooking and serving. In one such scene the boys got completely out of hand, demanding cups of coffee one after another while the girl was racing round in a frenzy. She finally gained control of the situation by announcing that there was no more coffee. Apparently it never occurred to her to sit down at the table herself and demand coffee from one of the boys.

Central to this representative incident, quoted by Colette Dowling in *The Cinderella Complex* (1981, pp. 100–01), is the role of mediation in constraining the social and personal roles – or more correctly, the strategies and tactics – of preschool girls and boys.

The mediation is not symmetrical: the boys mediate the girl's relationship to males, but she does not mediate their relationship to her. The boys, already literate in the brotherhood of 'boys will be boys', take control of the girl's relationship to them, and the girl, equally literate in 'co-operation' with boys, plays the game by their unstated rules. And when exhaustion and confusion strike, she does not contest the boys' strategy by one of her own, but settles for the 'tangential response' of 'it can't be done', 'it's out of my control' (there's no more coffee), abdicating even here any personal stand against the unacceptable behavior of the boys.

By colluding with their strategy of domination, she collaborates in her own humiliation. She follows the strategy of the victim – except that the strategy of the victim is not really a strategy at all, for it is identical to the tactical behavior defined and expected by the strategy of the victimizer.

No one respects a slave, and the more slavishly a slave tries to please, the more contemptuous the master becomes.

The hidden goal of the girl's collusion, Dowling argues, is to do the master's bidding in exchange for male protection. This is the heart of the Cinderella Complex, 'women's hidden fear of independence', the internalized acceptance of male supremacy that has held women down for at least ten thousand years and holds them down today. The Cinderella Complex is a

personal, psychological dependency – the deep wish to be taken care of by others – a network of repressed attitudes and fears that keeps women in a kind of half-light, retreating from the full use of their minds and creativity (p. 21).

Up until the age of 18, and sometimes beyond, as Elizabeth Douvan reports, girls show virtually no thrust towards personal independence, no desire to rebel against authority, and no insistence on 'their rights to form and hold independent beliefs and controls' (p. 101). Both mothers and fathers combine in creating this strategic helplessness, which is in complete contrast to the way they bring up boys.

The evidence is that dependency in women increases as they grow older.

Thus girls, from a very early age, are trained *into* dependency, while boys are trained *out* of it. Boys learn to compete for power, girls learn to compete for boys.

Boys are taught and encouraged to seek power in the world at large, and to learn how to use it effectively. Girls are taught to restrict themselves to the local community, and eventually to the home, and to retreat from power, exercising what power they have in trivial and non-threatening matters.

While this counter-adaptive strategy is undoubtedly at its most damaging and desperate in the lives of women, it is also part of every social relation where colonization has forced a caste, class, race, or sex into subservience, and then – this is the key – persuaded them that their subordination is 'natural' and 'deserved', because they 'really' are inferior. As the Brazilian educator Paulo Freire (b. 1921) said about the peasants of South America, if not in these exact terms: 'Beware of the words of the oppressor in the mouth of the oppressed.'

Divide and rule

The mediation of women's lives and attitudes by male power and control is based on the oldest imperial strategy, divide-and-rule. Just as many Africans in former colonies will tell you that they would rather work for a white man than for another African, so many women tell us that they would rather work for a man than for another woman.

In *The Pedagogy of the Oppressed* (1968), Freire had this to say about the strategy of divide-and-rule in society:

> As the oppressor minority subordinates and dominates the majority, it must divide and keep it divided, in order to remain in power. The minority cannot permit itself the luxury of tolerating the unification of the people. . . . Accordingly, the oppressors halt by any method (including violence) any action which . . . could awaken the oppressed to the need for unity. . . . It is in the interest of the oppressor to weaken the oppressed still further, to isolate them, to create and deepen rifts among them. This is done by varied means, from the repressive methods of the government bureaucracy to the forms of cultural action with which they manipulate the people by giving them the impression that they are being helped (p. 137).

Competition between women for the favors and approval of men has been legendary ever since the appearance of the jealous and vindictive Hera as the wife of Zeus in Greek mythology, following an earlier period when mythological mothers and sons united to curb the power and violence of father gods, and if necessary to kill them.

Competition between women is not the product of 'feminine psychology' or female genes, however, but rather of the mediation of male-female relations by competition between men. Competition between men is itself subdivided into the overlapping categories of caste, class, race, and sexual preference, as well as into competition between individual men within those groups. This competition, too, is the product of society and history, and not derived from 'naturally violent aggressivity' or male hormones or masculine genes.

Mediation is not to be condemned out of hand, however; like the code/message relation, legitimate mediation is a necessary, universal, and creative constraint on relationships. In human affairs, the perception of the past mediates between the present and the future, memory mediates between action and desire, values mediate between ideas and action, work mediates between love and play, morale and humor mediate between simply getting by and maintaining that touch of style and grace that makes uniqueness a welcome disruption of the usual pattern of events.

System and structure

Competition constrained and mediated by co-operation is essential to individual creativity and the well-being of society. It develops, extends, and sustains individual and social skills, personal and political wisdom, imagination and invention, and laughter, play, and self-esteem.

But in societies where co-operation is dominated by competition, as is our own, most mediation is a source of alienation, manipulation, violence, and indignity.

We co-operate to avoid competition at one level, only to face it again at another. People may co-operate at one level (as in a production team or a union), but that co-operation is mediated by the necessity to compete with other units at the same level (other production teams, other unions), and by contradictory conflicts (rather than by competition, which implies equal opportunity to compete) with other units at higher levels (the worker or the union versus the company).

In the case of monopolies and associations of semi-monopolies, called 'oligopolies' (like the US steel industry, or the US automobile industry before its market control was broken by the Japanese), co-operation to fix prices reduces competition at one level or in one

Examples of Co-operation:
[a]Cartels
[b]Manufacturers Associations
[c]Retailers Associations
[d]Labor Unions

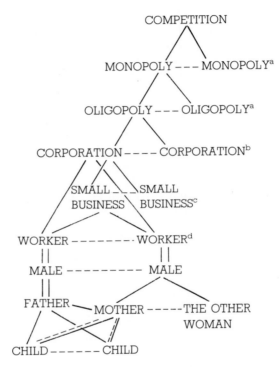

FIGURE 2.5 The general structure of competition and co-operation under capitalism, state or private, East or West. As in the triangle of mediation in Figure 2.3, the solid lines (or coding channels) represent the dominant-subordinate relationship between the mediator at the apex and the mediated at the base. Broken lines stand for relationships between the mediated (the message channels). The mediators at one level in the hierarchy become the mediated for the next higher level; the mediated at one level become the mediators for the next lower level. There is competition between the mediated at one level, competition between their mediators at the next higher level, and conflict or contradiction (not competition) between mediators and mediated at different levels. It is not to be assumed that all social, economic, or individual relations fit this pattern, only that this is the presently dominant structure of the capitalist and state-capitalist systems, where most co-operation is the product of attempts to reduce the effects of competition or contradiction.

economic sphere, but it does not reduce or eliminate competition at other levels or in other spheres.

A monopoly controls its market, and if 'vertically integrated' from raw material extraction to distribution, it may control prices at every level of production. But it will still find itself in competition with other monopolies outside its own field, whether for government funding of contracts, favorable tax and other legislation, the opening up of new markets, or the price of oil and money.

Competition in the system depicted in Figure 2.5 is not necessarily or solely economic, although that is the most important kind. It may be competition for political office, possession of material goods, sexual favors, love, attention, care, prestige. The general equivalent of exchange in this system, as in other imperial systems, is not ultimately money or exchange value, but power, and power in this system ultimately depends more on power over people than it does on power over things.

The potentially competitive and even pathological relationships set up in the modern 'nuclear' family by the mediation of the social context are more complicated than can be shown in the general structure of competition in Figure 2.5. The communication and exchanges between the child(ren) and the mother figure (who need not be female) are mediated by the father figure (who need not be male). At her subordinate level in the typical family system, the mother, mediated by the father (representing work and society), is herself a mediator (representing nature and the home) in relation to the children. The parents carry responsibility for their relationship with the children in proportion to their relative power to be responsible.

Introducing female workers into the model of the general structure of competition (Figure 2.5), or into that of the family structure, would of course result in changes in detail – as would the inclusion of single-parent families and working mothers. But these amendments would not change to any great extent the social and economic relationships between competition and co-operation presently dominant in our society, nor significantly alter their psychological, ideological, and behavioral effects on individuals.

Between children the social icon of the 'Boy (or the Girl) Next Door' plays a role – comparison and contrast, contradiction and conflict – similar to that played by the 'Other Woman' between the sexes (Chapter 3). In the family itself, even if they are of similar age and the same sex, children's relationships are not equally mediated by either or both parents; and in society in general, this is never the case for families with both boys and girls (Chapter 5).

There must be a mutual Cooperating for the good of the whole.
> Buchanan's *De Jure Regni*, translation of 1680.

Civilization is co-operation.
> Henry George: *Progress and Poverty* (1881)

2.5   New directions

Writing on symbiosis and co-operation in the August 1984 issue of *Discover* (the *Time-Life* science magazine with the largest English-speaking readership in the world), the philosopher and essayist Lewis Thomas begins by outlining the vast number and great diversity of symbiotic relations to be found in organic nature (including those at the origin of life). Turning to relations between human beings, he draws on the work of Robert Axelrod at the University of Michigan. Axelrod, says Thomas,

> set up an elaborate computer game, based on game theory, to determine what happens when two totally egoistical participants confront each other over and over again for long and indefinite periods of time in competition for essential resources.

The players have two choices for each encounter:

> to cooperate, in which case both benefit to a limited extent, or to defect, in which case one receives a much larger benefit at the other's expense – unless both players defect, which yields no benefit to either side.

With the help of some 75 colleagues, including experts in mathematical game theory, computer intelligence, and evolutionary biology, Axelrod set up a series of computer tournaments to see whether any particular strategy or strategies could consistently result in 'win/win' (rather than 'win/lose') (zero-sum) outcomes.

The results are published in Axelrod's new book *The Evolution of Cooperation* (1984, pp. 27–69). The 'hands-down winner', and the 'simplest strategy of all', says Thomas, was the program sent in by Anatol Rapoport, a philosopher, psychologist, and games theorist at the University of Toronto.

Rapoport's program – based on all players pursuing their own self-interest – is called Tit for Tat. The rules of the TFT strategy are two:

- Cooperate on your first move.
- Then repeat whatever move the other player makes.

If the other defects, then you defect; if the other cooperates, then you cooperate. True self-interest is self-and-other-interest.

Tit for Tat is regulated by the both-and relations of long-range survival, not by the either/or relations of short-range survival:

> Tit for Tat is not a strategy for any quick victory; it has no way of clobbering opponents; it does well by eliciting cooperation from the other players.

TFT strategists are never the first to defect. The TFT strategy, says Thomas, is 'nice' — but not too nice:

> It cooperates with cooperation, retaliates against betrayal, remembers, forgives, and can be trusted.

It is also a strategy that can spread swiftly through any community of players using other strategies, says Thomas:

> A cluster of Tit for Tat strategists can defend themselves against other, hostile or aggressive players. Once established within a sea of competitors — provided the game goes on for an indefinite period of time — it emerges as the only game in town.

He concludes:

> I never expected news like this from computer science. As an outsider, a non-player, I always thought computer games were contests between combatants bent on eating each other up or blowing each other up, exactly like what one sees in the behavior of human committees and, most of all, in the behavior of modern nation-states. Now I am all for the computers, and I hope the word gets around quickly.

One adds that what ultimately survives is not the fittest individual, population, nation, species (or whatever), but the fittest ecosystem: not the short-range survival of either 'system' or 'environment', but the long-range survival of the relationship between them, the survival of both 'system' (at one level) and 'environment' (at another) (Gregory Bateson).

Note also that taken to its logical, ecological, and long-range conclusions, the still-dominant ideology of the 'survival of the fittest' would inevitably result in the momentary survival of a single supreme species, followed by its complete extinction.

CHAPTER 3

Paradox: system, society, and sexuality

A statue conserves its shape, a plant performs it.
Jonathan Miller: *The Body in Question* (1980)

3.1 Double binds, useful

The Dobu of Melanesia live on several islands off the eastern tip of
New Guinea, immediately south of the Trobriand Islands and about
600 miles due west of Guadalcanal in the Solomons. They take part in
the 200-mile-wide system of symbolic exchange called the kula, which
accompanies economic and other exchange in the region (Figure 3.1)
(Malinowski, 1922, pp. 81–104). Around the many circuits of the
Kula Ring, valuables (*vaygu'a*) of two kinds, necklaces of red shell,
called *soulava*, and bracelets of white shell, called *mwali*, travel in
numerous circles, large and small, within villages and between villages,
inland and oversea, in opposite directions, each of the two kinds of
vaygu'a being exchanged for the other kind when they meet.

Kula valuables are exchanged in relations of protective and friendly
rivalry and honor between ranking male partners (and among the
Trobrianders, a society more stratified than most others in the kula,
also between a few women of very high rank) within and between
societies differing from each other in culture, language, and even race.
The Trobrianders are well known for their positive reciprocity and
mutual obligation; the Dobu, close by, are equally well known for
their negative reciprocity and mutual jealousies.

In the big kula expeditions overseas, the exchanges between kula
partners – a commoner may have one or two, a chief several hundred
– take place between 'kula communities': over a thousand kula
valuables may change hands at one time. The exchange system has its
rules of syntax: *mwali* bracelets move from left hand to right hand
and from north and east to south and west; *soulava* necklaces move in

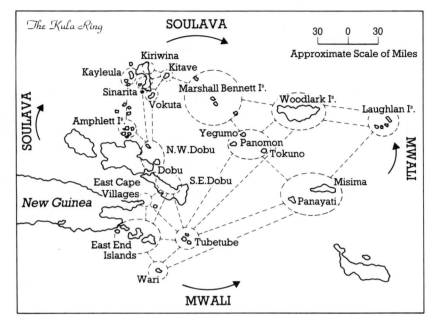

FIGURE 3.1 The Kula Ring in Melanesia, from Bronislaw Malinowski's *Argonauts of the Western Pacific* (1922). Symbolic exchange takes place within villages, between villages, and between kula communities (circles), consisting of 'a village or number of villages, who go out together on big overseas expeditions, perform their magic in common, have common leaders, and have the same outer and inner social sphere, within which they exchange their valuables'. In the kula, symbolic armshells (*mwali*) are exchanged for symbolic neckshells (*soulava*), one moving clockwise, the other counter-clockwise (arrows). It is quite probable that the kula exchange replaces warfare.

the opposite direction. Each kula partner thus has partners who give him white shell bracelets, to whom he gives red shell necklaces, and partners who give him necklaces, to whom he gives bracelets.

Every valuable has a personal name, a status, and a history (of its previous holders, for example); many are too big or too small to be worn and are simply displayed. Others are lent to male and female friends and relatives to wear, much more often than they are worn by their present trustee. The finest are worn only on ceremonial occasions of great importance. It may take from one to ten years for a particular valuable to complete the circuit of the Kula Ring.

The reason the valuables return is expressed by the rule: 'once in the kula, always in the kula'. Kula valuables never stop, but go round and round the ring. What has been received from one lifelong kula partner must always be handed on to another one, and no kula valuable is given or received in order to be used. A partner might cherish a particularly fascinating necklace or armshell for a year or so, but no kula valuable may legitimately become an object of possession, whether as private or as personal property.

Subordinate to the kula and its magic are the many other distinct 'spheres of exchange' in these societies, exchanges dominated by use values, such as the economic exchange between kinfolk called *wasi* by the Trobrianders, or the non-partnership bartering they call *gimwali* (where haggling is permitted). Some of the societies in the ring use money (not the Trobrianders, as it happens), but there is no 'general equivalent of exchange' (as money is for us) to make exchanges between distinct spheres of exchange possible.

The exchange value of a kula object is symbolic, and neither 'subjective' nor 'objective'. It is a matter of reputation and prestige in a two-way relationship mediated by what other people think of your charm, persuasiveness, and generosity.

The social codes of the societies in the Kula Ring do not exclude personal property. As Malinowski explains (p. 97):

> to possess is to be great, and . . . wealth is the indispensable
> appanage of social rank and attribute of personal virtue. But the
> important point is that to possess is to give. . . . The main symptom
> of being powerful is to be wealthy, and of wealth is to be generous.
> Meanness, indeed, is the most despised vice, and the only thing
> about which the natives have strong moral views, while generosity is
> the essence of goodness.

What is of supreme importance in the kula is the act, not the object, of exchange: it is the link – Greek *symbolon*, Latin *tessera* – with other people, not the link with things, that ultimately counts.

Throughout the Kula Ring the Dobu are feared as extremely dangerous sorcerers, and it is said that a Dobu feels safer on a kula visit to another group than a Dobu does at home.

As R.F. Fortune explains in *Sorcerers of Dobu* (1932), Dobu society is riddled with competition, jealousy, theft, threats, distrust, and bad magic. But in its deep structure, and unlike our own society, competition in the Dobu system is constrained by co-operation in the mutual obligation of givers and receivers. In the *pwatukwara* exchange between villages and family groupings, for instance, where givers and receivers alternate from year to year, the ritual formula used by the receivers to thank the givers represents a time-based double bind: 'If you kill me by witchcraft, how shall I repay you this gift?'

This ritual formula states the two related poles of advantage and prestige in Dobu society, magical power and economic abundance, but links them together in a paradoxical injunction like this:

> If you (the givers) wish to maximize advantage over us (the receivers), then you will use sorcery against us, as is the custom. If you use sorcery against us, we will not remain healthy enough to return the gift we owe you, as is the custom.

Thus, in any one cycle of this sphere of exchange, the givers' advantage can be fully maximized only if two conditions are simultaneously satisfied (besides your deep-seated belief in magic): (a) the receivers' productive capacities are crippled by the use of magic (hostile and damaging acts); and (b) the receivers are left alone so that the givers can recoup their gift in the next cycle. The two conditions are of course incompatible with each other – as one condition is satisfied, the other is undermined – and the socially coded necessity for givers and receivers to take both sides at once results in a safe and stable oscillation between them, governed by a useful double bind. This paradoxical injunction stands as a metaphor of the maintenance of structure in Dobu (morphostasis).

This interpretation is mainly due to Tim Wilson, a graduate student at Simon Fraser University, who insisted in 1976 that double binds are not necessarily pathological, abnormal, or representative of some deficiency or other – as they have often been assumed to be by therapists, ever since the discovery of the double bind (as an oscillation resulting from a confusion of logical types) in schizophrenic communication in the family by Gregory Bateson, Don D. Jackson, Jay Haley, and John Weakland, centered at Stanford University, between 1952 and 1956. Wilson is also the source of the Dobu example (first written up in Wilden and Wilson, 1976).

The dominant ideology of our society is in many of its aspects imaginary and oriented to short-range survival. In contrast, the general ideologies and grand strategies of band and village societies like the Tsembaga and the Dobu, while apparently imaginary, are in fact symbolic – symbolic of both-and, symbiotic, context sensitive, right-brain-dominated, and dialectical relationships between organism and environment and society and nature – real relationships of long-range survival co-evolved with nature and other people over centuries of time.

The recognition of structure gives the mind its ability to find meaning.

Susanne Langer (b. 1895)

3.2   Double binds, definition

A true double bind is not just an awkward situation in which we are 'damned if we do and damned if we don't', for this may involve no more than a choice between the 'lesser of two evils', without any actual or implied oscillation between them. Neither is it simply an opposition or a contradiction, for here too it is possible to make a stable choice between one side or the other (of an opposition), or between one level and another (of a contradiction), and the two alternatives may differ in symbolic, real, or imaginary value.

A true double bind – or a situation set up, coerced, or perceived as one – requires a choice between (at least) two states or situations that are so equally valued and so equally insufficient that a self-perpetuating oscillation is set off by any act of choice between them. A double bind is thus not a simple contradiction, but rather an oscillating contradiction resulting from the strange loop of a paradoxical injunction.

Like the unusual and unstable inversions of figure and ground (inversions leading to oscillations between levels) reported by Kurt Goldstein in the 1930s among people called 'schizophrenic', the oscillations of a double bind involve at least two levels of communication and reality. There is an oscillation between the level at which one alternative is the correct or necessary response and the level at which another is. (This oscillation between levels may be continuous or discrete.) A paradoxical command that can neither be obeyed nor disobeyed – Do not read this – defines an oscillation between the dominance of one alternative and the dominance of another – Disregard this line – in a system in which two or more alternatives are 'equally dominant' and perfectly symmetrical and commutative (Chapter 1), or treated as such.

A true double bind does not therefore imply a 'bankruptcy of choice itself', as Watzlawick, Beavin, and Jackson suggested in 1967 in *The Pragmatics of Human Communication*. The oscillation is the result of the fact that one must choose, and keep on choosing, throughout the oscillation. Here choosing to obey chooses to disobey and choosing to disobey chooses to obey.

The necessity of choosing is not, however, imposed by the double bind as such; it is imposed by the context that constrains one's relative freedom of response, one's relative diversity of behavior and communication, in dealing with the double bind. Once recognized for what it is, a double bind is always open to some kind of metacommunication or transcendence – it can be strategically enveloped or outflanked – provided the context allows such an innovation, or can be made to allow it.

The necessity of choosing is imposed by hierarchies of constraints (rules, metarules, meta-metarules) operating at more abstract levels than the double bind itself. In useful double binds these levels of rules constrain the competition between the poles of the double bind and the people involved in them; in pathological double binds they cut off or neutralize (or attempt to cut off or neutralize) the possibility of freeing oneself from the pathology by metacommunicative – strategic – action (Chapter 7).

Only under such conditions can the communicational closure necessary to the oscillation be maintained. Within the closed system thus set up, the two (or more) poles of the double bind will not only be incompatible with each other, but each alone will be incompatible with some essential aspect of the context.

Thus, what produces the oscillation in a binary double bind is that one is required to choose to satisfy *either* condition A *or* condition B within a set of metaconditions that can be satisfied only by *both* A *and* B. Although he symmetrizes a contradiction, Bateson's comment here is apt: 'A paradox is a contradiction in which you take sides – both sides. Each half of the paradox proposes the other' (Brand, 1972, p. 31).

Some double binds are universal – in the sense that 'I am lying' is a double-bound paradox for all users of analytic logic – whereas others are cultural or subjective, or peculiar to a class, race, or sex, depending for their efficacy on the way they are interpreted, or on the way a person has been taught or trained to interpret them (3.4 below).

The oscillations of a double bind may be discontinuous or digital (as with the paradox 'I am lying'), or continuous or analog (as with the 'more-or-less' oscillations of the business cycle: Chapter 4). Both digital and analog oscillations may in addition be independent of time (as logical paradoxes are) or time-dependent (as the business cycle is), and may include osciallations between distinct states or between thresholds.

In no case are these semiotic oscillations – oscillations governed by information – in any way comparable to the matter-energy oscillations of simple harmonic motion (the oscillations of a pendulum, a crystal, or a wave, for example).

Information is information, not matter or energy. No materialism which does not admit this can survive at the present day.

Norbert Wiener: *Cybernetics* (1948, 1961)

3.3   Pigs for the ancestors

The oscillations of the ten- or twenty-year ritual cycle of the Tsembaga of New Guinea are the product of a set of unstated double binds operating between thresholds over time in a cybernetic, ecologically regulated, political, social, and economic system.

The explicitly recognized factors in the Tsembaga cycle are war, ancestors, and pigs; the implicit factors are nutrition, neighbors, and the carrying capacity of the forested valley in which the 200 or so Tsembaga live.

The Tsembaga are a group of Maring speakers, egalitarian between men, bounded on the east by another Maring group, the Tuguma, with whom they are friendly, and on the west by the Kundagai, a Maring group against whom the Tsembaga waged war four times in the fifty years before 1962 (Rappaport, 1971).

In the Maring cosmology there are two sets of spirits, those of the high ground, the Red Spirits and the Smoke Woman who dwells with them, and those of the low ground, the Spirits of Rot (and growth) and Koipa Mangiang who dwells with them.

The Red Spirits, hot, dry, hard, strong, and prone to anger, associated with men, the high valley sides, and the upper body, are said to be the spirits of people killed in war. Marsupials are said to be their pigs. Dwelling with them is Smoke Woman, who was never human, through whom the living communicate with the dead by the medium of shamans. After smoking extremely strong cigars of local tobacco, the shaman goes into a trance during which Smoke Woman comes into his head and speaks through him. The spirits of the high ground are the spirits of war and its rituals and taboos.

Residing with the spirits of the low ground, the Spirits of Rot, is Koipa Mangiang. Like Smoke Woman, Koipa was never human. Just as marsupials are the pigs of the Red Spirits, eels are said to be the pigs of Koipa Mangiang. The Spirits of Rot, cold, soft, and wet, associated with women, the valley floor, the lower part of the body, fertility, pigs, and death (as part of the cycle of birth and growth), are said to be the spirits of people whose deaths were not the result of war. The spirits of the low ground are the spirits of fertility and its rituals and taboos.

As Rappaport points out, the relationship between these two apparently opposed sets of spirits is mediated by the Maring themselves, for the Red Spirits and the Spirits of Rot are kinfolk, no matter how they died. More significant, however, than this 'logical mediation' is the 'dynamic mediation' of the ritual cycles, 'for it is in terms of this mediation among supernatural entities that the actual material variables comprising the ecosystem are regulated' (p. 254).

When warfare is initiated it is necessary to segregate the two sets of spirits and everything associated with them as much as possible, and to identify the community with the Red Spirits, i.e. with the men. In an elaborate ritual 'fighting stones' are hung from the central post of a ritual house. Hot and cold, dry and moist are segregated by a taboo on sexual intercourse and on men eating food prepared by women. The living are separated from the dead by heavy obligations, for the spirits govern success in war. These obligations are owed even to the spirits of the low ground, who have little to do with war, for they are asked to strengthen the warriors' legs.

Fighting may go on for weeks. It rarely results in actual rout or defeat, it is not based on conquest of territory, and it usually ends by agreement between the antagonists that there has been enough killing and wounding for the time being. The fighting ground is prepared by both parties before the battles, which stop for ritual observances every time someone is wounded or killed. No one fights when it rains. One ritual element that reduces the severity of the daily battles is that the warriors are required to eat salt pork in the morning and forbidden to drink liquids all day (so as not to put out their 'fire'). Hostilities for the day thus tend to taper off from growing thirst by mid-afternoon.

In the worst engagement in living memory, on a day when the Tsembaga's allies did not appear, the Kundagai and their allies the Kanump-Kaur made a sudden charge (flanking movements are unknown) and killed eighteen people, six of them women and children, and wounded many others (Rappaport, 1968, p. 139).

With the termination of warfare the reintegration of the Maring universe begins. Provided a group has not abandoned its territory (a rare occurrence), the men go through the ritual of planting a sacred shrub called *rumbim*, with each man grasping the plant as it penetrates the soil, signifying and confirming his membership in the group and its relationship to growth, nature, and fertility. The planting of the *rumbim* is a message 'to whom it may concern': it signifies a digital and either/or change from a state of war to a state of truce. Along with other taboos, those against sexual intercourse and food cooked by women are lifted.

The planting of the sacred shrub is followed by a wholesale slaughter of the group's adolescent and adult pigs, in recognition of the aid of the spirits in the war. (In 1962–3 over 100 animals were killed.) The spirits are said to devour the spirits of the pigs, while the living consume their flesh – an essential source of high-quality, nitrogen-rich protein in a largely vegetarian diet.

But this sacrifice of pigs is not enough to meet the group's obligation to the spirits. Many taboos still remain, including dealing with the enemy, and a sanctified truce exists while the pig population is allowed to grow to a size sufficient to meet the symbolic debt to the ancestors, with which a new sequence of the ritual cycle can begin.

The truce may last from six or seven to twenty years.

Beside their central ritual function, pigs are important in Maring societies in many other ways. Pigs will eat anything, and they are the most efficient of animals for the conversion of plant matter to meat. Domesticated pigs may not be killed except on ritual occasions and in cases of illness or injury; their high-quality protein is thus kept always in reserve, but used in emergencies. Pigs are penned up in abandoned gardens, where by rooting up unharvested tubers and plants, they probably hasten the return of the forest. In the village they act as garbage collectors, disposing of all waste matter, including human feces. The care of pigs falls to the Tsembaga women (who work harder than the men); pigs are fed from the gardens, each consuming about as much as an adult Tsembaga male.

It takes at least ten years for the pig herd to return to its former size. When it was at its maximum during Rappaport's field work, 170 pigs were consuming 36 per cent of the produce of the gardens. At this point in the cycle the women begin to complain of overwork, and, by invading other people's gardens, the pigs cause arguments and annoyance. Long before the pigs and their owners approach the carrying capacity of the territory, the pigs pass through the boundary of the nuisance capacity of their owners.

There is no constituted authority among the Tsembaga; they avoid meetings to avoid confrontations; and the idea of voting is unknown. The decision that there are now 'more' rather than 'less' pigs, that there are now enough pigs to sacrifice to the ancestors to settle the symbolic debt, is made by consensus.

A complicated series of ritual events introduces the next part of the cycle. After the Tsembaga have ritually planted stakes at the boundaries of their territory – messages 'to whom it may concern', like ringing the bounds of a parish – certain taboos are lifted. Within a month or so, in an important ritual, the *rumbim* planted after the last fight is uprooted. During this ritual a number of pigs are killed, reducing the symbolic debt, and an important reintegration of the cosmos is begun. The communion entered into years before by the men when they took the Red Spirits into their heads is now concluded. The Red Spirits are asked to take the pig offered them and leave (p. 259).

The spirits of the high and low, long separated, are now drawn closer together by a number of rituals, and the year-long pig festival, the *kaiko*, the culmination of the entire ritual cycle, begins.

Along with various rituals, friendly groups are now invited to be entertained at elaborate dances, and the young men and women begin to size each other up as marriage partners. About six months after the uprooting of the *rumbim*, when the taro has begun to open in the gardens, the fighting stones are lowered, eels are trapped, and presentations of taro (for the Maring the most important of foods) are made to the visitors being entertained. Through further rituals, all residual taboos between the Tsembaga and their friends – now their allies – are abrogated, and all quarrels among the Tsembaga themselves are settled.

> The renunciation of these taboos permits the locals to perform the rituals which are the climax of the entire ritual cycle. Performed at sacred places in the middle altitudes, and accompanied by the slaughter of great numbers of pigs, the rituals call to mind the sexual act (p. 260).

At the same time the Smoke Woman and Koipa Mangiang have been called; their presence together signifies that the reintegration of the sacred universe is now complete.

The next day there is a massive distribution of pork to all, and friends and allies smash through the ritual fences separating them and dance together on the dance ground. No restrictions now separate the Tsembaga from their allies, and their symbolic debts to both the living and the dead have been repaid. The sanctified truce is ended, and, had the Australian government not forbidden it in the late 1950s, the Tsembaga and their allies would be free to declare war once again.

I'll return to the question of warfare later. For the moment, consider the cybernetics of this ritual cycle. Like the canaries kept in coalmines to warn the miners – by dying – of noxious gases, the number of pigs is the system-sensitive variable, the information about the matter-energy relations of the local ecology, with which all other events are connected.

When the pig herd is increasing during the truce, the system is in 'positive feedback'. Positive feedback, meaning 'the more there is, the more there will be', may be useful or it may be dangerous. It is characteristic of organic growth to maturity, population increase, compound interest, cancer, arms races, and escalating arguments. The output of a system in positive feedback is added to its input, the greater output then resulting is added to the input again, in an increasingly escalating system of exponential growth, like inflation. (In exponentially decreasing systems, positive feedback means 'the less there is, the less there will be'.) Exponential growth is generally measured in doubling times: the doubling time is approximately equal to 70 divided by the growth rate. At 7 per cent inflation, for example, prices double every ten years.

The arguments about pigs invading gardens and the women's complaints of overwork are the information sensors in the system. The pig population increases in an ever-steepening curve until the uprooting of the sacred plant, the *rumbim*, sends a digital signal that the state of the system is about to be altered. The killing of the pigs is negative feedback – the more (or the less) there is, the less (or the more) there will be – which is characteristic of all cybernetic control systems, organic, social, or engineered.

The essential of feedback is 'difference' – the difference between desired output and actual output. In engineered negative feedback systems, the system is controlled by comparing what it is doing with what it was doing. Thus if a stationary steam engine is subjected to a load and its speed falls, the flyweights on the centrifugal governor fall inwards, opening the steam valve to provide more power. If the load is removed and the speed suddenly increases, the weights fly outwards, closing the steam valve to reduce speed. As the engine oscillates along an analog continuum between 'too slow' and 'too fast', the weights oscillate in and out, acting digitally every time they change direction.

Positive feedback amplifies differences; it is 'deviation amplifying'. Negative feedback reduces differences; it is 'deviation reducing'. (Here the meaning of the terms is unrelated to their colloquial sense.) Positive feedback thus goes along with what the system is already doing; negative feedback, as the name implies, opposes or transcends it.

Systems open only to positive feedback are self-expanding. If not brought under control by negative feedback at the same or a higher level, they become unstable 'vicious circles' or spirals that threaten the survival of their environments, and thus their own survival. As a number of academics pointed out in a letter to the *Guardian Weekly* of September 26, 1982, the arms race is based on exactly this kind of instability, on the paradox of deterrence, which 'requires each adversary, in order to prevent the nuclear holocaust, to prepare to engage in that holocaust'. The nuclear paradox is not even a potentially stable condition. Not only does it continuously develop over time, but it destroys the conditions of its own credibility – and credibility is the essence of its supposed effects. In Bateson's terminology it is a binary system of escalating 'symmetrical competition', like Hitler and Mussolini cranking themselves upwards in the barber's chairs in Charlie Chaplin's *The Great Dictator* (1940).

The Maring-Tsembaga system displays an analog-digital oscillation controlled by negative feedback. The change of state between 'more' rather than 'less' pigs is communicated by the either/or, digital signal of the *rumbim*.

As Rappaport summarizes the system (p. 252):

The operation of these cycles helps to maintain an undegraded biotic and physical environment, distributes local surpluses of pig throughout the region in the form of pork, and assures people of high quality protein when they are most in need of it.

The cycles also limit warfare to frequencies that do not endanger the survival of the regional population. When, as occasionally happens, one group is driven away from its territory and goes to live with allies, the land is considered inhabited by their spirits, and not taken over by the victors until it is clear that the others will not be coming back. Thus the cycles allow war occasionally to redisperse people over land, and land among people, tending to correct discrepancies of population densities among different local groups.

The system directly protects the Maring from possible parasitism or competition for resources by their pigs, and along with their gardening practices protects the local environment. Sexual taboos limit population increase. The many taboos on eating different animals at different times conserve the fauna of the area. The ritual system mitigates the severity of warfare and facilitates exchanges of goods and intermarriage between different Maring groups.

With the exception of natural catastrophes or the coming of the white man, the Maring-Tsembaga system, co-evolved with nature, is quite capable of lasting to the end of time. At the root of it all is a useful double bind:

> Once you have gone to war, you must repay your obligation to the ancestors.
> Once you have repaid your obligation to the ancestors, you must go to war.

The stability of the system is the result of 'order through oscillation'. This is not a matter-energy oscillation, but rather a semiotic one, an oscillation governed by information (Chapter 1).

'Tis said that Beauty ne'er in any age
Has been at peace with Chastity . . .
For she is powerless 'gainst Beauty's force . . .

> May wolves devour the flesh, dogs gnaw the bones
> Of those by whom I am so cuckolded.
> Foul woman, ribald hussy, lecherous bitch,
> By you and your vile ways I'm put to shame . . .
>   All women are, have been, and e'er will be,
> In thought if not in deed, unvirtuous . . .
> Scolding and beating will not change their minds;
> He'd rule their bodies who could rule their wills.

Let's talk no more of things that ne'er can be!
Jean de Meung: 'The Jealous Husband Recounts how Women have
      Deceived Men': *Le Roman de la Rose*, Part Two (1275–80)

3.4   Double binds, beguiling and bewitching

In their excellent review of double binds in literature and philosophy, the authors of *The Pragmatics of Human Communication* (1967, pp. 230–1) cite the conclusion of the Wife of Bath's Tale in the *Canterbury Tales* of Geoffrey Chaucer (?1340–1400).

The Wife of Bath's Tale is the story of a young knight of King Arthur's Court, guilty of raping an unprotected peasant maid, but saved from execution by Queen Guinevere and her ladies on the condition that within a year and a day he find the answer to the question: 'What thing is it that wommen most desyren?'. Or as Freud put it, severely vexed by 'the woman question', as it once was called: 'What is it that women want?'.

The knightly rapist travels far and wide:

> Somme seyde, wommen loven best richesse,
> Somme seyde, honour, somme seyde, jolynesse;
> Somme, riche array, somme seyden, lust abedde,
> And ofte tyme to be widwe and wedde.
> Somme seyde, that our hertes been most esed,
> Whan that we been y-flatered and y-plesed . . .
> And somme seyn, how that we loven best
> For to be free, and do right as us lest . . .

Christine de Pisan (?1364–?1430), the celebrated poet and defender of her sex, daughter of an Italian physician at the court of Charles V in France, would no doubt have chosen the last proposal,

> For to be free and do right as us lest

('To be free and do right as we wish'), as the true answer, but the Wife of Bath's Tale rejects them all.

On the last day the knight is returning empty-handed to his execution when his way is barred by a witch (a 'foule olde wyf'), ugly beyond all imagination, who promises him the answer if he will do whatever she next asks of him, provided it is within his power.

Before the Queen and the assembled ladies of the court he tells what the old crone has told, and the answer is a power inversion:

> 'My lige lady, generally', quod he,
> 'Wommen desyren to have sovereyntee

As wel over hir housband as hir love,
And for to been in maistrie him above;'

('Women in general desire the sovereign place, to be masters over their husbands, and to have their own way in love'.)

The answer is accepted by the feminine court, the rapist is reprieved. The old witch then claims her due: marriage. On their wedding night the young man cannot overcome his revulsion at her ugliness. She then offers him two alternatives: either accept her ugly as she is, and she will be a true and humble wife, or reject her, and she will turn herself into a fair young maid, but never be faithful to him.

We see that if he chooses one alternative, he will wish he had chosen the other, and so on *ad infinitum*. But his answer is to say that he places himself under her wise governance: she should choose what she thinks best:

I do no fors the whether of the two.

By his response that he does not care for either of the two, he refuses to make a choice, escapes the proffered double bind, and deprives it of its power. That is not all, of course: his hideous bride turns into a beautiful young maiden, becomes a faithful, true, and obedient wife, and the two of them live happily ever after.

Figure 3.2 depicts this double bind between the young beauty and the old crone as a paradoxical figure like those of Chapter 1, as an oscillating contradiction between alternating patterns (inversion of figure and ground). Most people see the fair young lady first and the ugly old hag later (some people do not see it until it is pointed out), after which the image oscillates slowly between the two. (The young woman's chin is the old woman's nose.)

As Fred Attneave tells us in his 'Multistability in Perception' (1971), the original picture was created by the cartoonist W.E. Hill and published in *Puck* in 1915. It was brought to the attention of psychologists by Edwin G. Boring in 1930. Hill called it 'My Wife and My Mother-in-law'. It is a classic variation on the theme of purity and danger, beauty and ugliness, virtue and wickedness, as seen, for example, in Walt Disney's first full-length animated feature, *Snow White and the Seven Dwarfs* (1937), where the alter ego of the Evil Queen, mad with jealousy at Snow White's beauty, is the Ugly Witch.

Jean de Meung (d. ?1305), the thirteenth century male supremacist and author of the second part of the immensely influential French narrative and philosophical poem, *The Romance of the Rose* (1275–80) – whose attack on women in that work was refuted by Christine de Pisan (d. ?1430) in her *Epistle to the God of Love* (1399)

FIGURE 3.2 The paradoxical figure of the fair young lady and the ugly old witch, created by W.E. Hill for *Puck* in 1915 and titled: 'My Wife and My Mother-in-law'. The young woman's chin is the old woman's nose.

and her *Essay on the Rose* (1400) – had this to say about mothers-in-law (the Jealous Husband inquires after the source of his wife's new dress):

> ... You swore
> By Saint Denis and holy Filibert
> And by Saint Peter 'twas your mother's gift,
> Who sent it to you out of love for me,
> As you gave me to understand, that I
> Might save my money while she spend her own.

> If those were not the very words you used,
> I'll see her burned alive, the dirty whore,
> Old prostitute, vile bawd, and sorceress —
> And you along with her, as you deserve.

This was no idle threat. As Barbara Ehrenreich and Deirdre English show in *Witches, Midwives, and Nurses* (1973), many thousands of peasants, including children, midwives, and healers, were hanged or burnt at the stake as witches from Germany to Scotland between the fourteenth and seventeenth centuries. Eighty-five per cent of the victims — the scapegoats of the male establishment — were women.

This use of physical and psychological terrorism to divide and rule the peasantry by torturing and murdering peasant and artisan women — Susan Brownmiller gives the long history of this strategy in *Against Our Will* (1975) — was contemporary with the rise in the cost and power of labor following the Black Death (1347–51) during what Barbara Tuchman calls 'the calamitous fourteenth century' (seeing there a 'distant mirror' of our own); with the social upheavals of early commercial (mercantile) capitalism; with the teachings of John Wycliffe (?1320–1384) in England and the martyrdom in Bohemia of the Czech leader and rector of the University of Prague Jan Hus (1372–1415); with the fourteenth- to sixteenth-century Protestant attacks on the corruption of the Church; with Reformation and Counter-Reformation; with the peasant rebellions in England and especially in Europe (where the Hussite peasant generals invented the armored vehicle); and with the early struggles of the emerging middle class, the future bourgeoisie ('townspeople'), allied with the monarchy against the feudality and the landed aristocracy.

As in the anti-female aspects of the Book of Genesis, enlarged on by the misogyny of St Paul and the later Fathers of the Church (see Joachim Kahl's *Misery of Christianity*, 1968), not to mention Luther or Calvin, women are regarded in Christian tradition as the principal medium through which the devil works his evil upon the world, this being effected largely by his appeal to woman's 'inherent and insatiable lust'. (All humans are said to be equally tainted with the 'original sin' of Adam and Eve, but women are more equally tainted than men.) As Ehrenreich and English recount, female 'witches' were accused of every conceivable sexual crime against men; they were accused of being organized; and they were condemned to torture and death, not only for supposedly doing evil, but also for actually doing good.

We saw in a previous section the employment of useful double binds to maintain the structure of social, economic, and ecological relations, notably among the Tsembaga and the Dobu. We may now turn to examine the use of other double binds to maintain a pathological structure: male supremacy (patriarchy).

Whereas pathological double binds in pathological families and other institutions merely draw general support from their social environment, the double bind in the following male supremacist example maintains the context of (temporarily) essential aspects of that social environment itself. The following remarks were published in Paris in an anonymous article in the second issue of *Le Torchon Brule* ('That's torn it!') in 1971:

> Within this system of [patriarchal and competitive] values, the woman's choice is to identify herself *either* with the image of the Mother (the saint, the virgin, the procreatress, the responsible influence, the housewife, Mum . . .), *without* a vagina, *or* with the image of the Harlot (the slut who sells herself, the seductive doll, the vamp, the groovy chick . . .), *with* a vagina. Her choice creates a conflict which gives rise to fluctuating attitudes. The woman's role as a woman will be to oscillate between these two static models.

The paradox between the (Virgin) Mother and the Whore has been particularly remarked on in Catholic countries, but it is by no means confined to people of that faith.

This analysis, arrived at without benefit of the double-bind theory, is a precise example of it. It is not simply the two socially coded and incompatible roles that set off the pathological oscillation, but rather the *act of choice itself*, for it is the constraints requiring that a choice be made between the alternatives that makes them into a true double bind, a closed system of oscillation *ad infinitum*.

Nothing of any similar intensity, universality, or pathological power applies to men. As the American Protestant writer Mrs Hugh Fraser recorded in her autobiography, *A Diplomatist's Wife in Many Lands* (1910), in remarking on the social code of the village of Rocca di Papa in the Alban Hills of Italy, in 1861:

> The parish priest was the great authority and he kept his flock in splendid order, permitted no quarrels, no gaming – and no scandals. The great preoccupation in the 'Castelli', as the mountain villages are called, is to keep the girls out of harm's way; I have heard the preacher say to the women, 'Never mind about the men – they were made of different stuff to you! They can be sometimes bad and sometimes good – but you cannot! A woman must be either an angel or a devil – and there is no place between for *her*!'

Of the either/or double bind between the 'sexless' (Virgin) Mother and the 'insatiable sexuality' of the Whore, one would emphasize the following features:

> the significance of contextual information (rules and metarules) to the maintenance of the double bind: information spoken by no particular person or group, but constantly communicated by all (including the victims);
> the binary-digital choice between static, imaginary, and either/or images, neither of which is a person;
> the all-pervasive constraints of the context requiring that a choice be made, thus setting off the oscillation;
> the competitive and destructive jealousy between women encoded in their mediation by unspoken social constraints, a jealousy not 'innate' in the victims, nor in their genes, but in their environment, ruled by men;
> the victim's subjection to the oldest imperial strategy, divide-and-rule.

Above all one notes that each imaginary image is for the other exactly what is implied by the social signifier 'the Other Woman' (as in Joanne Woodward's role in *The Three Faces of Eve* (1957), Eve White and Eve Black).

At an even deeper level of relationship, the double bind between the unsexed Mother and the oversexed Whore is operative in the context of the woman in relation to other women: a competitive battle between 'self' and 'other', mediated by the Other (Figure 3.3). It is

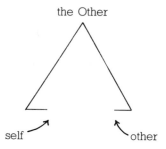

FIGURE 3.3   Self and Other: The mediation of the relationship between 'self' and 'other' by 'the Other', representing a dominant class, caste, race, or sex – the White Anglo-Saxon Protestant Male, or WASP, for example – or by a dominant person or persons in the subject's life, including parents, doctors, bosses, therapists, teachers. . . . The mediation of the Other may be necessary, legitimate, and beneficial (as in true parenthood and liberating education), or arbitrary, illegitimate, and harmful (as in the petty tyrants of the workplace).

also operative in the context of the woman in relation to herself: a schizoid splitting between 'mind' and 'body' and 'reason' and 'emotion' – a conflict between an 'I', as subject, and a 'me', as object (Jean-Paul Sartre), a conflict between a 'true self' (hiding away) and a 'false self' (striving to make life's ends meet), neither of which is a person (R.D. Laing).

The dominant mediator in this structured divide and rule is competition between men (not competition between women, actual as that may be), and this in turn is mediated by competition between commodities and corporations in our society (cf. Figure 2.5).

The situation is similar to that of non-whites under domestic or foreign colonialism, summed up by Frantz Fanon in *Black Skin, White Masks* (1952, pp. 109–40, 161–4) as 'Turn white or disappear'.

Learn the ABC, it's not enough, but
Learn it. Don't let it get you down!
Get on with it! You must know everything.
You must take over the leadership . . .
Search out the school, you homeless.
Secure yourselves Knowledge, you who are frozen!
You who are starving, grab hold of the book: It's a weapon.
You must take over the leadership.
Bertolt Brecht (1898–1956): In Praise of Learning

3.5 Double binds, context

Double binds may be universal, as in 'I am lying' in analytic logic; cultural, as in a paradoxical figure like the imaginary triangle (Figure 1.13); subjective, as in 'Jailbound' (Figure 1.6); amusing, as in the T-shirt joke ('You didn't like the other one?'); useful, as in the cybernetic regulation of the Tsembaga cycle; terrifying, as in 'Don't be so obedient!'; and pathological, as in the preceding section.

Modifying the definition of the double bind in schizophrenic communication in the original article of 1956, which is reprinted in Bateson's *Steps to an Ecology of Mind* (1972, pp. 201–27), and that given in *The Pragmatics of Human Communication* (1967, pp. 211–19), the conditions necessary to a pathological double bind – which is dependent on power – can be outlined as follows (none of them is necessarily conscious):

1   Two or more persons in an intense relationship that has a high degree of physical and/or psychological survival value for one, several,

or all of them, with at least one of them designated as the 'victim'. The victim is defined by those with the power to do so as either 'mad' or 'bad' or both. Typically intense relationships where power is or may be abused are parent-child interactions; friendship or love; infirmity or material dependence; contexts bound by repressive social norms; loyalty to a creed, cause, or ideology; captivity and brainwashing; and torture or psychotherapy.

2   The acceptance of a primary injunction, communicated by the context of the double bind (often by non-verbal means), that if the victim does not please the victimizer(s) punishment will follow. This may include physical violence, verbal violence, confinement, humiliation, expressions of anger or hate, the withdrawal of love, disconfirmation ('for me you don't exist'), or the expression of an utter inability to help the victim in any way (this is especially devastating when expressed by parents).

3   The acceptance of a secondary injunction, also communicated by the context of the double bind, often by non-verbal means, that what is happening to the victim is *not* the result of the demand of the double binder, not the result of orders or prohibitions, not the result of threatened punishment, not a contradiction of the love of the victimizer for the victim, and in fact not the result of any rules, constraints, metarules, or power relations at all, but simply the freely chosen behavior of the victim, behavior for which the victim is entirely responsible. This level of implicit communication becomes more complex when the double bind is inflicted not by one person, but by two. One parent (or in another context, the 'good cop') may negate at a more abstract level the injunctions of the other (the 'bad cop'), thus constructing the conditions for the double bind out of two contexts, or two aspects of the general context, rather than one.

4   Next, the imposition of a particular double bind on the victim, that is to say, an assertion that makes an assertion about itself such that the two assertions are mutually exclusive – 'Disregard this sign' – so that the message must be disobeyed to be obeyed and vice versa. If it is a definition of self or other, as in the case of the (Virgin) Mother and the Whore, then the paradoxical message defines the person as being such and such (e.g. the Mother) if and only if the person is not (the Mother), and as *not* being such and such (e.g. the Whore) if and only if the person is (the Whore). The message and its definitions are undecidable: the key to the pathology is that the victim believes them to be decidable, and believes that safety, security, and sanity depend on making the right decision between them.

5   A third contextual injunction preventing the victim from stepping outside the frame of the situation, an injunction preventing any attempt at comment, metacommunicative action, withdrawal, or escape. The victim thus cannot *not* respond to the double bind, but at

the same time no appropriate response – within the context imposed – is possible.

6   In some cases, the use of existential, universal, or simply logical double binds as well, paradoxes defined by the nature of language, negation, communication, and the human condition, rather than by pathological relations.

7   Quite commonly, especially in families, a situation in which the 'sanity' and the personal relations of the victimizer(s) depend on the presence of the victim. Once the victim is packed off to hospital, as apparently desired by the Others, every effort is made to get the victim back again.

8   Finally, repeated experiences of double binds and closed contexts by the victim, such that a complete double bind is no longer necessary: almost any part of one may precipitate panic, rage, despair, or self-destruction. At this level pathological double binds may become so completely internalized, and so split between a 'true self' and a 'false self' (R.D. Laing), that they become self-imposed: communicated to the victim by hallucinatory voices, telepathic messages, the 'influencing machines' of the doctor's case books, or God himself – a state of affairs indicating that the victim has been driven completely mad, and perhaps irreversibly so.

Wives be subject unto your own husbands, as unto the Lord. For the husband is the head of the wife, as Christ also is the head of the church, being himself the saviour of the body. . . . Even so ought husbands also to love their wives as their own bodies. He that loveth his own wife loveth himself . . .
>   The Epistle of Paul the Apostle to the Ephesians

3.6   *Zzzzz*

Zzzzz, a one-hour teleplay about men, women, and bees in the US network series *The Outer Limits* (American Broadcasting Corporation, 1963–64), tells the story of an attempt by the bees (women) to take over the universe (men), while seeing to the destruction of the 'jealous rivals' (wives) who stand in the path of their evil and secret ways.

In *Zzzzz*, the worker bees – who talk like midget men – attempt their takeover of the world by sending one of their Queen Bees, in the 'mutated' form of a beautiful dark-haired lab technician, to seduce a (dedicated) researcher working on translating the 'language' of the bees, Professor Field (whose marriage is childless), in order to propagate their kind by the millions. Regina, the mutant, is young enough to be the scientist's daughter (as the script has his wife point out). The failure of the couple to have a child is presented as a failing of the wife, with the implication that she is not a 'real woman'. There is never any doubt, however, that her husband is a 'real man'.

As is customary in 'science fantasy', Regina – the imaginary personification of the Alien Other, the Other Species, in female form – is shown to be heartless and ruthless. As with the supposedly emotionless Mr Spock of *Star Trek* – his inventors having failed to note that his dedication to his form of logic is not logic, but emotion – Regina's heartlessness is represented as the (sociobiological) result of genetics – the genes that she lacks being the same old kind as most Alien Others lack in most science fiction: those for 'love' and 'joy' and 'love of God'. (She may also be lacking the gene for marriage.)

Many sci-fi writers, Freudian or not, build their plots around psychoanalytical categories of Good and Evil, Reason and Emotion, Rationality and Animality. Regina is at one moment Instinctual Id trying to take over Rational Ego (the 'perfect' scientist) – imaginary Body trying to take over equally imaginary Mind – and at another, a cold-blooded biological Robot, a deadly Iron Maiden, trying to take advantage of Professor Field's supposed 'male frailty'.

She is depicted as every variation of what men define as the primal Eve, the submissively sexual Playmate, the childlike Temptress, the dangerous Seductress, the female Threat who – like blacks, hispanics, unions, 'Marxists', radicals – is Trying to Take Over.

As the story unfolds Regina becomes the Woman slaving behind the Man, the Holy Mother, the Virgin Queen. Indeed, in her relationship with what the carefully-crafted script calls the 'exacting and perfect' scientist and her bees (which he thinks are his), she is Snow White, the House Mother, the Evil Queen, and the Wicked Witch all rolled up into one.

All wide-eyed 'male innocence', the scientist employs his 'orderly and organized mind' in encouraging competition between his wife Francesca and this Other Woman, taking time to reassure his wife that her jealousy is perfectly all right, since she is a 'normal wife'. (The director consistently places the three in visual triangles.) But Regina uses the bees in the Professor's laboratory to kill Francesca – she dies of fright in the garden – whom she has viciously and cleverly attacked from their very first meeting.

The Professor becomes grief-stricken and sees the Error of his Ways. By now he knows that Regina, the Imaginary Other, the Threat to Men, is a so-called mutant. When she suddenly appears in the bedroom doorway wearing his wife's bridal veil like a department-store mannequin, he launches into a verbal assault on her about the 'love' and the 'God' and the 'human ritual' of marriage (once and for always) that she can never know.

Calling her 'inhuman', he advances threateningly towards her. Regina then suffers the standard dramatic punishment reserved for all her kind ('Thou shalt not suffer a witch to live!'): backing away in terror she conveniently falls over a balcony to her death on the patio below, whence she returns to being a bee hovering menacingly at the Professor's window. The Aliens have been defeated once again – but we all know that one day they'll be back.

An apt summary of this quite complex tale of female stereotyping, among thousands of others, is provided in a book published in 1979:

> It was in February 1944 . . . that I first saw her and knew how fascinating she would be. She carried herself with a graceful arrogance. Although she was slim, there was a toughness about her, a lethality, and also the unmistakable air of the coquette. An aristocrat with the tendencies of a wanton. She exuded primal power; yet, properly handled, she would be obedient, a vestal virgin consecrated to Mars and to a spectacular duty: death to the King's enemies. It was perhaps this knowledge that gave her an aura of vindictiveness. Some fusty man [at] the Admiralty had given her an appropriate name – *Vixen*. The Royal Canadian Navy had bought her from the Royal Navy; she was, after all, only a chattel to be bought and sold and used. [Now] she had been given a new name which emphasized her latent ferocity. This was His Majesty's Canadian destroyer *Sioux*.

The source is Hal Lawrence's book, *A Bloody War: One Man's Memories of the Canadian Navy 1939–1945* (1979, p. 114).

To men a man is but a mind. Who cares
What face he carries or what form he wears?
But woman's body is the woman. O
Stay thou, my sweetheart, and do never go.
                    Ambrose Bierce: *The Devil's Dictionary* (1906)

3.7   The female combatants

(Virgin) Mother, Wife, Whore, and Witch (Bitch) – these six terms and the pairs of imaginary opposites derived from them make up the basic lexicon of the code of stereotypes from which the individual messages used to humiliate, terrorize, and control individual women in our society are selected and combined.

The stereotypes of this 'code of the Other' are not restricted to

Western society, however – if the *ad feminam* attacks by the Party on Chiang Ching of the Shanghai 'Gang of Four' in 1976 and later are any guide. (In China, the Witch is also the Evil Empress.)

Richard Wilhelm writes in his commentary on the second hexagram, K'un, the Receptive, Earth, in the *I Ching* or *Book of Changes*:

> ... the Receptive [Yin] does not combat the Creative [Yang] but completes it. It represents nature in contrast to spirit, earth in contrast to heaven, space as against time, the female-maternal as against the male-paternal.

The principle of this complementary relationship between dominant and subordinate is also found in the relationship between prince and minister and between father and son.

> Indeed, even in the individual this duality appears in the coexistence of the spiritual world and the world of the senses.

Strictly speaking, however,

> there is no real dualism here, because there is a clearly defined hierarchic relationship between the two principles. In itself of course the Receptive is just as important as the Creative, but [Yin's] attribute of devotion defines the place occupied by this primal power in relation to the Creative. For the Receptive [Yin] must be activated and led by the Creative [Yang]; then it is productive of good. Only when it abandons this position and tries to stand as an equal side by side with the Creative, does it become evil.

(Note here that in Christianity, although the Virgin Mary is the 'Mother of God', she is not 'God the Mother' equal to 'God the Father'.)

The Mother and the Wife, each an ideal slave, are placed on a pedestal with the Virgin all the more easily to be put down. The Whore, Witch, and Bitch, each an expression of the male terror of female power, are placed 'beyond the pale', like the Catholic Irish, or treated as another species, like the people of color and the 'lower classes', or regarded as a 'danger to civilization', like the 'communists' and the 'Marxists' – all the more easily to be regarded as animals or objects, and thus to be made the targets of verbal, mental, and physical violence, without troubling the consciences of those who use them so.

In the terminology of scapegoating, stereotyping, and symmetrization used in the analysis of colonization in *The Imaginary Canadian* in

1980, the 'normal' status of the 'second sex' is that of a despised *'other'* subordinated to 'dominating Others' (male supremacists and their female partisans). In symmetrizing this illegitimate hierarchy of power, the dominating male Other is reduced (in the imaginary) to the status of the subordinated female *other*. In inverting the illegitimate hierarchy of power, the female *other* is elevated to the status of an Imaginary Other, a Regina supposedly dominant over men.

Symmetrization and inversion used in combination permit the sufferer (as in psychosis) to maintain mutually exclusive, logically or factually contradictory attitudes on the same subject at the same time. As the men say: 'Ballbreakers all, always sniping from below'.

Brigitte Helm plays each of the six stereotyped roles in Fritz Lang's *Metropolis* (1926) – each role acting as the Other Woman for the others. Marlene Dietrich plays them step by step in a narrative circle of trespass and redemption in Josef von Sternberg's *Blonde Venus* (1932), where she also appears dressed as an ape at the beginning of the nightclub number 'Hot Voodoo', accompanied by Cab Calloway and his band, as she takes on the role of the Whore (becoming Cary Grant's mistress to save her husband's life), and where the women of the chorus appear as black 'savages' carrying shields decorated with shark-like mouths (the *vagina dentata* of psychoanalysis) (Figure 3.4). Joan Crawford, the star of *Queen Bee* in 1955, rang the changes on these roles for forty years in every kind of film.

Fritz Lang's *Metropolis* (1926), a melodrama of subtly anti-semitic 'expressionism' (subjective relativism), written by Lang and his spouse Thea von Harbou, later an enthusiastic supporter of Hitler, is a classic epic of colonization by class and sex. Metropolis is a huge and futuristic city of aristocrats and managers living in towering skyscrapers and fleshly roof gardens, supported by workers who attend and regulate a vast machine driven by the Demon Steam (they are its brains) – a machine equated by Lang/Harbou with Moloch, the Hebrew deity to whom child sacrifices were offered in the days of the Biblical kings – as they toil like trogdolytes among the cruel works of pistons, cogs, and wheels without wheels far beneath the surface of the earth.

Brigitte Helm, an astonishing 18-year-old actress, plays the role of Maria, a worker's daughter. She first enters the film by appearing above ground (to the *jeunesse dorée* hero, son of the Master of Metropolis) in the role of mother to the workers' 'neglected' children, whom she refers to as the hero's 'brothers' (ignoring his 'sisters'). There is no doubt about her virginity.

The workers are portrayed as idiots and brutes incapable of doing anything for themselves. Maria offers them a spiritual deliverance from oppression by means of a 'mediator' ('the heart', meaning herself, if not Christ), who will intervene between the industrialists ('the brains') and the workers ('the hands'). This she does in a vaulted cave deep in the catacombs, like the Christian catacombs of Rome, complete with altar, candles, and crosses.

At the bidding of the Master of Metropolis, the Mad Scientist Rotwang (implicitly Jewish) chases Maria through the caverns, carries her off to his laboratory adorned by a symbolic star and straps her down in his electric machine. He has constructed a robot to replace the workers, which in all but one respect, its breasts, is the original of C3PO in *Star Wars*. Maria is symbolically raped by Rotwang in a series of fantastic electrical effects that transform the metal robot into her double in flesh and blood.

The Robot-Maria then plays the vamp with the Master of Metropolis in front of his son, who is in love with the real Maria. The Master sends the Robot-Maria into the catacombs as an *agent provocateur*, to stir the workers into self-(and-other)-destructive violence.

After this, in a visually amazing scene the Robot-Maria plays the harlot for the upper-class men of the clubs in the city above the ground, appearing as the Medusa-like Goddess of Lust, the irresistible Femme Fatale, the all-powerful Empress of Evil.

The Robot-Maria drives men mad. She incites the upper class to further depths of (1920s) decadence and the workers to revolt. The workers begin destroying the machines. In line with the general absurdity of the several plots, and the disgusting portrayal of the workers, the rebels smash the water pumps, thus flooding their underground city and threatening their children (left alone, of course) with drowning. Predictably, the children are saved at the last moment by the real Maria and her lover, the upper-class hero, son of the Master of Metropolis.

In the climax of the film the rebellious workers are incited by their foreman, whose brutish tyranny they abjectly accept, to find a scapegoat for their troubles – a witch. They capture the Robot-Maria, believing it to be the real one, and dance around the funeral pyre while they burn her at the stake. As the flames mount higher around the panic-stricken figure of Maria, the evil Robot reappears through the flames and melts away.

Following another 'chase-the-woman' sequence (up the cathedral in this case) Rotwang tries to kill the real Maria, but is toppled off the roof of the cathedral by the hero. Led by their foreman, the workers then beg forgiveness of the Master of the Metropolis as he stands reprovingly at the open cathedral door, and the film ends with the real Maria ready to marry into the bourgeoisie.

Men often respond to the analysis of the stereotyping of women by

FIGURE 3.4   Man and woman, war and peace. (a) The opening scene of 'Hot Voodoo' ('I don't know right from wrong') in *The Blonde Venus* (1932). (b) An RKO publicity still for the film. The war shields play a striking visual role in 'Hot Voodoo', where they form the moving ground for the static figure of Dietrich as she sings. Von Sternberg never does anything accidental in black and white. If you force yourself to invert the figure-ground relationship so that the shark-faced shields in the hands of the (savage) women become the figure instead of the ground, the sensation of unbridled violence is overpowering. (c) Dietrich, now an independently famous artist and no longer seeing Cary Grant, singing in a Paris nightclub, only to find him next to her in the audience, with all the sexual ambiguity that implies.

In *Ideology and the Image* (1981, pp. 98–32), Bill Nichols analyzes the conflict between Dietrich using Cary Grant to save her sick husband's life and support her child, and her 'final redemption' as a 'perfect wife and mother', now that her husband is cured, at the end of the film. The action is dependent on (subjective) double bind:

If I am to preserve our family, I must earn money.

But if I earn money, I cannot preserve our family.

Many a mother in the workforce today faces the same paradoxical injunction. Figure 3.4(a) and 3.4(c) are reprinted from: Homer Dickens: *The Films of Marlene Dietrich* (1968).

FIGURE 3.5 *The Female Combatants*, an American pamphlet of 1776. Here the Anglo-Saxon and the Teuton, white, confront the Amerindian, non-white. Britannia (for whom Britons, such as the American Colonists, ought never to be slaves) declares: 'I'll force you to Obedience, you Rebellious Slut!' America, the Noble Savage, responds with a right cross and declares: 'Liberty, Liberty for ever, Mother, while I exist!' Colonies and other subordinate entities are typically depicted as wives, daughters, or mistresses of the dominant power. (Today, Canada, the wealthiest of the Anglo-American colonies, daughter of Great Britain and elder sister of Australia and New Zealand, is said to be in

symmetrization or inversion, saying that they are equally stereotyped by women, or more so, e.g. as macho studs.

The response is, first, that there are many dozens of stereotypes of men; second, that they do not necessarily involve double binds; third, that unlike the mainly negative images of women, most male stereotypes are those of irresistible, independent, commanding, and adventurous figures, i.e. heroes; and lastly, that male stereotypes are originally imposed on men, not by women, but by other men.

The femininity of the Robot in *Metropolis* fits the stereotype of Her Majesty's Canadian Ship, the destroyer *Sioux*. For men, machines are mechanical and electronic slaves designed – as they should be – to be mastered and controlled. It is this mastery – strategic control of the machine – that has allowed men to make machines traditionally feminine. (Says Richard Pryor to Gene Wilder as they steal a car in *Silver Streak* (1976): 'That Chev's a jerk-off, man! This here Jag's p-u-r-e pussy!')

Figure 3.5 tells another tale of witchery and savagery in 'the female of the species'. No doubt the Savage and the Primitive – the non-white Savage associated with Evil and the Witch; the Primitive, with Innocence and the Virgin – form another stereotypical pair.

There is no reason to suppose that this code of stereotypes came into being automatically with the emergence of human society from animal social groupings – wherever and however often that occurred. But to a greater or lesser degree, we find the same basic stereotypes of women in most societies – and the same symmetrization, inversion, oppression, and rationalization of oppression (blaming the victims and teaching them to blame themselves) as in our own.

These stereotypes are not a product of capitalism, state or private, Russian, Chinese, European, or American, but rather of imperialism. They are the result (and the rationalization) of the colonization of women by men, the original act of violence by means of which women became the original working class, the class whose mental, manual, and emotional labor supports the labor of men.

---

bed with the United States, which has effectively controlled the Canadian economy since the 1960s, while Quebec, the neglected wife, is said to be seeking a divorce.) As Elaine Pagels notes in *The Gnostic Gospels* (1979, p. 57), this use of family metaphors to represent domination and subordination is of venerable origin. The God of Israel is depicted as husband and lover in the Old Testament, his spouse being the community of Israel (Isaiah 50 : 1–8; Jeremiah 2 : 2–3; 20–25; 3 : 1–20; Hosea 1–4, 14), or the land of Israel (Isaiah 62 : 1–5).

FIGURE 3.6   An early American lithographic poster by Matt Morgan (1881).

These imaginary stereotypes are maintained in men and women's individual imaginations, attitudes, and ideologies by what Colette Dowling has aptly called 'the Cinderella Complex' – that learned but hidden fear of individuality and independence by means of which dominant social codes induce most girls and women, but relatively few boys or men, to sabotage their own originality (1981, p. 103) (Chapter 5).

Dowling's description of her early attempts to declare her independence of the Other is an account of a double bind (pp. 97–8):

At the age of twelve or thirteen I began to pursue what was to become a lifelong ambition: to get my father to shut up. . . . I did not believe myself capable of . . . Real Thinking. . . . Real Thinking was for professors, fathers, priests.

. . . I had little experience in learning to develop a rational position on anything. Even in college I was more a jouster than an independent thinker. The kind of mental and emotional development that comes in isolation, when one is up against oneself alone, was something I was too frightened to engage in for almost twenty years. I would try to gain clarity by differentiating myself from some strong and forceful Other – anyone, male or female, on whom I could project that internalized image of my father. The 'clarity', needless to say, would be short-lived. I would pull from the Other like a rubber band, glimpse my differentiated self for a brief moment, then snap back again when the tension of separateness became too great to endure.

For I am the first and the last.
I am the honored one and the scorned one.
I am the whore and the holy one.
I am the wife and the virgin . . .
I am the barren one, and many are her sons . . .
I am silence that is incomprehensible . . .
I am the utterance of my name.

> *Thunder, Perfect Mind* (c. 100 CE). Quoted by
> Elaine Pagels in *The Gnostic Gospels* (1979)

3.8   One flesh, one person

Spoken by a female divinity and probably first written down about 100 CE, the extraordinary words quoted above voice what may best be called 'the Other Woman Paradox' as precisely as any other or later text.

Some of the paradoxical injunctions – report, command, and question – implicit in the male discourse about women can be gleaned from the following selection of male bywords in male gossip, taken from *PsychoSources*, a psychology resource catalog edited by Evelyn and Barry Shapiro in 1973 (p. 40):

A clever woman knows how to keep a man — *Smart women are emasculating* — All women think about is their looks — *A woman's place is in the home* — If she can't get along on what I give her she can get herself a job — *Women can't handle money* — I let my wife do all the bookkeeping — *Why can't she do anything right?* — With her looks she doesn't need brains — *Women are only suited for monotonous work* — Just like a woman to change her mind — *All women want is to get married* — Men create things, women create life — *Once they get married they sit around and get fat* — A man works from sun to sun but a woman's work is never done — *Women like to be raped* — It's a smart broad who holds out for a license — *All women do is gossip* — Women basically dislike other women — *Women are always so emotional* — Frigid bitch — *Career women are too damned independent* — Women cling like vines — *Women don't think* — Conniving female — *If she goes to college she'll never get a man* — They're all alike — *I can't figure women out* — Never trust a woman — *Behind every great man is a woman . . .*

In *The Family, Sex and Marriage in England 1500–1800* (1977), Lawrence Stone, an authority on the English Revolution of the seventeenth century (1642–88), explains the status of wives at that time as follows (p. 195):

> As Widow Blackacre put it in Wycherley's *Plain Dealer* [a play of 1674 based on Molière's *Misanthrope* of 1666], 'matrimony to a woman [is] worse than excommunication in depriving her of the benefit of the law'. Defoe's *Roxana* [1724] was even more critical of the legal impotence of a wife: 'the very nature of the marriage contract was . . . nothing but giving up liberty, estate, authority and everything to a man, and the woman was indeed a mere woman ever after — that is to say a slave.'

This legal subjection of women to husbands or fathers was the reason why suffrage was always restricted to male householders. (English women over 30 were given the vote in 1918; women over 21 were given it in 1928.) That 'universal' suffrage should be manhood suffrage alone was never questioned by the Chartists (the radical Workingmen's Associations of the 1830s), nor by the Levellers, the radical democrats of the seventeenth century — men like John Lilburne (?1614–1657) who, if less radical than the Diggers (who were persecuted by everybody), were put down by Cromwell, Parliament, and the Army.

In another 1977 book, *Women in Canadian Law*, Linda Silver Dranoff explains the theological and common law doctrine of 'one flesh . . . one person':

In one biblical account, Eve was said to have been created from the rib of Adam, and was thus seen as an aspect of his wholeness.

(The story of Adam's Rib in Genesis 2: 21, the commonly accepted account – enshrined in the imaginary equality between Spencer Tracey and Katherine Hepburn in the 1949 movie of that name – was written into later versions of Genesis by the priestly class, changing the past and its myths to fit the present like Orwell's Newspeak. It is contradicted by the earlier account, faithful to ancient mythical traditions, in Genesis 1: 27: 'God created man in his own image, in the image of God created he him; male and female created he them'. Here 'man' stands for the people of Israel, there is no subordinate or secondary creation of woman, and God is both male and female. In Genesis 1: 26, where God says 'let us make man in our image', there is more than one God.)
Dranoff continues:

The biblical concept of marriage as a sacrament, in which the husband and wife became one flesh, seems to have been a reuniting of Adam and Eve into one person. This 'one flesh' concept was institutionalized in legal systems: the common law of England, the civil law and Napoleonic Code of France, and then Canadian law.

(The 'one flesh' concept is apparent in St Paul's Epistle to the Ephesians (5 : 22) already quoted: The husband is the head of the wife, whom he loves 'as his own body', and 'the twain . . . become one flesh'.)
Under these conditions,

marriage had enormous legal consequences for a woman, for she was absorbed into her husband's identity and they became in law 'one person'. In effect, this 'one person' was the husband.

As for the imaginary power of women over men, the fifteenth-century *Hammer of the Witches* (1486) – written in Latin by Friar Heinrich Kramer and Friar James Sprenger, accepted as gospel by Church, Inquisition, parish priests, local magistrates, and men (and women) in general, and translated into English by Montague Summers in 1928 – has this to say about women's 'diabolical operations':

It is asked whether witches can with the help of devils really and actually remove the [male] member, or whether they only do so apparently by some glamour or illusion . . .
    Answer. There is no doubt that certain witches can do marvellous things with regard to the male organs . . .

What is to be thought of those witches who . . . sometimes collect male organs in great numbers, as many as twenty or thirty members together, and put them in a bird's nest, or shut them up in a box, where they move themselves like living members, and eat oats and corn, as has been seen by many and is a matter of common report? . . . For a certain man tells us that, when he had lost his member, he approached a known witch to ask her to restore it to him. She told the afflicted man to climb a certain tree, and that he might take which he liked out of a nest in which there were several members. And when he tried to take a big one, the witch said: You must not take that one; adding, because it belonged to a parish priest.

All of these things are caused by devils through an illusion or glamour . . . by transmuting the mental images in the imaginative faculty.

In his *Politics of the Family and Other Essays* (1971), R.D. Laing gives an account of the complicated confusions of self-and-sexual-identity produced by the family relations of a young man of 23. Simplifying enormously, says Laing, the young man experienced himself in the following way:

Right side: masculine.
Left side: feminine.
Left side younger than right side.
The two sides do not meet.
Both sides are rotten, and he is rotting away with them to an early death.

Psychoanalysis and other information revealed that his mother and father separated when he was 5:

His mother told him he 'took after' his father.
His father told him he 'took after' his mother.
His mother said his father was not a real man.
His father said his mother was not a real woman.

From Paul's point of view they were both right.

Consequently, on the one hand (or, as he would say, on his right side), he was a female male homosexual, and on the other hand (his left side), he was a male lesbian.

The issue of being a real or not-real man or woman had been a longstanding family conflict:

In his view of his mother's view of her father, and his mother's view of her mother's view of *her* husband; and his father's view of his mother, and his father's view of his father's view of *his* wife, there had never been a real man or woman in the family for four generations.

Through this internalization of these tangled contradictions, these strange loops in relations between relations, Paul was effectively immobilized:

> His body was a sort of mausoleum, a haunted graveyard in which the ghosts of several generations still walked. . . . The family had buried their dead *in each other*. . . . This young man was tied in a knot; it had taken at least four, perhaps five or more, generations to tie it.

Finally here, on nature and nurture and personal and social identity, sexual and otherwise, the following list of terms will serve to illustrate the correspondences between four sets of increasingly violent metaphors used first to label with exaggerated politeness, and then to stereotype, degrade, and humiliate non-white, non-male, non-heterosexual, non-Christian people in our society.

Black	Woman	Gay	Jew
Negro	lady	homosexual	Hebrew
colored	shady	queer	non-white
boy	girl	'can't tell'	jew-boy
darkie	chick	fruit	?
?	gold-digger	?	sheeny
savage	harpy	sodomite	alien
indolent	irrational	unnatural, immoral	inhuman, medieval
oversexed	insatiable	promiscuous	avaricious
violent	hysterical	sick	dirty
ape	bitch	freak	monster
devil	witch	pervert	Christ-killer
rapist	ball-breaker	child-corrupter	child-killer
nigger	whore	faggot	kike

POSTSCRIPT: FILM STEREOTYPES OF AMERICAN WOMEN*

Milton Berle: 'Wait a minute. Are you knocking this country? Are you saying something against America?'

Terry Thomas: 'Against it! I should be positively astounded to hear of anything that could be said for it. Why, the whole bloody place is the most unspeakable matriarchy in the whole history of civilization. Look at yourself. And the way your wife and her *strumpet* of a mother [Ethel Merman] push you through the hoop. As far as I can see American men have been totally emasculated. They're like slaves. They die like flies from coronary thrombosis, while their women sit under hairdryers eating chocolates and arranging for every second Tuesday to be some kind of Mothers Day.'

Stanley Kramer's *It's a Mad, Mad, Mad, Mad World* (1963)

In an important article Joseph W. Baunoch and Betty E. Chmaj of Wayne State University have identified sixteen strategic stereotypes of women in American films, providing us with a semiotic dictionary of the 'nature of woman' according to Hollywood from the 1930s to recent times (before Rambo and Rambolina).

These stereotypes are by no means confined to Hollywood, of course. As ideological and working images necessary to the colonization of women by men (most of whom are colonized by other men), they appear in one form or another wherever women are oppressed.

(On the exploitation of young women by young men in the United States in the 1960s, see Marge Piercy's 1969 piece, *The Grand Coolie Dam*.)

(In 1969 the politics of certain young French Maoists included the classically European anti-American image of the 'matriarchy' espoused by the English actor Terry Thomas in *It's a Mad, Mad, Mad, Mad World* (1963). Unlike the 'submissive' and 'henpecked' American males, said the French activists (the question arose when two North Americans volunteered to do the dishes), Frenchmen (and European men in general) were 'real men' who would never permit themselves to be dominated by women.)

In what follows I am summarizing Baunoch and Chmaj's article, omitting the numerous films they cite as examples.

Their categories are:

The Pillars of Virtue: the Sweet Young Thing, The Perfect Wife, the Gracious Lady, Mother/Mammy/Mom/Ma

---

* Reprinted from 'Montage Analytic and Dialectic: The Right Brain Revolution' in *The Rules Are No Game: The Strategy of Communication*, 1987.

The Glamour Girls: the Femme Fatale, the Sex Goddess, the Showgirl, the Cool Beauty
The Emotive Woman: the Long-Suffering Lady, the Vixen, the Sexually-Frustrated Neurotic
The Independent Woman/The New Woman: the Career Girl, the Regular Gal, the Durable Dame, the Brassy Modern, the Liberated Modern

The details follow.

A   The Pillars of Virtue

1   The Sweet Young Thing

As sacred as Mom – in America – she is 'a chaste charmer, whether child, waif, girl next door, or Pollyanna. Warm and wholesome, she looks at the world with wide-eyed innocence. The eternal girl-woman and apple-pie symbol of all that is good.'
Representative stars: Janet Gaynor (1929–38), Shirley Temple (1934–40), Doris Day (1948–69), June Allyson (1944–53), Julie Andrews (1964–69).

2   The Perfect Wife

'Often the elder sister to the Sweet Young Thing,' she is 'more chic and sophisticated in the thirties and forties than later', but 'remains throughout film history the supportive, enduring, good-humored, comely (though not often overtly sexy – less so, certainly, in later decades) complement to her mate and bastion of the American Home.'
Representative stars: Myrna Loy (1934–52), June Allyson (1954–59), Eve Marie Saint (1957-present).

3   The Gracious Lady

Although sharing many of the attributes of the Perfect Wife, 'she was something more: the focal point of her dramas rather than a supporting peg. Virtuous, compassionate, intelligent, witty, and in her own elegant, genteel way, always able to face whatever crisis confronted her'. She could be 'strong and independent, freely giving of her strength to sustain her man without loss of dignity'.
Representative stars: Irene Dunne (1930–52), Greer Garson (1939–55), Deborah Kerr (1947–present).

4   Mother/Mammy/Mom/Ma

'Aproned, over-forty, and beyond sex, another bastion of the American Home, usually bolstering from the background.' She is 'the quintessence of strength, constancy, approachability, and integrity who would sacrifice all for the family. Not until the fifties and sixties does this tower of selflessness give way in film to the "Great American Bitch"' (e.g. Angela Lansbury) 'moms who blight instead of brace.'
Representative stars: Fay Bainter (1934–35), Hattie McDaniel (1932–48) (also Ethel Waters), Jane Darwell (1930–56) – who played the role in over three hundred films.

B   The Glamor Girls

1   The Femme Fatale

'Dietrich, as a *femme* at her most *fatale* in *The Devil is a Woman* [1935], tells the hero, "I came to see if you were dead. If you loved me enough, you would have killed yourself". Although most film *fatales*, including Dietrich herself, aren't really such lethal witches, even the most Americanized carries a hint of destructiveness. A woman of mystery and allure, she is the exotic conqueror of the submissive male in a world of romance, intrigue, and shadows.'
Representative stars: Marlene Dietrich (1930–57), Rita Hayworth (1941–57), Hedy Lamarr (1938–57), Ava Gardner (1946–64).

2   The Sex Goddess

'Another temptress, but open rather than mysterious, straightforward rather than devious, brassy rather than sinister. Her guise is whorish but her heart is often as generous as her proportions.' 'By the forties the brassiness gives way to cuddliness and by the sixties (as a reflection of an alienated, automated age?) it sometimes descends to a zombie-like, plastic, super-womanishness.'
Representative stars: Mae West (1932–40), Jean Harlow (1930–37), Lana Turner (1941–55), Marilyn Monroe (1950–62), Raquel Welch (1966–present).

3   The Showgirl

'The Sweet Young Thing with spangles. Although glamorized and greasepainted, she is essentially a "good kid": affable, wholesome, reliable, with "the-show-must-go-on" in her blood. Curiously, a less overtly theatrical personage than many of her performing sisters, she

often experiences a metamorphosis from chorus kicker or cheap honky tonk singer or the prettier part of a song-and-dance team into Lady and Star at the film's end. When backstage musicals fade in the fifties, she fades with them.'
Representative stars: Ruby Keeler (1933–37), Alice Faye (1936–43), Betty Grable (1940–55), Judy Garland (1940–54).

4   The Cool Beauty

'The "white" lady, the goddess on a pedestal: aristocratic, imperturbably and impeccably groomed. Often an heiress or a princess', she draws respectful glances 'rather than leering appraisals from men. Copulation with such a creature, if at all imaginable, could cause frostbite. After the fifties, the Cool Beauty, too, disappears.'
Representative stars: Constance Bennett (1929–39), Gene Tierney (1940–55), Alexis Smith (1940–59), Grace Kelly (1951–56).

C   The Emotive Woman

1   The Long-Suffering Lady

'The noble martyr who tearfully but courageously suffers the slings and arrows. Her agonizing is usually the result of the abusiveness and/or infidelities and/or weaknesses of a man (or men); on other occasions her antagonist might be a thankless child, malicious gossip, or disease (physical or mental). Popular with feminine audiences, she "complies with woman's image of herself as long-suffering" (Leslie A. Fiedler). Interesting and paradoxically, many stars who made the type a specialty were equally adept at portraying her opposite, the Vixen.'
Representative stars: Greta Garbo (1930–37), Bette Davis (1937–64), Joan Crawford (1945–62), Barbara Stanwyck, Susan Hayward, Olivia de Havilland, and others (1940s and after), Katherine Hepburn (1951–present).

2   The Vixen

'Overpowering and destructive, a more lethal antagonist than the *femme fatale*, the neurotic, vindictive, castrating bitch-woman.'
Representative stars: Bette Davis (1934–1970s), Joan Crawford (1931–1967), Barbara Stanwyck (1930–56), Susan Hayward (1942–61), Elizabeth Taylor (1963–present).

3   The Sexually-Frustrated Neurotic

'The perennial outsider, the misfit, the unfulfilled woman, whose lonely, empty life is vitalized almost solely by her own hysterical outbursts.'
Representative stars: Miriam Hopkins (1936–43), Agnes Moorehead (1942–60), Mercedes McCambridge in *All the King's Men* (1949), Rosalind Russell in *Picnic* (1955), individual roles by Ingrid Bergman, Bette Davis, Shelley Winters, and others.

D   The Independent Woman (at times the 'New Woman' or the 'Modern Woman')

1   The Career Girl

'Ambitious and productive, tailored and crisp; triumphant in a dismayed man's world (until her final-reel conversion into a lovestruck, "fulfilled" female). The Career Girl as a star type, along with most of her Modern Woman sisters, all but disappears after the forties.'
Representative stars: Jean Arthur (1935–48), Katherine Hepburn (1933–52), Claudette Colbert (1939–46), Rosalind Russell (1940–52).

2   The Regular Gal

'Earthbound and salty, another female who holds her own in the male world but men like her better; the wise-cracking "good Joe", comfortable "pal" or "buddy"'. The masculine terms used to describe her are assumed to be complimentary.
Representative stars: Joan Blondell (1930–56), Ginger Rogers (1930–50), also Anne Sheridan, Patricia Neal, and Eve Arden (in supporting roles).

3   The Durable Dame

'Behind her battleaxe exterior beats the proverbial heart of gold (or, in recent caricatures of the type, as with Bette Davis, a "one hundred percent camp" malignancy).' 'A lovable, earthy old rock, too tough to be a relic and too honest for the prescribed niceties', she 'weathers the world, one way or another, and only death can demolish her.'
Representative stars: Marie Dressler (1930–33), Marjorie Main (1937–57), Bette Davis (1961–1970s).

4   The Brassy Modern

'As brash as the Regular Gal but bouncier and more volatile; a bombshell – likeable, rambunctious, and non-stop in her quest, whether for a man or anything else, comes on strong but makes them laugh.'

Representative stars: Ethel Merman (1934–53), Betty Hutton (1942–52), Barbra Streisand (1968–present).

5   The Liberated Modern

'The newest of the types, good-looking in her own way', she appeared in the mid-1960s. '"Liberated" in any of several ways, she may be prominent as a career woman of a newer kind (whether as teacher, model, tramp)', and '"free" in a new way (free of stereotypes, for instance).' 'Unlike most American Dreaming sisters, she sets her life-goals beyond the husband-and-home-in-the-suburbs.' 'Usually self-reliant, razor-sharp, alienated, and tough but pretty.'

Representative stars: Jane Fonda (1965–present), Julie Christie (1965–present), Faye Dunaway (1967–present), Glenda Jackson (1970–present).

CHAPTER 4

Paradox: ecology, ideology, and political economy

HOW MUCH MORE OF
THE PRESENT DO WE
HAVE TO SIT THROUGH
BEFORE THE FUTURE
COMES ON?

Pot-Shots (c. 1975)

4.1 The paradox of prosperity

Paradoxical relations of distinctly different content from the ideological and psychological warfare behind the pathologies noted in the last chapter, but of similar paradoxical form, play an important, if unintended, part in the regulation of the modern economic system, and may in the future become significant as the proximate sources of fundamental change.

The capitalist revolution that began in earnest with the organized piracy of the age of discovery and the commercial revolution of the sixteenth century did not invent merchants, markets, media, monopolies, racism, sexism, imperialism, wage labor, the class structure, alienation, ideology, poverty, male supremacy, or the petty bourgeoisie – all of these could be found, in one form or other, under the 'oriental despotism' of the 4000-year-old imperial city-state of Babylon, mythical locus of the Tower of Babel, instrument of the Jewish captivity, and one of the wonders of the ancient world.

But capitalism did invent the business cycle – periodic recessions and depressions produced not by external factors such as piracy or the weather, but by its own activities – as well as the dominance of commodity production by wage labor over all other kinds of creative activity.

According to Arthur F. Burns, Chairman of the US Federal Reserve in the 1970s, in his Keynesian account 'Business Cycles' (1968), written for the *International Encyclopedia of the Social Sciences*, the system-generated oscillations of the short-term business cycle – two to ten years long – appeared in Britain, France, and the United States only some two centuries ago.

At that time Britain and its Empire, the pioneer capitalist system, was developing from the state-sponsored and regulated mercantile capitalism of the seventeenth and eighteenth centuries – the heyday of political, economic, and military monopolies like the East India Company – into the first fully capitalist economy.

Capitalism also invented the systematic employment of wage labor and technological innovation to increase the capacity of the system to produce. Systematic growth in productive capacity is not a functional aspect of capitalism, to be used or enjoyed at will, it is a structural necessity through which the system maintains its (temporary) stability, economic, social, and political.

State and private capitalism is thus an inherently unstable economic system, dependent on expanding into every available environment, not excluding outer space. The necessity for expansion makes many kinds of imperialism (military, economic, social), which long antedates capitalism, into structural features of the system too.

On the political side the capitalist economic revolution and the resulting political struggle between the rising middle class (later the industrial bourgeoisie) and the landed aristocracy resulted in the invention of capitalist democracy in the seventeenth and eighteenth centuries, of which the United States remains the most advanced example.

The challenge to perform

Capitalism is a many-leveled, adaptive, open, semiotic, cybernetic system – not a machine, not a physical system, and not an organism – controlled by information and limited in its possible behaviors by hierarchies of natural, social, economic, and often political and national constraints, some of which are variable – such as the rate of profit, the 'acceptable' level of unemployment, or the role of warfare as an economic activity – and some of which are not – such as the limited capacity of nature to act as a 'waste sink' to recycle and detoxify the system's industrial and agricultural wastes.

The economic activities of the system depend on the combination of competition (at certain levels) and co-operation (at others), and its daily activities are coordinated and controlled, and often disordered and disrupted, not by physical forces, but by the feedback of information about its past and present and probable future states – including that represented by wages, prices, profits, output, sales, inventories, interest rates, and so on – between its many millions of goal-seeking parts.

The goal of every subsystem within the constraints of the whole is (at least) short-range survival, and for any business corporation to survive, it must not only make a profit, but also protect its capacity for future profitability. The result is the necessity to reinvest profits in corporate growth. The 'challenge to perform' – and to keep performing – represented by the goal of continued profitability is the key to the relationships between corporations and their various environments (other corporations, governments, people, nature, the future).

Under capitalism considered as a system (as distinct from the activities of any particular corporation, national economy, or economic sector), the goal of production is more production.

In the productive industries (as distinct from wholesale or retail distribution, the service industries, or the financial services of banks) labor uses capital goods (tools, machines, computers, assembly lines, plants, refineries, mills) to create consumer and other capital goods, with exchange value, out of energy and raw materials.

To realize the profits contained in the exchange value added by labor in the process of production, commodities – whether consumer or capital goods – have to be exchanged for money in the market. Money, however, is only the medium of exchange (the general equivalent), the means of expressing information such as prices. While money (so long as it is respected) can represent and store quantitative value (just as a computer represents and stores information), money cannot create value. As liquid capital (imaginary capital) money is dead value until it is reinvested in real capital and labor in the production of new use values and exchange values – and in the system as a whole, with its dependence on growth, some part of the profits realized in money must ultimately be invested not in utilizing the productive capacity of existing enterprises, but in the expansion of productive capacity itself.

Capitalism thus involves two basic kinds of growth:

> the short-term expansion of the production of commodities at the level of the surface structure (wages, price, and profit), regulated by fluctuations in the short-term business cycle which increase or reduce economic activity;
> the long-term expansion of productive capacity at the level of the deep structure (use value, exchange value, and surplus value), continuing in spite of expansions and contractions in the short-term business cycle.

These two levels of growth – surface structure and deep structure – are shown schematically in the diagram in Figure 4.1 (4.3 below).

Consumer goods and capital goods

The two most important levels of production and consumption in the system are the circuit of consumer goods and services and the circuit of capital goods and services. In the industrialized countries the circuit of consumer goods includes non-durable goods such as food and clothing, durable goods such as cars, computers, appliances, audio and video systems, and of course houses, as well as services such as entertainment, medical care, police, plumbers, mechanics, and undertakers. The circuit of capital goods and services (serving the system's productive capacity) includes every component required to produce new consumer and capital goods, including the purchase of machine tools, the building of factories, and investment in labor power.

The expectation of profit

John Maynard Keynes (1883-1946), the millionaire financier, is often credited – along with the Second World War – with saving capitalism by recognizing the necessity of the expansionary policies being devised in several nations to save the system from the depression of the 1930s. In his view, the crucial factor in the capitalist economy, with its repeated inability to avoid deep depression and massive unemployment (Robinson, 1948, pp. 111-13), besides the amount of government spending, is the level and rate of the investment of capital in new or unused productive capacity – labor, resources, factories – or more simply put, the rate of capital investment.

(To invest in labor is to purchase control over the expression of an individual's creative capacity.)

That capital investment is the key to the system is the view elegantly outlined in Keynes's *General Theory of Employment Interest and Money* (1936). When investment in capital goods and labor remains high or increases the economy booms, when capital investment falls (when capital strikes) the economy busts (Clarke, ed., 1978, pp. 99-101).

The boom-and-bust cycle can be moderated and manipulated to a degree by government spending, often on non-productive commodities, such as weapons and warfare (beginning most recently with the tiny defense industry whose public dangers Eisenhower warned against when he labeled it the 'military-industrial complex' in 1961), as well as by budgetary and monetary policies affecting business profits, wages, employment, the currency, the money supply, interest rates, and so on.

The amount of activity in the economic system (its relative prosperity measured as a quantity) is equal to the rate at which the consumer and capital goods and services it is producing are consumed, i.e. purchased.

The rate of investment depends on the capitalist's expectation of profit (the inducement to invest), which is partly a matter of fact (gathered from economic indicators), partly a matter of available supply and actual demand, partly a matter of monopolies (corporations controlling their markets), partly a matter of perceived corporate needs, and partly a matter of psychology, based on conscious and unconscious desires, hunches, and estimates about what consumers, other corporations, or the economy will do in the future.

The level of capital investment is thus related by the feedback of information to the expectation of profit (the inducement to invest), which in its turn depends on the present and expected trend of economic activity. In this way the level and rate of economic activity depend on the level and rate of investment, the level and rate of investment depend on the expectation of profit, and the expectation of profit depends on the level and rate of economic activity in various sectors, markets, and other spheres – a typically cybernetic (and non-Newtonian) circuit of reciprocal, informational causality, regulated by positive and negative feedback between inputs and outputs (Tustin, 1952; Mayr, 1969).

The importance of investment in capital goods and labor, especially for governments following Keynesian expansionary policies to reduce unemployment, is that a relatively small input at this level will be amplified via the consumer goods circuit into a much larger change in total incomes (wages and profits). At times of high unemployment, this multiplier effect (recognized by Richard F. Kahn in 1931) can in certain sectors be as much as ten times the original investment.

There is of course no one kind of capital or labor and no completely typical cycle of expansion and contraction in the irregular and generally unpredictable business cycle: some industries may be expanding in recession (or contracting in expansion). Within the limits of their own economy, state capitalist countries can considerably restrict such oscillations by planning.

These oscillations are not products of matter-energy relations, as are the simple harmonic oscillations of a pendulum, or a sine wave, or AC current, or a quartz crystal. They are governed not by 'economic forces' (these are imaginary); nor by capitalism's supposed 'laws of motion' (the Newtonian slip by which Marx torpedoed the grounds of his own theory); nor by 'tensions' (the system is neither an organism nor a spring system); nor by the 'swing of the pendulum' (everybody's favorite analogy for action and reaction); nor by the 'ebb and flow' of tidal waters (an analogy that hardly needs refuting); nor by 'Eros and Civilization' (in Marcuse's unhappy words); nor by the 'interpenetrating forces' or 'unity of contradictions' of imaginary constructs like yin and yang (a cyclic and almost 'instinctual' system closed to context, novelty, evolution, and radical change); nor by the action and reaction of mechanics (the system is not a solar system or a steam engine); nor by 'pressures' (the economy is not a fluid); nor by the relative solidity of the 'social cement' preferred by some writers (others speak of 'bricks and mortar'); nor by 'attraction and repulsion' (gravitational, electrical, magnetic, or otherwise); nor by bioenergetic 'vibrations' or 'fields of force' (like Peter Finch in Paddy Chayefsky's *Network* (1976), directed by Sidney Lumet) – the capitalist system is not governed by any of these largely inanimate physical causes, but by information, relation, feedback, adaptation, flexibility, and the constraints of its diverse environments (symbolic, imaginary, and real).

This said, the basic character of the short-term surface structure business cycle can be set out quite simply.

Expansion

The level and rate of production – governed by the inducement to invest (the expectation of profit) – is the strategic constraint on the economic system as a whole. Within the system of production the strategic constraint is the capital goods circuit. An expansion of production may result from an increase in spending on capital goods and labor by business firms, or from innovations in technology, or from increases in consumer spending encouraging increases in investment, or from arms budgets, government 'pump priming', or new tax policies, or from sources outside the domestic economy – just as the American war in Indochina stimulated the Canadian and other economies (at the cost of worldwide inflation) – or some combination of these.

At the beginning of the expansion (during the recession), wages, interest rates, prices of capital goods, and construction costs will all be relatively low, creating a favorable climate for investment.

(Until the Second World War, real wage costs were commonly reduced during recession and depression by reductions in the actual sums paid out; more recently the same reductions are being achieved with less fuss by letting wages lag behind inflation; now the system is also back to the wage reductions of the last great depression, while an illusory boom in the United States in 1985 was financed by the right wing's use of Keynesian policies – in this case government defense spending of paranoid proportions and budget deficits of unparalleled size and cost: Under Ronald Reagan the US public debt doubled to two trillion dollars in just four years.)

Expansion begins when changes in the constraints on the costs of production enable leading corporations to commit themselves to new production. They hire more labor, place new orders for materials and equipment, and usually finance some of their outlays by loans from banks or by selling bonds or new share issues, which increase activity in the financial sector, resulting in increased profits and commissions – this too favoring increased spending and investment.

Retail sales and services will be stimulated by the new investment in wages, and more consumers will buy more products. Eventually demand for 'big ticket' or 'durable' goods commonly purchased on credit, such as cars, appliances, and new housing will also increase. As production and sales rise, the profits of most firms will tend to rise also, and if their productive capacity is used more efficiently because of increased output or better allocation of resources, then costs per unit of production will fall. As a result the productivity of labor and the rate of profit will both increase.

(The productivity of labor is constrained primarily by capital – by the quality and efficiency of plant layout, technology, and management – and only secondarily by actual mental, emotional, and physical effort.)

Other corporations proceed to join the general trend. The bandwagon effect further increases the level of economic activity and the inducement to invest. Some corporations will take the opportunity to expand or modernize their productive capacity, increasing the demand for construction, machine tools, mainframe computers, and so on. New businesses will be created, new projects will be floated, and public spending will tend to increase, while budget deficits may fall, corporation and high bracket income tax rates may decrease, along with increases in the money supply, easy credit, and relatively low interest rates.

But as the expansion spreads, it generates a condition as essential to its immediate continuation as to its eventual termination: confidence that the expansion will continue. The paradox of the business cycle is that expansion creates the conditions for contraction, and contraction creates the conditions for expansion.

As production and consumption rise during expansion and as more and more firms, including brand new enterprises, join in, the increased demand for capital goods, raw materials, new construction, labor, and credit eventually sets off a general rise in prices, including the rate of interest. (High employment under capitalism is usually accompanied by inflation.)

These increases in the costs of production would alone be enough to check the continued expansion of investment even if profits were spread uniformly among the various firms. This is not the case, of course, and the uneven spread of profits is another major factor in impeding the continuation of expansion (Burns, 1968).

As economic activity begins to decline, uncertainty replaces confidence, shortages are relieved, inventories increase, sales fall, prices tend to stabilize, expenditures on capital goods and durable consumer goods decrease, production is reduced, and unemployment rises. The inevitable recession has begun.

Unemployment

The social effects of unemployment, even in mild recessions, are devastating. Harvey Brenner of Johns Hopkins University has shown that for every percentage point that unemployment rises in the United States the death rate increases 2 per cent. (The suicide rate rises 4.1 per cent.) Deaths from heart attacks, strokes, liver disease (alcoholism), mental illness, crime, and murder increase. The 1.4 per cent rise in unemployment in 1970 in the United States, sustained over six years, resulted, according to Brenner's figures, in an extra 51,000 deaths (*The Reckoning*, The World in Action: Granada International Television, 1980). Brenner has demonstrated similar increases in mortality in Britain, and the same increases in the death rate are believed to be occurring in other industrialized countries as well.

The danger of unemployment is that it does not simply make life hard, insecure, and dull, but it also undermines the sense of identity, creativity, equality with others, and self-esteem of those who cannot find work. Newspaper reports suggest that divorce, desertion, crime, rape, and child abuse and other violence within the family also increase in hard times, but I have not yet seen any specific studies on this topic.

The *New York Times* reported on June 8, 1986 that each time the US recovers from a recession the unemployment rate is higher than before the economic decline (as in the back-to-back recessions in the first half of 1980 and from mid-1981 to late 1982). This is structural unemployment. At the end of 1985, despite three years of economic expansion, the goods-producing sector of the [US] economy had recovered only 80 per cent of the jobs lost earlier in the decade. Many of the new service industry and information jobs pay less than the poverty line, others are part-time (20 percent of all US workers), others are temporary – with no employee benefits (p. 20).

Hodding Carter III begins a 'Viewpoint' article in the *Wall Street Journal* (July 24, 1986) by quoting *Time* magazine on 'the New Age of Capitalism'. Says *Time*: 'While some players may founder, the system shows no sign of sinking.' Carter comments:

> There, in one smug phrase in the current issue, the heir of Henry
> Luce encapsulated the moral myopia of most of the complacent,
> 'morning in America' commentary that dominates the national
> dialogue. Even as the evidence grows steadily stronger that we are
> building a class-ridden society of ever-sharper contrasts between

haves and have-nots, we are treated to long treatises on the triumph of capitalism and the American dream.

Time's 'neat phrase' came in an issue that ignored 'the single most significant piece of economic news' of the week:

The Census Bureau published a study that found that the net worth of the median white household was 12 times more than that of the typical black household and eight times higher than Hispanic households.

Similarly, though they are better than the figures for black wealth, black income has been frozen at roughly 60 per cent of white income for 20 years and the wage gap is increasing. The America of assimilation, upward mobility, and opportunity, says Carter, 'is becoming a thing of the past'.

(*Newsweek* (July 28, 1986) reports that whereas only 8.4 per cent of white families had no net worth or owed more than they owned, the figure for blacks was 30.5 per cent.)

But 'race is not the only determinant in the push toward the permanent creation of a two-nation society', says Carter. Between the booming East and West coasts, near or on which over two-thirds of the population lives, 'there is economic stagnation and despair'. Agriculture in the Mississippi Valley is 'a wasteland'; there is 'no meaningful revival' in smokestack America.

Moreover, the Education Commission of the States reported some time ago that

15 per cent of youngsters between the ages of 16 and 19 are unlikely to become productive adults because of drugs, delinquency, pregnancy, unemployment and lack of education. About 2.5 million of them are 'at risk' of becoming 'disconnected' from society.

The problem is that

we are structuring a country in which Third World conditions coexist side by side with prosperity; in which too few have far too much (12% of American households control 38% of all personal wealth) and too many have far too little. That describes many places, but not the American ideal. It is also social dynamite.

This might as well be news from Mars as far as middle America is concerned, he adds. The 'visible minorities' are becoming invisible again. Said John Herber in the *New York Times* three years ago, commenting on the enrichment of the suburbs at the expense of the cities:

With some exceptions, 'the other side of the tracks' is no longer visible to 'society hill'.

Commentators point to a similar decay and polarization in Britain in the 1980s: the 'two nations', where South (largely Southeast) dominates North.

According to the revised report of the Congressional Joint Economic Committee, as reported in the *Wall Street Journal* for August 22, 1986, the rich continue to get richer while most other people continue to get poorer. The top 10 per cent of American families controlled 67.9 per cent of total household wealth in 1983, up from 64 per cent twenty years earlier; the remaining 90 per cent of families controlled a mere 32.1 per cent of the same, down from 36 per cent in 1963.

Positive feedback

During the expansion, then, there are higher sales (with less effort), general optimism, a high expectation of profit, a high level and rate of investment in capital goods and labor, high production, consumption, and employment, and a high rate of profit – a deviation-amplifying process of *positive feedback* in the expectation and rate of profit – the more there is, the more there will be – resulting in increases in economic activity at many levels. The result of this mutually reinforcing process of expansion, however, is higher prices, higher interest rates, a tendency to overshoot actual consumption at the peak of the expansion (overproduction), resulting in high inventories of unsold goods, and a general increase in production costs – all of which sets the stage for recession.

Negative feedback

Recession begins with lower sales (with more effort), a lower rate of profit, general uncertainty, a lower expectation of profit, a lower level and rate of investment, and a lower level of production, consumption, and employment – a deviation-reducing process of *negative feedback* in the expectation and rate of profit – the more there is, the less there will be – resulting in decreases in economic activity at many levels. (The downturning process of negative feedback may become a downturning spiral of positive feedback – the less there is, the less there will be.) The result of this mutually reducing process of contraction is an all-round reduction in the costs of labor time, capital goods, raw materials, and money – all of which sets the stage for the recovery in the next cycle as the expectation of a higher level and rate of profit encourages new investment in capital goods and labor time.

Recession and depression

The major difference between a depression and a recession is the extent and depth of the downturn and disruption. In the normal course of events, expansions may last from a year to three or four years, but rarely longer; recessions tend to last from twelve to eighteen months (Burns, 1968). (There were recessions in 1957-8, 1960-61, 1969-70, 1973-5, and 1981-2.)

Whether the recession develops into a depression depends on many factors. The most important are the scale of speculation during the expansion, the amount of credit extended, the costs of bad loans, bankruptcies, and repudiations of debt, the extent to which markets were saturated by production before the decline, the amount of now excess productive capacity, the balance of international payments between debtor and creditor countries, the stability and prudence of the financial system, the aptness of government actions, and the reduction of economic activity resulting from 'protective tariffs' in international trade (notably 'domestic content' legislation).

If there is a financial crisis – a crisis involving the stock market, bank failures, exchange rates, interest rates, or runaway inflation (or some of all five) – depression becomes that much more inevitable, severe, and likely to last. And at some point the moneyed classes will demand increased unemployment rather than continuing inflation.

Recessions tend to be confined to particular countries, economies, industrial sectors, or areas. Thriving or expanding economies in other areas help to overcome them. (In August 1986, 31 of the 50 states – half of the US population – were in recession.)

Depressions in contrast are worldwide recessions in which the weaknesses of national economies or regions or industrial sectors in one area tend to amplify the weaknesses of others, resulting in a (downturning) spiral of positive feedback, as weak activity in one sphere feeds into weak activity elsewhere, and eventually feeds back on itself.

Recessions are generally shorter and less intensive than expansions. A number of factors commonly mitigate the severity of a recession, as well as preparing the way for recovery. In the first place the whole system is structurally oriented towards continued growth. Wise corporations will choose growth over profits in difficult times, so as to keep together the managers and technologists that they cannot afford to lay off as they can their ordinary employees. Besides that, in recession optimism and the ingenuity of individual entrepreneurs make the best of available opportunities, people work harder and use savings to avoid reducing their standard of living, competition between workers and between firms becomes much sharper, and improvements in production, products, and marketing, as well as the elimination of 'uneconomic waste', can increase profitability even in bad times. At the same time population and productive capacity are still growing and government action may decrease the severity of the decline.

Regulation by double binds

Contraction thus creates the conditions for expansion, and expansion creates the conditions for contraction. The challenge to perform – the challenge of the rate of profit – demands the simultaneous satisfaction of two incompatible conditions related by a double bind: high economic activity (a high rate of growth), on the one hand, and a high rate of profit (low costs of production), on the other.

But as one condition is satisfied the other is undermined, and there is no position of stability between the two.

The key to the many paradoxical injunctions that constrain production and consumption in the business cycle is that whether production is expanding or contracting, there always exist thresholds of economic activity beyond which either successful expansion or unavoidable contraction will each destroy the conditions necessary for their own continued existence.

The double binds that constrain within unpredictable but nevertheless effective limits the irregular oscillation between expansion and contraction in the business cycle are time-dependent, threshold-sensitive, analog-digital double binds. They are also useful – paradoxical injunctions that (unintentionally) regulate the short-term stability of production and consumption in the system over time.

The capitalist economic system is thus self-regulating in relation to some of its environments – self-regulating, that is, provided it can continue to expand – but only at an appalling cost in physical, psychological, and ecological damage and distress for the populations of the planet earth.

Nowhere has the liberal philosophy failed so conspicuously as in its understanding of the problem of change.

Karl Polyani: *The Great Transformation* (1944)

4.2 Economics, imaginary and real

What is missing from this simple analysis of the short-term business cycle is the fact, manifest in the 1930s and explained by Keynes, that capitalism can attain a (relatively) stable state in the business cycle with very high unemployment, 'structural' unemployment.

This is in complete contradiction with the doctrine of the founder of classic political economy, the Scotsman Adam Smith (1723-1790), whose *Wealth of Nations* of 1776 promised bounteous employment. It equally contradicts revered neoclassical economists like Albert Marshall (1842-1924), whose theories were in fact discarded in the 'Keynesian Revolution' between the 1930s and the 1960s (much appreciated by Marxists), led in large part by economists advising the Democratic Party in the United States, and including at least twenty years of war.

Even if Keynesian expansionary policies have often been abandoned in the unprecedented structural economic instability in which we live today, the reason they don't work is that Keynes is right.

The classical and neoclassical economists were proponents of Say's so-called 'Law of Markets', named after J.B. Say (1767-1832): that production and consumption (like Newtonian action and reaction) are always equal and opposite. They maintained the utterly discredited view that under capitalism the 'hidden hand' of supply creates its own demand (this is 'supply side theory', complete with its imaginary talisman, the 'Laffer curve') (Stockman, 1986). Thus, they said, capitalism when left alone and unregulated (laissez faire capitalism) makes overproduction (depression) impossible and always leads to full employment.

But the business cycle can oscillate as easily with 10 per cent unemployment as it can with 4 per cent (the latter is the American definition of 'full employment'). Keynes saw this inherent, structural instability (political and social, as well as economic) as the great danger at the heart of capitalism (the other is inflation).

American and other employers were saying in 1985-86 that they can achieve the same output as before the depression of the mid-1970s and 1980s with at least 10 per cent fewer employees.

The uneasy state of overextended banks, the massive inflation of the service industries in the United States (industries that create no real wealth), the recent massive corporate mergers, creating corporations of a relative size not seen since the days of the East India Company, the pyramids of paper corporations, the constant attacks from within the capitalist system by speculators, economic terrorists, corporate kidnappers, and business buccaneers in general (the corporaton as commodity), especially the pirates of the air waves – these are all reasons for alarm. Nothing is more dangerous than an empire in decline.

The *State of the World Atlas* (Kidron and Segal, 1981) uses United Nations figures to show graphically the forecasts of greatly increasing unemployment up to the year 2000 and beyond, especially but not only in the Third World – where massive unemployment and under-employment (50 to 60 per cent in some countries) have persisted for most of the present century (and never worse than in the 1980s).

Except for the Far East and parts of the US, most of the industrialized countries had persistent serious unemployment at the time of writing, and there exists in many nations whole 'lost generations' of young people who have never held a job and cannot expect to, either.

> The Laws of Commerce are the Laws of Nature and therefore the Laws of God.
>
> Edmund Burke (1729-97)

Say's Law

On page 32 of *The General Theory of Employment Interest and Money* (1936), Lord Keynes notes the nineteenth-century victory of the economics of David Ricardo (1772-1823) – based on 'free trade', the new market-dominated economy, and the eighteenth-century doctrine of uninterrupted progress towards perfection (unlimited growth) – over the more accurate views of Parson Malthus (1766-1834):

> Not only was [Ricardo's theory, and with it, Say's Law of Markets] accepted by the city, by statesmen and by the academic world. But controversy ceased; the other point of view completely disappeared; it ceased to be discussed. The great puzzle of Effective Demand with which Malthus had wrestled vanished from economic literature. . . . It could only live on furtively, below the surface, in the underworlds of Karl Marx, Silvio Gesell or Major Douglas.

The theory of supply and demand in classical economics (based on 'perfect competition') is Cartesian and Newtonian mythology, not science. Whereas Say's Law is imaginary, Keynes's principle of 'effective demand', and his (cybernetic) theory of the amplification of total incomes by the 'multiplier' effect of investment in the capital goods circuit, are real.

The advantage of the imaginary aspects of the classical and neoclassical theory, says Keynes, is that once you accept Say's imaginary Law (that supply creates its own demand), then the entire classical construction follows – however illogical it was (and is), and however often events have proved it false – the depression of 1837-48, for instance, or that of 1873-96.

(In the 1960s progressive neoclassicists freely admitted that their equations and curves had no known application to reality.)

The completeness of the Ricardian victory, says Keynes, is something of a curiosity and a mystery.

That it reached conclusions quite different from what the ordinary uninstructed person would expect, added, I suppose, to its intellectual prestige. That its teaching, translated into practice, was austere and often unpalatable, lent it virtue. That it was adapted to carry a vast and consistent logical superstructure, gave it beauty. That it could explain much social injustice and apparent cruelty as an inevitable incident in the scheme of progress, and the attempt to change such things as likely on the whole to do more harm than good, commended it to authority. That it afforded a measure of justification to the free activities of the individual capitalist, attracted to it the support of the dominant social force behind authority (pp. 32-3).

(Keynes's Newtonian metaphor of 'force' in this passage is easily translated into the cybernetic metaphor of power.)

'Effective demand' for consumers is plain English for what and how much people will actually end up buying, i.e. real demand. In the capital goods circuit it simply means what return on investment people will actually accept.

As Keynes noted, the capitalist system oscillates fairly rapidly:

> ... [Another] condition ... provides not so much for the stability of the system as for the tendency of a fluctuation in one direction to reverse itself in due course; namely, that a rate of investment, higher (or lower) than prevailed formerly, begins to react unfavourably (or favourably) on the marginal efficiency of capital [the rate of profit] if it is continued for a period which, measured in years, is not very large (p. 251).

This is an instance of what was recognized in Chapter 1 as 'order through oscillation' in open systems; and Keynes's system is open where classical economic theory is closed.

(On the problems of the Keynesian concentration on short-range factors, see the Postscript to this book.)

In contrast, in the static and mechanical view of the classical economists,

> an increase of investment, however small, would set moving a cumulative [positive feedback] increase of effective demand until a position of full employment had been reached; while a decrease of investment would set moving a cumulative [positive feedback] decrease of effective demand until no one at all was employed (pp. 251-2).

In the first case prices would escalate to infinity; in the second, the economy would come to a stop.

But the outstanding feature of our actual experience, says Keynes, is

> that we oscillate, avoiding the gravest extremes of fluctuations in employment and in prices in both directions, round an intermediate position appreciably below full employment and appreciably above the minimum employment a decline below which would endanger life (p. 254).

(Ricardo's 'iron law of wages' (1817) or 'natural price of labor' in the newly invented 'labor market' is 'that price which is necessary to enable the labourers, one with another, to subsist and perpetuate their race, without either increase or diminution'.)

But, Keynes continues, we must not conclude that 'the mean position is determined [i.e. conditioned and constrained] by "natural" tendencies' or supposed 'laws of necessity' (p. 254). Not at all. The 'unimpeded rule' of the conditions he has explained, is 'a fact of observation concerning the world as it is or has been, and not a necessary principle which cannot be changed.'

Wages, prices, profits

The account of Keynesian economics in Donald Clarke's *Encyclopedia of Great Inventors and Discoveries* (1978, pp. 99-101) does not recognize that the economic system and the Keynesian theory are cybernetic, as Tustin did in 1952, but we can still draw on it for a reliable summary of the Keynesian view:

> Keynes argued that the aggregate [total] supply of goods and services could indeed be suppressed even if there was spare [productive] capacity in the economy, if the aggregate demand was too low. Firms would not offer employment if there was no expectation of selling their products.

Therefore, what constrains and conditions the total amount of employment offered (and therefore the level of unemployment) is the level of total 'effective demand'.

> And the level of effective demand was in turn determined [i.e. conditioned and constrained] principally by its three main constituents: consumers' demand, businessmen's demand for more investment, and the government's expenditure.

The previous economic orthodoxy would (and did) argue that

> if there is unemployment then this means that wages are too high;

therefore unemployment was caused by unions who refused to allow wages to fall. Keynes argued that wages were not too high anyway, since depressions were caused not by union wage policies but by fluctuations in the level of investment.

Moreover, argued Keynes,

if wages were lowered this would lead to lower demand (because workers would have less money to spend) and lower prices, but would not solve the unemployment problem.

The Keynesian theory

produced a clear-cut policy for governments to adopt: increase government spending to avoid unemployment. (Also the converse is true: if aggregate demand was too high, decrease government spending to avoid inflation.) And in fact this produced a neat justification for what governments had by 1936 already begun to do.

Two previous policies resulting in significant increases in effective demand were the transformation of the laboring poor into laboring consumers by the end of the nineteenth century, and the invention of credit cards in the 1950s.

A third stimulus to effective demand is arms races – such as that beginning in the 1890s (following the Great Depression of 1873-96), which led straight into World War One, the opening campaign in the Twentieth Century War. H.G. Wells (1866-1946) recognized the Keynesian paradox. As he said in 1933, in *The Shape of Things to Come*:

Without this cancer growth of armies and navies [at the end of the nineteenth century], the paradox of overproduction latent in competitive private enterprise would probably have revealed itself in an overwhelming mass of unemployment before even the end of the nineteenth century. A social revolution might have occurred then. Militarism, however, alleviated these revolutionary stresses, by providing vast profit-yielding channels of waste. And it also strengthened the forces of social repression.

Pride in risk

There is a formal similarity between the 'challenge to perform' behind the oscillations of the business cycle and the oscillations produced by the 'pride in risk' and the 'challenge' to the self peculiar to some forms of addictive alcoholism (and probably gambling also), as analyzed by Bateson in 'The Cybernetics of Self' (1971), reprinted in his collection of essays, *Steps to an Ecology of Mind* (1972, pp. 309-45).

The definition of an alcoholic, says Bateson, drawing on the work of Alcoholics Anonymous, is the definition of an 'alcoholic personality', and that is a person who cannot conceivably win a battle, much less a war, with the Demon Drink – it is in fact that very symmetrical, competitive, either/or, dualistic, mind-body battle between 'self' and 'other' (between self and bottle), between 'mind' and 'matter', and between oneself as a person and drinking as a thing existing 'outside' the self, that makes any ordinary attempt at a cure practically impossible.

The alcoholic's pride in performance and 'self-control' – the failure to recognize (as Alcoholics Anonymous insists) that he is absolutely powerless to control his drinking – is undermined by the social and psychological effects of alcohol. In order to reassert and reaffirm this pride, the alcoholic must stop drinking. But so long as the constraints and values under which the alcoholic operates do not change (essentially the values of Western society, as Bateson argues), the very act of stopping drinking sets up a double-bound oscillation between being 'on the wagon' and being 'on the bottle'.

The act of stopping drinking removes from the relationship the 'other' (or the Other), represented by the bottle, with which the alcoholic's 'self' is in symmetrical (escalating) competition. Success in meeting the challenge of not drinking destroys it; it is replaced by the challenge of drinking. Pride in performance and self-control measured against the 'other' can now be reasserted only by taking the 'one little drink' that will set the whole oscillation going again. As Bateson puts it, 'the contextual structure of sobriety changes with its achievement', for 'symmetrical effort requires continual opposition from the opponent' (p. 322).

As Bill W., one of the founders of Alcoholics Anonymous, explains, he 'hit bottom' when diagnosed as a hopeless alcoholic by Dr William D. Silkworth in 1939. 'Hitting bottom' and recognizing that 'once an alcoholic, always an alcoholic' (one's utter helplessness in the face of alcohol) are the preconditions of any attempt at curing oneself. Quoted by Bateson (p. 331), Bill W. adds that it was Silkworth who

supplied us with the tools with which to puncture the toughest alcoholic ego, those shattering phrases by which he described our illness: *the obsession of the mind* that compels us to drink and *the allergy of the body* that condemns us to go mad or die.

Thus whereas the oscillations in the business cycle are underlain by an escalation of the conditions of economic growth, the oscillations of the alcoholic are underlain by an escalation of the conditions of psychological and eventually biological death.

It goes without saying that the paradox of reality is also expressed in linguistic paradoxes, which contradict commonsense. . . . The contradictions which arise from the fact that under commodity production . . . relations between people manifest themselves as relations between things, and relations themselves are represented as things – these contradictions lie in what we are studying, and not in its verbal expression.

Karl Marx: 'The Disintegration of the Ricardian School' in
Theories of Surplus Value (1861-3)

4.3   The paradox of growth

In an unlimited environment, the capitalist system of the maximization of exchange values could continue to oscillate interminably at one level and continue to expand productive capacity indefinitely at another.

But the growth that may have been profitable and functionally adaptive in one historical and ecological context can become counteradaptive in another over time. The adaptivity and flexibility of our social and economic system (its unused potential for future change) is turning into counteradaptivity and rigidity, not because of its responses to natural processes in its environment (including random and even catastrophic change), but rather because of its own activities, including the destruction of soil fertility by overfertilization, overgrazing, and irrigation (soil salting); the pollution and damage to soil, air, rivers, groundwater, and human and other organisms by toxic products and 'byproducts', including radioactivity, biocides, heavy metals, asbestos fibers, coal and cotton dust, runoff from beef feedlots, noxious gases, industrial chemicals, and acid rain, some of which (if past experience is any guide) have yet to be detected; and changes in the atmosphere and world climate with as yet unknown but almost certainly disruptive effects.

The great danger of increasing counteradaptivity is that it is a positive feedback relationship, tending to accelerate with time, and that, like inflation and government deficits, it results in the exploitation of the system's future and its own generations to come.

Our system is not the first to fall into this trap, but it is the first to be caught in it by its own economic logic (as distinct from population increase or technological failure or other factors outside the economy).

It is also the first world-wide economic system, a system in which changes in one or two countries can affect most of the rest of the world. It is further the first system to create new varieties of organisms, such as drug-resistant bacteria resulting from the over-production and overuse of antibiotics, threatening increases in untreatable diseases (in Mexico, in 1972-3, 20,000 people died in an epidemic of drug-resistant typhoid), and pesticide-resistant insects, threatening future agricultural productivity.

Energy efficiencies

It is furthermore the first economic system in which the most powerful of the national economies, that of the United States, depends for much of what is called economic efficiency (the rate of profit) on (increasing) inefficiencies in the use of energy, especially in agriculture. According to David Pimentel of Cornell University, the energy available from a can of corn (270 calories) costs 2790 calories of energy to produce, package, and distribute. Energy conversion inefficiencies in the production of meat are even more staggering: 100 grams of beef (270 calories) cost 22,000 calories to produce, package, and distribute (cf. Harris, 1977, p. 284).

(Barry Commoner points out in *The Closing Circle* (1971, p. 148) that in 1968 US farmers applied five times as much nitrogen fertilizer to their crops as they did in 1949, for exactly the same crop yield. Not only was there a five-fold decrease in the efficiency of fertilizer use in these twenty years, but the excess nitrates remained in the soil and groundwater, polluting the local ecosystem.)

In North America it has long been claimed that one farmer feeds forty or fifty people. However, when one considers the matter, energy, and information budget of the system of food production from tillage to consumer – treating the farmer in context – we need to take into account the raw materials, the physical energy (from renewable and non-renewable sources), and the human labor time that go into manufacturing farm equipment and tractors, ploughing and tilling the fields, irrigating where necessary, manufacturing and applying ferti-lizers, herbicides, and pesticides, transporting farm materials, bringing livestock and produce to wholesalers and retailers, processing and packaging the products, getting them on to the store shelves, and finally into the kitchen cupboard – which suggests that besides non-renewable natural resources, there may in fact be forty or fifty people feeding the farmer who is then subsidized by public money to maintain high prices by not producing food.

State and private capitalism is also the first economic system in history with the power to extinguish all or most of the world population, whether by war or pollution or both.

It seems impossible that the present economic system can survive in the long run without a change of structure, a morphogenesis, an economic and social revolution in its deep structure.

Growth in productive capacity

The apparent inevitability of some such restructuring may in its turn be related to the double bind theory. If the world economic system – including China and the Soviet Union – is dependent on quantitative growth for its stability over time, then it cannot afford to *cease* growing. On the other hand, in a limited environment, it cannot afford to *continue* growing as it has in the past. *Without* continued growth in productive capacity it faces stagnation and depression and possibly collapse. *With* continued growth in productive capacity it faces further pathology and perhaps self-extinction. The conditions required for continued short-range stability and survival in one sphere of existence are incompatible with those required for long-range stability and survival in another.

So long as the economic system does not run up against the limits imposed on it by the carrying capacity of its human and natural environments – note that it is less likely that these limits will be defined by the future availability of resources than by the limited capacity of nature to act as a 'waste sink' for the entropic disorder society pumps into it – then the incompatibility between the system and its environment is merely an unresolved contradiction. Should the system begin to approach those limits, however, the incompatibility becomes a paradox (Figure 4.1).

Whereas a contradiction can always be put in order in one way or another, and whereas those with the power to do so can choose one aspect or another of a contradiction, a paradox cannot be resolved, nor one 'side' preferred to the 'other side', so long as one remains bound by the constraints that create and maintain it.

The visual double bind of a paradoxical figure can be overcome by simply looking away. A logical paradox can be resolved by laughing at it, or by mentally stepping out of its constraints and talking about what makes it paradoxical (metalanguage). A double bind in communication and action can be defeated by breaking through the constraints governing its paradoxical closure and communicating about the rules and metarules it depends on (metacommunicative action). A system paradox can be resolved by a structural change creating a system in which the paradox no longer has any effect (the creation of a metasystem). Each of these solutions involves a strategic envelopment of the situation creating and maintaining the double bind.

Figure 4.1 is a schematic representation of the positive-negative

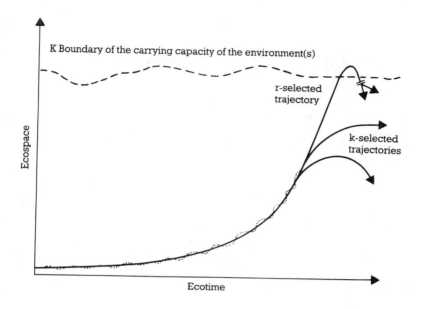

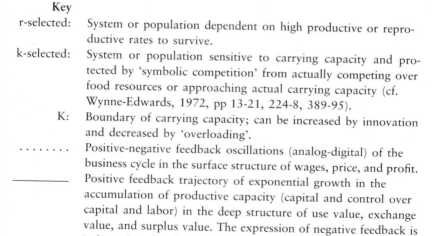

FIGURE 4.1   The accumulation of productive capacity.

Key

r-selected: System or population dependent on high productive or reproductive rates to survive.

k-selected: System or population sensitive to carrying capacity and protected by 'symbolic competition' from actually competing over food resources or approaching actual carrying capacity (cf. Wynne-Edwards, 1972, pp 13-21, 224-8, 389-95).

K: Boundary of carrying capacity; can be increased by innovation and decreased by 'overloading'.

. . . .   Positive-negative feedback oscillations (analog-digital) of the business cycle in the surface structure of wages, price, and profit.

————————   Positive feedback trajectory of exponential growth in the accumulation of productive capacity (capital and control over capital and labor) in the deep structure of use value, exchange value, and surplus value. The expression of negative feedback is indicated in the diagram by the flattening out or reversal of the J-curve.

feedback of the surface-structure business cycle, superimposed on the (so far) positive feedback curve of exponential growth in productive capacity in the deep structure of state and private capitalism.

By 'ecospace' is meant all those ecosystem variables that act as constraints on the subsystems in the ecosystem, such as types and forms of food supply and energy transformations, cycles of material nutrients, the patterning of ecological niches, the organization and levels of the food 'chain' or food 'web', the 'resource environment' and the 'waste sink' environment, and so on.

By 'ecotime' is meant the kinds of biological, ecological, and social time in which the reproduction of the past in the present affects the future of the system – the ecosystem as information projected into the future, as Margalef has said (1968, p. 2).

'Carrying capacity' should be understood as a dynamic and interdependent factor, defined both by the resources and recycling capacities of the environment, as well as by the capacities – biological and technological – of the systems within it to make use of that environment. Carrying capacity can be expanded by innovation – as in the divergent evolution of competing species in nature, or the technological inventions of society – and reduced by overloading, both qualitatively and quantitatively. The break in the 'r-selected' trajectory in the diagram is intended to indicate the catastrophic effects of passing beyond the constraints of carrying capacity.

The only cause of depression is prosperity.
Clement Juglar: *Les Crises commerciales et leur retour périodique en France, en Angleterre et aux Etats-Unis* (1862)

4.4 Adaptivity and counteradaptivity

In a 1976 article 'Wolves', Barry Lopez explains that in 1966 William Pruitt discovered by accident that wolves signal their prey – caribou in this instance – if they are intent on attacking. L. David Mech, author of *The Wolves of Isle Royale* (1966), observed that at least one wolf pack in his Minnesota study concentrated their hunting in a different part of their territory each year, thus contributing to their own survival by contributing to that of their prey.

Moreover, adds Lopez,

of the 160 moose Mech saw from the air on Isle Royale and judged to be within the range of hunting wolves, 29 were ignored, 11 discovered the wolves first and eluded them, and 24 refused to run and were left alone. Of the 96 that ran, 43 got away immediately, 34 were surrounded and not harmed, 12 made successful defensive stands, and 7 were attacked. Of these seven, six were killed, and one was wounded and abandoned.

The outcome of the hunt, says Lopez, 'is usually settled in the first moment, the moment of eye contact between the animals':

Immediately after a one-minute stare the moose may simply walk away, or the wolves may turn and run, or the wolves may charge and kill the animal in less than a minute. What transpires in these moments of staring . . . is probably a complex exchange of information regarding the appropriateness of a chase and kill.

A prey-predator relationship is a co-evolved, mutually adapted relation between two (or more) species – 'What but the wolf's tooth whittled so fine the fleet limbs of the antelope?' wrote Robinson Jeffers (1887-1962) – in which the size of each population is constrained by a feedback relation with the other. (The prey, generally herbivores, are also constrained by their own sources of food.) The result is a generally stable (if unpredictable) oscillation of both populations around a position of stability, neither becoming either large enough or small enough to endanger the other.

The feedback is 'negative' because it opposes whatever the system is doing (deviation reduction). More predators permit the survival of fewer prey; fewer prey permit the survival of fewer predators. Fewer predators permit the survival of more prey; more prey permit the survival of more predators . . . and so on, if undisturbed, *ad infinitum*, each population contributing to the long-range survival of the other.

Since the predator kills weakened, diseased, or crippled prey more often than healthy prey, and since similarly weakened predators are unlikely to hunt and reproduce as successfully as others, the relationship between the two also maintains the useful and requisite diversity of their gene pools, thus contributing to their long-range survival in another way.

But if a random mutation or recombination of genes were to produce a group of predators better adapted to catching the prey, the new adaptation, however successful it might be in the short range, would in the long run threaten the survival of the predators by threatening the survival of their prey. (The same would be true if the prey became better adapted to escaping the predator, for the increase in the prey population would threaten their own source of food.)

A successful adaptation in the short range can thus become counter-adaptive in the long range as a result of its own effects.

The 'Green Revolution'

The 'Green Revolution' that began in the 1950s – based on single-crop hybrid plants dependent for their high yields on imported chemical fertilizers and requiring protection from their local environment by herbicides and pesticides – has proved both adaptive and counter-adaptive. It has greatly increased crop yields in many areas, such as the Punjab: it has permitted double and even triple cropping elsewhere; it has made India almost self-sufficient in food; and it has almost always resulted in larger marketable surpluses (cash crops).

At the same time, however, the new technology has decreased the diversity of available local nourishment, especially in proteins; it has replaced diverse and long-adapted local plant strains by energy-, chemical-, and irrigation-dependent hybrid varieties; it has vastly increased material and non-biological energy costs; it has increased by its capital costs and quick profits the already huge gulf between rich and poor in Third World countries; and it has created farming systems structurally and technologically dependent on the agribusiness in the industrialized countries.

(On this and related issues Susan George's *How the Other Half Dies: The Real Reasons for World Hunger* (1976) is a reliable and well documented source.)

Salt and silt in Mesopotamian irrigation

A historical example will elaborate the point. By about 4000 BCE, the Sumerians of the temple communities in southern Mesopotamia, the land of the fertile crescent between the Tigris and the Euphrates, were using the traction plough and had invented irrigation. The system of water allocation that developed here was a crucial factor in the origin of centralized eastern despotism.

By 3000 BCE the Sumerians had also invented wheeled vehicles, sailing ships, metallurgy, turned and fired pottery, and civilization itself: a priestly bureaucracy, later the dictatorship of kings, a system of writing, the study of the heavens, the class structure, and the state. They had also produced one of the earliest recorded dominant ideologies: the reason the Sumerian people existed, said the priests, was to save the gods from having to work for a living.

Their relatively simple 'braided stream' irrigation system was based on short canals leading directly into the fields from the river banks, and required little maintenance. But as the archeologists Thorkild Jacobsen and Robert M. Adams showed in 1958, by about 1000 BCE this system of irrigation had destroyed the soil it had once made fertile, principally by swamping (waterlogging) and salting. (Salting in this area is a positive feedback relationship: the more salt there is deposited on the soil surface by evaporation, the less easily water can penetrate the soil, and the more quickly the next pool of water evaporates and deposits more salt.) The swamps and salt pans abandoned in southern Mesopotamia at that time can still be seen in Iraq today. For the adaptivity of this technology to become counter-adaptive nevertheless took 3000 years.

Farther upstream – the strategic center, with communication on interior lines – irrigation based on the same system continued under Mesopotamia's successive imperial states: the Akkadians, the Babylonians, the Assyrians, and others.

Between 150 BCE and 650 CE Parthian and Persian engineers greatly increased the size and technological complexity of the system in northern Mesopotamia. They designed a 'branching' system requiring tunnels, weirs, dams, sluices, bridges, and aqueducts – and constant cleaning, dredging, and mechanical attention – and above all mile upon mile of newly dug canals. Outside of China this system and its technology was unequalled among the wonders of the ancient world. The Nahrwan Canal (5th century CE), for example, ran through the desert for nearly 200 miles in a great curve around Baghdad, crossing two major rivers on its way.

As it happens the Tigris carries five times the silt of the Nile. (The Nile irrigates without long canals, and for natural reasons works nearly as well today – disturbed as it is by the Aswan Dam – as it did for the Ancient Egyptians.) The new system on the Tigris suffered from severe silting, requiring a centrally controlled labor force (including at various times no doubt artisans, free peasants, prisoners of war, serfs, and slaves) to keep it working. The silt was piled in spoil banks along the canals, from which it was spread by the wind over the fields, eventually raising the soil level above the water level in the canals, which became useless.

The system-generated disorder (or entropy) of the irrigation system continued to increase under the Islamic Caliphate of the Abbasids (750-1258 CE). Canal flows dwindled to mere trickles, and town life along the banks shrank and disappeared. Invading Mongol horsemen under Hulagu Khan first surveyed the resulting devastation when they overthrew the Caliph in 1258 – and they have been unjustly blamed for causing it ever since (Jacobsen and Adams, 1958, p. 393). For the adaptivity of this more complex technology to become counter-adaptive took perhaps 600 years.

Mesopotamia never recovered. Half the arable land of modern Iraq is estimated to have been rendered useless by the entropy of swamping, salting, and silting. The irrigated area in Iraq today is perhaps a tenth of the ancient fertile area, and the crop yields remain a poor fraction of what the Sumerian temple states enjoyed 5000 years ago.

Most irrigation systems in the world today are also destroying the fertility of the soil they irrigate through salting. The Colorado system serving the vast agricultural output of Southern California is a glaring example: its salt-laden runoff is not only damaging the soil and poisoning the groundwater in California, but it is also destroying farmland in Mexico as it flows across the border. For the adaptivity of this system to display counter-adaptivity has taken less than 50 years.

Long-range survival

In 'The Part Played by Labor in the Transition from Ape to Man' in *The Dialectics of Nature* (1872-1882), Frederick Engels (1820-95) considers the intimate connections between the development of the human hand with opposed thumb, the rise of co-operative work between 'humans-in-the-making', and the origin of speech, communication, and society. He goes on to examine the relationship between society and nature:

> Animals . . . change the environment by their activities in the same way, even if not to the same extent, as man does, and these changes, as we have seen, feed back on and change those who made them. In nature nothing takes place in isolation.

The distinction between animal and human in relation to nature, he suggests, is that the animal merely *uses* the environment (there is no exploitation of the environment in nature), whereas in modern society we seek to *master* it through mental and manual labor:

> Let us not, however, flatter ourselves overmuch on account of our human victories over nature. For each such victory takes its revenge on us. Each victory, it is true, in the first place brings about the results we expected, but in the second and third places it has quite different, unforeseen effects, which only too often neutralize or go beyond [*aufheben*] the first.

Drawing on the work of C. Fraas on climate and plant life (1847), he continues:

> The people who, in Mesopotamia, Greece, Asia Minor and elsewhere, destroyed the forests to obtain cultivable land, never dreamed that by removing along with the forests the collecting centers and reservoirs of moisture they were laying the basis for the present forlorn state of those countries.

Thus:

> At every step we are reminded that we by no means rule over nature like a conqueror over a foreign people, like someone standing outside nature – but that we, with flesh, blood, and brain, belong to nature, and exist in its midst, and that all our mastery of it consists

in the fact that we have the advantage over all other creatures of being able to learn its laws and apply them correctly.

(Society is part of nature, and nature is part of society, but they are not the same parts. If by flesh, blood, and brain we belong to nature, by body, soul, and mind we belong to society.)

The greater our knowledge of science, he continues, the better we can perceive 'both the more immediate and the more remote consequences of our interference with the traditional course of nature'.

As a result of the great advances in science in the nineteenth century, he says, 'we are more than ever in a position to realize, and hence to control, even the more remote natural consequences of at least our day-to-day production activities' – unlike the present situation, he adds, when 'the harmony of supply and demand is transformed into its polar opposite, as shown by the course of each ten years' industrial cycle.'

(Here Engels is referring to the crash and economic crisis of May 1873, which began the Great Depression of 1873-96.)

Moreover, he concludes, the more our understanding of nature progresses,

the more will human beings not only feel but also know their oneness with nature, and the more impossible will become the senseless and unnatural idea of an opposition [*Gegensatz*] between mind and matter, humanity and nature, soul and body, such as arose after the decline of classical antiquity in Europe and obtained its highest elaboration in Christianity.

In *The Source of Civilisation* (1935), G. Heard spoke of adaptation and efficiency – or, in Bateson's terms, of the necessity for living and social systems to maintain their flexibility, their potential for adaptive responses to future change – in similar terms:

A creature which has become perfectly adapted to its environment, an animal whose whole capacity and vital force is concentrated and expended in succeeding here and now, has nothing left over with which to respond to any radical change. . . . It can therefore beat all competitors in the special field, but equally on the other hand should that field change, it must become extinct. It is this success of efficiency which seems to account for the extinction of an enormous number of species.

As Darwin noted, extinction is the commonest event in evolution. It is estimated that the two million or more species presently existing are a mere 0.1 per cent of all the species that have existed over the past 600 million years (Lewontin, 1978). That makes some two billion extinctions.

FRONTISPIECE René Magritte: *Les Liaisons dangereuses (Dangerous Relationships)*, 1936. Reproduced from Harry Torczyner and Bella Benard, *Magritte: Ideas and Images*. Tr. by Richard Miller, New York: Concise New American Library.

CHAPTER 5

In the penal colony: the body as the discourse of the Other

PARENTS. The News is Edited to omit Atomic and other Horrors during the Disney Season.
– Notice outside Cameo Cinema, Charing Cross Road, 1953
Sight and Sound (Autumn 1982)

5.1 No quarter

At 3 a.m. on March 13, 1964 in a Queens neighborhood in New York City, thirty-eight people heard or saw Kitty Genovese screaming for help for half an hour as she was being stabbed to death on the street and in the lobby of her building. Not one moved to help her. Not one called the police. They didn't want to get involved.

In 1974 16-year-old Corney Naisbitt arrived at an Ogden, Utah, emergency room with a bullet in his skull, a terminal case. He was also 'spewing blood from his lungs nearly three feet into the air'. No one knew why. The reason was that after his killers had tied and gagged him and four other people in the basement of the store they had come to rob, they had made their captives drink liquid Drano, a caustic alkali for clearing drains of grease, before they shot them. The idea came from a Clint Eastwood movie. They raped one woman, hanged another victim, and drove a ballpoint pen through his ear drum. He survived: the woman did not. The details can be found in Gary Kinder's book about the crime, *Victim*.

'If I could have wings, I would fly like a bat,' said Betty Chikove, an elderly African woman displaced by the black war of independence in Zimbabwe (1965-80), speaking to Norman Lockman of the *Boston Globe* (*Vancouver Sun*, September 3, 1980). 'We suffered in the war,' she said: 'That child there was tortured by electricity by the security forces' of the white-dominated regime.

> It took an African interpreter a few minutes to break through the old woman's circumspection to determine that the young woman, then a teenager, had been raped with an electric cattle prod.

'She has no mind now,' the woman said.

On Sunday, March 6, 1983, in Big Dan's bar in New Bedford, Connecticut, fifty miles from Boston, a 21-year-old woman was held down on a pool table and repeatedly raped by four men. By itself, says Ellen Goodman of the *Boston Globe* in 'Saturday Night Live at Big Dan's' (*Vancouver Sun*, March 17, 1983), this assault would be just one more example of police-blotter male violence.

> But this rape occured in the presence of at least a dozen other men, maybe 15 men, maybe 20. We are told that these men did nothing to help the woman. We are told that these men watched. These men cheered. For two-and-a-half hours.

Goodman also recalls the murder of Kitty Genovese in 1964. The brutal refusal of her neighbors to do as much as lift the phone came as a great shock at the time. In those days, of course, we could be shocked by newsfilm of American soldiers torching the homes of innocent Vietnamese peasants. (It shocked the US Army too. The CBS correspondent who filed the original story, Morley Safer, was suddenly slipped off to London.)

In the communication between Kitty Genovese and her neighbors a basic democratic principle was at stake. Thirty-eight people were apparently too fearful, too 'alienated' (as was said), too ignorant, and apparently too misguided to act in their own self-interest by rendering mutual aid, which defines danger to the individual in a democracy as danger to the community as well.

The highest obligation of the citizen of a democracy is to preserve the community, and the highest obligation of the community is to preserve the citizen. Every other political right and duty derives from these.

It would not have taken much. One man shouted from an upstairs window, 'Leave that girl alone!', and that scared off her assailant, a 29-year-old business machine operator. But the man who had shouted shut his window and the assassin came back to finish the job.

What I never remember hearing about the killing of Kitty Genovese is that she was raped by her murderer as she lay dying.

The public killing of Kitty Genovese was one of many signs in the 1960s telling us that the codes of accepted behavior in American society were changing in dangerous, violent, even cynical ways. In 1967 Hollywood told us this was so with a stylish, stunning, violent new film called *Bonnie and Clyde* – but its bullet-ridden climax would shock no one today.

The great danger of violence is that the more we are exposed to it – whether it be physical or verbal, mental or material, printed or pictured, symbolic, imaginary, or real – the easier it is to get used to it.

The events at Big Dan's in 1983 tell us (as if we don't really know) that if there is one class of individuals who cannot rely on their community for self-defense, it is women – and after them, teenage girls and children. The reason is that for women and children it is their own community that attacks them. Most rapists and child molesters, whatever their class or race, are men the victim knows.

Timothy Beneke reports in *Male Rage* (1982), excerpted in *Mother Jones* for July 1982:

In a random sample of 930 [American] women, sociologist Diana Russell found that 44 per cent had survived either rape or attempted rape.

In this survey, rape was defined as sexual intercourse physically forced on a woman, or coerced by threats of bodily harm, or forced on her while she was helpless (asleep, for example).

Beneke continues:

In a September 1980 survey conducted by *Cosmopolitan* magazine to which 106,000 women anonymously responded, 24 percent had been raped at least once. Of these 51 percent had been raped by friends, 37 percent by strangers, 18 per cent by relatives and three percent by husbands. Ten percent of the women in the survey had been victims of incest; 75 percent of the women had been 'bullied into making love'.

Joni Miller of Vancouver reported in 1981 that one Canadian woman in four can expect to be raped eventually, and that in Canada a woman is raped every 17 minutes and one is sexually assaulted every 6 minutes. She added that 75 per cent of the women calling for help from Vancouver Rape Relief were raped by someone they know or trust, or both. Many rapes are never reported, however, and few of the men are charged. Besides,

it is usually futile to try to bring charges against a rapist father, grandfather, uncle, boss, ex-boyfriend, husband's best friend, or the 'nice' guy down the street. Usually the 'authorities' will not believe you. . . . The men who are jailed for acting out the macho myth are typically poor non-white immigrant or working class (*Vancouver Sun*, June 23, 1981).

Either/or

In a second article on the 'team game' and the 'spectator sport' at Big Dan's (August 2, 1983), Ellen Goodman describes a 'photo fantasy' from the January 1983 issue of Larry Flint's *Hustler*, sent to her by a teacher in High Falls, N.Y. It depicts the gang rape of a waitress on a pool table. The woman is depicted as enjoying it.

We also learn that at about the same time as the assault in New Bedford, in a working-class neighborhood, five or more fraternity brothers at the University of Pennsylvania gang-raped a woman student at a party.

Goodman continues:

One inch under the veneer of changing sexual mores lingers the most ancient vision of woman as either virgin or whore. The woman who willingly, even lovingly, has sex with one, becomes a target for any.

The either/or is important. You will recall the words of the Italian parish priest who summed it up in 1861 with Mrs Hugh Fraser, the diplomat's wife, in the congregation (3.5): Men may be more or less good, bad, or indifferent, he said, but for women the choice is either innocence or depravity: 'A woman must be either an angel or a devil – there is no place between for *her*!'

Male axioms

The same imaginary opposition between the 'good girl' and the 'bad girl' appears in the memory device used by British radio technicians to remember the color code of the resistors:

Bad boys raped our young girls, but Violet goes willingly.

Violet is about to become the Whore. Her existence and identity for others is going to be constrained by four utterly imaginary male axioms – an axiom in this sense is a statement so apparently true that it requires no evidence, argument, or proof – two of them general, two of them particular:

1   Women like to be raped (they are masochists).
2   Women who get raped were 'asking for it' in any case (they provoke it).
3   Women who run around with more than one man are whores anyway, so it serves them right if they get raped (they invite punishment).
4   When prostitutes and 'women like that' say 'no' they really mean 'yes', so they can't be raped anyway (they lie back and enjoy it).

FIGURE 5.1 Sylvia chats with her extra-terrestrial visitor. Reprinted from: Nicole Hollander: *That Woman Must Be On Drugs* (1981).

(Note that for St Paul (I Corinthians) and for a good many other men, all women are whores. Male fear and hatred run deep. Says a medieval Latin couplet: 'Woman pollutes the body, drains the resources, kills the soul, uproots the strength, blinds the eye, and embitters the voice'.)

> Man's discovery that his genitalia could be used as a weapon to generate fear must rank as one of the most important discoveries of prehistoric times.
> Susan Brownmiller: *Against Our Will* (1975)

Terrorism

In her analysis of the New Bedford rape, Ellen Goodman draws on Susan Brownmiller's *Against Our Will* (1975):

> Men who commit rape have served in effect as frontline masculine shock troops, terrorist guerrillas in the longest sustained battle the world has ever known (p. 209).

It is more than a battle, of course, it is history's longest war.

The ever-present threat of male violence against women is a ruthless assault on women's freedom to think and do and be as they are and run their own lives. The threat of rape makes growing up a recognition of subordination and life a state of siege. As the reality behind the threat, the rapist forces women to depend on other men – fathers, brothers, boyfriends, husbands, sons, police – for protection. The rapist is thus the man who enforces and perpetuates the male supremacy of every other man, whether we realize it or not.

The conspiracy among men about rape does not exist because it is deliberately intended, but rather because men who share the dominant values of our society benefit (in the short range, at least) from the way things are. The result is that from ideology and ignorance men deny the reality of rape, deny its history, deny its nature, deny its importance, and deny its violence. Men do not see rape as a physical and mental attack on the body and soul of another human being, but rather as a crime against property, as the devaluation of a man's assets, as the invasion of a man's territory, as the violation of the possessor through the possessed.

Rape is not a sexual act, it is a crime of power, a mark of fascism. To be raped is to be tortured, to be degraded, to be at the mercy of a madman who sees you as a victim, not as another human being. Says Brownmiller: 'Rape is the act of a conqueror' (p. 58).

> I saw one case where a woman was shot by a sniper, one of our snipers. When we got up to her she was asking for water. And the lieutenant said to kill her. So he ripped off her clothes, they stabbed her in both breasts, they spread her eagle and shoved an E tool up her vagina, an entrenching tool, and she was still asking for water. And they they took that out and used a tree limb and then she was shot.

(This testimony is from the *Winter Soldier Investigation* by the Vietnam Veterans Against the War (Boston: Becon Press, 1972), reprinted in Arlene Bergman's *Women of Viet Nam*, 1975, p. 71, and more fully in Brownmiller, 1975, p. 108.)

Rape is also a means of communication between men. Of the five-day gang-rape in 1966 of a 20-year-old South Vietnamese villager, Phan Ti Mao, kidnapped by an American reconnaissance patrol (the men were court-martialed), as reported with assumed names, for the men by *New Yorker* writer Daniel Lang, Susan Brownmiller observes:

> Of the five men in the patrol only one, Private First Class Sven Eriksson, did not participate in Mao's rape and murder. As Lang described the ordeal, individual acts of superfluous cruelty practiced on Mao appeared to be competition for a masculine pecking order. Eriksson, for refusing to take his turn in Mao's gang rape was derided by the patrol leader, Sergeant Tony Meserve, as a queer and a chicken. One of the followers, Manuel Diaz, later haltingly told the military prosecutor that fear of ridicule had made him decide to go along with the rest (p. 102).

These young men made Mao into a despised and degraded *other* (whore, witch, or bitch), into a slave acting as the medium for the body messages of her masters, the Others, a living tablet of flesh upon which they inscribed every detail of their crime.

On the fifth day they killed her. The combat report read: 'One Viet Cong, killed in action'.

These four men thus qualified as 'double veterans' in Vietnam. A double veteran, explains Mark Baker in *Nam* (1981), was a soldier who had sex with a woman and afterwards killed her.

As the men say: 'All's fair in love and war'. Or in Cervantes' words, from *Don Quixote* (1605):

> Love and War are the same thing, the stratagems and policy are as allowable in the one as in the other.

The My Lai massacre of between 350 and 550 old men, women, and children by Charlie Company of the American Division on March 16, 1968 was followed by rape and rape-murder. To Seymour Hersch's questions about rape at My Lai, quoted by Brownmiller (p. 105), a squad leader replied: 'That's an everyday affair. You can nail just about everybody on that – at least once. The guys are human, man.'

> 'They only do it when there are a lot of guys around,' veteran George Phillips told writer Lucy Komisar. 'You know, it makes them feel good. They show each other what they can do – "I can do it", you know. They won't do it by themselves.'
>   'Did you rape too?'
>   'Nope.'

'Why not?'

'I don't know. I just got a thing. I don't – Of course it got around the company, you know, well, hah, "the medic didn't do it".'

'Did anyone report these incidents?'

'No. No one did. You don't dare. Next time you're out in the field you won't come back – you'll come back in a body bag. What the hell, she's only a dink, a gook, this is what they think' (p. 107).

'I hate gooks', said a veteran of My Lai quoted by Robert Lifton in *Home from the War* (1973), reprinted in *Women of Vietnam* (1975):

and of course the only way you could determine who hated them the most was how many times you beat them or killed them or raped them or something like that.

The 2.7 million American troops who served in Vietnam were assisted by troops from Thailand and South Korea, by about 8000 troops from Australia and New Zealand, and by about 15,000 Canadians serving with the US military – whose Green Berets used the Montagnards (despised by the Vietnamese) as mercenaries. Sixty thousand American veterans have committed suicide since coming home from the war.

Along with liquor, looting, and destroying whatever it suits you to destroy, the male lust for the pathology of power means the power to do whatever you like with the women and children of the defeated enemy men.

The opportunity to exercise such power, the power of a god, has for centuries been the richest prize offered by brutalizing generals to brutalized men.

In apparently endless wars of conquest and colonization, wars of religion, wars against 'witches' and 'heretics', wars against non-whites, wars against 'barbarians' or 'savages', wars against mutinies and rebellions, wars against workers and peasants – in every war waged against people regarded by the victors as uncivilized, subhuman, 'primitive', 'savage', mere animals or organisms, mere objects or things, and usually as the incarnation of evil besides, the warlords have written out their hatred of humanity in other people's flesh and blood.

Atrocity breeds atrocity: Russians excused Russian rape in Berlin in 1945 and after by saying: 'This is what the Germans did in Russia.' Here again the bodies of women are being used as a medium of communication between men.

In El Salvador women tortured and then murdered by government forces or freelance death squads have been found with their husband's or boyfriend's head sewn up inside them.

Brutalization breeds brutality. In Zimbabwe, following six years of ruthless war and three years of uneasy political independence, it was reported in 1984 that the 5000 men of the North-Korean trained Fifth Brigade of the Shona-controlled army were pillaging, beating, torturing, killing, and raping members of the country's minority Ndebele tribe, who had risen in insurrection. Between 1200 and 3000 deaths were estimated.

Speaking now of rape associated with mob violence, Brownmiller says that as far as women are concerned,

> it is worth noting the similarity of experience . . . between such disparate events in time and place as the Ukrainian pogroms [against the Jews] and, for example, the Mormon persecutions [in the United States] and the periodic outbreaks of white mob violence against blacks. In each historical interlude a mob of men, sometimes an official militia, armed itself with an ideology that offered a moral justification − 'for the public good' − to commit acts of degradation on women.

(Of the Russian pogrom of 1880 an account reprinted in the London *Times* in 1881 recorded that Russian Orthodox peasant women held Jewish women down while other Christians − their fathers, husbands, neighbors − violated them.)

In the three examples of mob violence cited by Brownmiller, there was a campaign of terror, whose goals included the annihilation of a people, and this provided a license to rape

> In each interlude the symbol of the mob's hatred and contempt became its exuberant destruction of *other men's property*, be it furniture, cattle, or women.

It mattered little to the rapists among the mob how 'attractive' their victims were, which argues that sexual appeal, as normally understood, has little to do with rape.

> A mob turns to rape as an expression of power and dominance. Women are used almost as inanimate objects to prove a point among men (pp. 124-5).

Gratuitous acts

Rape may also involve what an Australian law professor called 'gratuitous acts and extravagant defilements . . . often excretory in nature' (p. 196). Menachem Amir deals with what he calls 'sexual humiliation' in his 1971 study of patterns of forcible rape. According to Brownmiller such acts as urination, ejaculation into the victim's face or hair, and other defilements were ignored by Amir – perhaps the Philadelphia police reports gave no information – but he does deal with fellatio and anal penetration. Including repeated intercourse in his definition of 'sexual humiliation', Amir found that in over a quarter of his cases the victim was subjected to some form of 'extra insult' beyond the rape itself. Sexual humiliation ran higher in group rapes than in individual rapes (p. 196). The *coup de grâce* may be the ramming of a stick, bottle, or some other object into the victim.

It appears that an even more basic male axiom may underly the four male axioms already noted:

1   women like to be raped
2   women ask to be raped
3   women invite rape as punishment
4   women can't be raped anyway (they lie back and enjoy it).

This more basic male axiom, as imaginary as the others, is that sex is an act of violence.

Brownmiller cites the example of Colin Wilson, whom I knew as the self-taught author of *The Outsider* (1956), a brilliant and erudite theory of morbid existential alienation centered on 'being and nothingness' in 'a world without values', much read in literary and university circles in the 1960s. Wilson is apparently one of the many admirers of Jack the Ripper as an example of the 'heroic rapist' (p. 295). In Wilson's later book *A Casebook of Murder* (1969), which is a compendium of sex slayings, only one such killing really disgusts him, he says, a lesbian murder of two children. But, says Brownmiller,

> of the rest of his gallery of heterosexual and male homosexual rapists, necrophiliacs, disembowelers, axe murderers, breast eaters, kidney devourers, etc., he displays no queasiness.

Wilson considers these to be of proper interest to the 'sexually normal'. On page 220 he writes:

> The sexual act has a close affinity with murder . . . Murderer and victim are in the same sort of relation as the male penetrating the female.

Here Wilson crosses the boundaries of class, race, and country to give us the ideals of the police-blotter rapist under the guise of philosophy. He is in fact confessing that he cannot tell the difference between erotic sexual love and fear, hatred, and domination masquerading as sex, by which I mean pornography.

Pornography is violence, physical and not, as obscene as napalm, but tricked out in the language of slaves.

In the summer of 1973 a 28-year-old Quaker pacifist named Robert A. Martin, a former seaman with a background in journalism, held a 'stunning' press conference in Washington, D.C. Arrested during a peace demonstration in front of the White House, he had gone to jail rather than post a $10 bond (Brownmiller, 1975, pp. 258-9).

After a week he was transferred to a cell-block of 'predominantly young black prisoners, many of them in jail for serious crimes of violence'. During his first evening recreation period in the new tier, he was lured into a cell on a pretext:

> 'My exit was blocked and my pants were forcibly taken off me, and I was raped. Then I was dragged from cell to cell all evening.'

Two of his violators then promised him protection from further assaults.

The next night his 'protectors' initiated a second general round of oral and rectal rape. The pair stood outside his cell and collected packs of cigarettes from other prisoners wanting a turn.

He eventually managed to escape and alert a guard.

When a skeptical reporter asked where the prison guards had been during his two nights of multiple assault, in which Martin estimated he had been ganged by 45 to 50 men, he replied in all honesty, 'That's a good question'.

There is no doubt that Martin was deliberately transferred to this particular cell-block, in full knowledge of what would happen: 'getting even with Whitey'. (Homosexuality is not significant here: as in the rape of a woman, 'masculinity' in male rape is defined by the aggressor, not by sex.)

The blood lust

In 1982 during the Falklands War it was reported from Washington sources (*Vancouver Sun*, June 2) that a British paratroop commander, Lt.-Col. Herbert Jones, had been machine gunned to death at Goose Green after Argentine troops had waved a flag of surrender. Some 250 Argentines were reported killed on that occasion. The official British report differs, but according to the American source, with access to British military information:

The 2nd Battalion was so enraged by the loss of its commander that it erupted into a fury of killing. The reaction was so emotional that consideration initially was given to removing the 2nd Battalion from further action . . .

This is the 'blood lust', the hot-blooded complement of cold-blooded killing and cruelty.

Why men fight

'There is an exhilaration in combat that is not evident in any other life experience,' said Major L.H. 'Mike' Williams, Deputy Commander of Grey's Scouts, a much-feared mounted infantry unit deployed against the Nationalist guerrillas in Rhodesia, during Zimbabwe's war of independence (1957-1980), in *Merc* (1979) by Jay Mallin and Robert K. Brown, Lieutenant Colonel (retd.) in the US Special Forces and editor and publisher of *Soldier of Fortune*, 'the journal of professional adventurers'.

Perhaps it stems from the realization that you can survive in spite of chaos, confusion and noise. Each time you do come out it leaves you with a tremendous desire to stay away from it, but this is soon replaced with an equally intense feeling of wanting to try it again (pp. 120-1).

In the September 1983 issue of *Soldier of Fortune*, which reports the conclusions of the team of experts sent by the magazine to train, evaluate, and share combat with E1 Salvador's government forces in April 1983, the magazine's military small arms editor, Peter G. Kokalis, writes:

While forever attracted to its implements, god, how I loathe war. And yet . . . no wine gives fiercer intoxication, no drug more vivid exaltation (p. 69).
"(He has obviously never flown a plane, fallen in love or finished a book)."

Defining GI jargon in his *Vietnam War Wordbook* in the October issue, Thomas Edwards writes:

BEAUCOUP DINKY DAU: Bastardized Vietnamese meaning 'You are very, very crazy'. After some weeks in 'Nam, it was a pretty apt description of most U.S. troops' mental state.
    As one ex-paratrooper pointed out, 'Serving in 'Nam was like being parachuted into an insane asylum. You knew you were okay, but you had to act as crazy as everyone else to keep them from turning on you'. Dinky dau. Right.

Matching in intensity the exhilaration of combat is the spiritual bonding between men who serve together under fire. In an article of 1921 on medieval chivalry, the Dutch scholar Johan Huizinga (1872-1945) quotes from *Le jouvencel* (*Youth*), the biographical romance by Jean de Bueil, Joan of Arc's companion in arms before her immolation in 1431:

> One loves one's comrade so in war. When one sees that one's quarrel is just and one's blood is fighting well, tears rise to the eye. A sweet feeling of loyalty and pity fills the heart on seeing one's friend so valiantly exposing his body in order to do and fulfill the command of our Creator. And then one prepares to go die or live with him, and for love not to abandon him. And out of that rises such a delectation that he who has not essayed it is not man enough to say what a delight it is. Do you think that a man who does that fears death? Not at all; for he feels so strengthened, he is so elated that he does not know where he is. Truly he is afraid of nothing.

When Nanking, the capital city of the Nationalist Chinese forces of General Chiang Kai-shek, fell to the Japanese on December 12, 1937 after six months of incessant battle, says Colonel Roy M. Stanley II in *Prelude to Pearl Harbor* (1982), an account of the events between 1937 and 1941 during the Japanese invasion and occupation of Manchuria and much of China (1931-1945),

> Japanese troops went berserk with elation. In an orgy of arson, rape, looting, and massacre, over one hundred thousand Chinese were killed and large parts of Nanking destroyed (p. 106).

From newsreels current during World War Two I vividly recall scenes of Japanese troops burying women and children alive, stamping the earth down over their heads and around their protruding hands.

It was the policy of the Japanese commander, General Matsui, to permit unrestricted rape and looting as the 'spoils of war' and to let his men 'unwind' after battle. He was hanged by the Americans as a war criminal in 1948.

The Rape of Nanking incensed even some Japanese journalists. A reporter for the *Osaka Daily* wrote that 'no words can describe the deterioration of discipline among Japanese soldiers . . . their cruelty is beyond description' (pp. 107-8). Colonel Stanley comments in a note (p. 108):

> While in no way excusing the Japanese excesses at Nanking, it is important to understand them. Just as extremes of anger or emotion will cause some people to burst out laughing in a misdirected release

of emotion, troops sometimes go wild as a release. Once begun, the mad frenzy will often spread like wildfire. If well directed or fortunate in its timing, the result can be an overwhelming, if mindless, attack such as the 24th Wisconsin charge that took Missionary Ridge at Chattanooga in November 1863. When vented on a helpless populace it becomes Nanking. It is important to remember that the Japanese considered the Chinese to be inferior and defeated – and, to the Japanese, the defeated are without rights or honor . . .

The unfortunate city, he adds, had undergone an only slightly less violent ordeal of looting and rape when Chiang Kai-shek's Kuomintang or Nationalist troops took the city during the Chinese civil war in March 1927, a few weeks before Chiang's betrayal and massacre of the workers of Shanghai, recorded for posterity by André Malraux in *La Condition humaine* (1933).

Reuter reported on August 15, 1985 that China marked the anniversary of the end of the Second World War by reminding the world that Japanese troops killed more people in the Rape of Nanking than died in the atomic attacks on Japan.

The report continued by saying that the Japanese forces took Nanking, the former Chinese capital, on December 13, 1937, and immediately began a six-week orgy of killing, burning, looting, and raping in which 340,000 people died. An article in the official *People's Daily* said:

More than 190,000 of our compatriots were killed and their corpses disposed of collectively. Another 150,000 were killed separately.
The total is greater than the number of deaths caused by the atomic bombs dropped on Hiroshima and Nagasaki.

Culloden

In 1745, led by Bonnie Prince Charlie, the Stuart claimant to the throne of England and Scotland, most of the Highland clans rose in rebellion against George II. After initial successes in England and their two victories at Falkirk and Prestonpans, they faced the royal troops again on Culloden Moor, April 6, 1746.

A musket volley followed by a raging, blazing, screaming charge with target (shield), claymore, and dirk was the principal and winning battle tactic of the Highlanders at this period. A century later the headlong charge was still the primary tactic of their Celtic descendants on the Confederate side in the American Civil War (1861-65).

At Culloden, outnumbered by 9000 royal troops to their 5000, deficient in cavalry and artillery, ill-organized, tired, hungry, outgeneraled, poorly-positioned, and badly-led, the Highland army was first decimated by a torrent of fire from the royal artillery, then smashed itself to pieces in a series of charges against the Hanoverian, British, and Scots troops led by the Duke of Cumberland, George II's 29-year-old son, who had devised a tactic to neutralize the power of the Scottish onslaught (Chapter 6). The battle lasted all of forty minutes. The Scots lost over 2000 killed or wounded; the English lost 50 killed and 200 wounded.

After the defeat the French and Irish fighting with the rebels were admitted to quarter and made prisoner. In his *History of the Rebellion of 1745-6*, Robert Chambers describes what happened next:

> Immediately after the conclusion of the battle, the men, under the command of their officers, traversed the field, stabbing with their bayonets, or cutting down with their swords, such of the wounded of the defeated party as came under their notice. This was done as much in sport as in rage, and as the work went on, the men at length began to amuse themselves by splashing and dabbling each other with blood. They at length looked, as one of themselves has reported, 'more like so many butchers than an army of Christian soldiers' (p. 303).

Here the lust for blood was expressed as cold-blooded murder, the Highlanders being 'mere savages' as far as the British and Hanoverians were concerned.

This was the victory celebrated by Handel with 'Hail the Conquering Hero Comes'.

Fleeing in confusion towards Inverness after the battle, the defeated warriors and the local inhabitants were ruthlessly pursued by the British cavalry, who cut them down without quarter or remorse. For four miles the bodies of the victims lined the road.

The next day it was discovered that some of the wounded on the battlefield were still alive. By Cumberland's direct order – he was called the 'Butcher' ever aferward – seventy of these men were carried off and dispatched by firing squads, who were ordered to administer the *coup de grâce* to any rebels still alive by beating their brains out with musket butts.

At least a hundred other men sheltering in nearby houses were murdered shortly after, 32 by being shut up and burnt to death. The prisoners taken were confined without heat or clothing for months in prison hulks at sea, where most of them died of malnutrition, disease, or exposure.

Brownmiller records the startling fact that the battle itself was accompanied by the 'sexual mutilation of women on Culloden Moor', but gives no details (p. 38).

The rape of Highland women began as a matter of opportunity. After Lord George Sackville's troops had been attacked by a few desperate clansmen, who got away with some provisions and horses, Sackville

> allowed his men to take revenge at the next hamlet, where the women were first raped and then held to watch the shooting and bayonetting of their husbands, fathers, brothers and sons (p. 38, quoting John Prebble's *Culloden* [1961]).

Rape continued as a matter of policy. In volume II of Cassell's *British Battles* (c. 1885) James Grant records:

> The women . . . were subjected to brutal violation, and then turned out naked, with their children, to starve on the barren heath. One whole family was enclosed in a barn, and consumed to ashes. Those ministers of vengeance were so alert in their office, that in a few days there was neither house, cottage, man, nor beast to be seen in the compass of fifty miles; all was ruin, silence, and desolation (p. 37).

Thus ended the last battle to be fought on British soil.

The English campaign of pacification in the Highlands after Culloden is distant in time from Vietnam in the 1960s, but the English campaign to wipe out Scottish independence and to destroy the Highland way of life, was predicated on the same kind of strategy as the American attempt to permanently colonize South Vietnam.

In *Attack and Die* (1982), an account of the disastrous military tactics of the predominantly Celtic Confederacy against the largely Anglo-Saxon Union in the American Civil War, the authors Grady McWhiney and Perry D. Jamieson note the racism of the Anglo-Saxons towards the Celts, whether in Scotland or Carolina, and summarize the results of the defeat on Culloden Moor (p. 178):

> After Culloden the English sought to destroy the clans. [Rebels] were hunted down, their houses burned, and their cattle stolen. The English adopted laws that declared a number of clan leaders traitors, disarmed the Highlanders, proscribed their dress, confiscated the estates of all attained persons, and abolished the traditional relationships between clansmen and their chiefs. More destructive yet to the Celtic way of life in Scotland were the changes in tenancy, animal husbandry, and work patterns. Traditional ways and social customs were outlawed to be replaced by the ways of a 'money economy'.

McWhiney and Jamieson say nothing about the killing of the wounded or the raping of the women, however.

More than 20,000 Scots emigrated to North America between 1763 and 1775. In the United States, while New England remained largely Anglo-Saxon, from Pennsylvania south and west the population became increasingly Celtic, with Celts in an overwhelming majority throughout the South. The argument of *Attack and Die* is that by employing the same Celtic tactic, the headlong charge, in battle after battle in the Civil War, and consistently losing more men than the Union, who outnumbered them anyway, the Confederacy made its defeat inevitable. 'It was not war', said General Daniel H. Hill of the reckless Confederate attacks on fortified Union positions, 'it was murder.'

Conquest

The rape of the defeated side's women by the winners, along with the slaughter of their children, is the ultimate humiliation for the defeated men, the stamp of total conquest. In Bangladesh (originally East Pakistan), for example, between 200,000 and 400,000 Bengali women were raped by West Pakistani soldiers in nine months of terror during the civil war that followed its declaration of independence from West Pakistan in 1971.

Following the custom of making victims responsible for their victimization, a custom not restricted to Islamic countries, most of the raped women were afterwards disowned by their menfolk and their families.

Of rape and conquest Brownmiller concludes:

The body of a raped woman becomes a ceremonial battlefield, a parade ground for the victor's trooping of the colors. The act that is played out upon her is a message passed between men . . . (p. 38).

The message may not be defeat but vengeance. Following the independence of the Congo in 1960, large numbers of white women of all ages were raped by Congolese soldiers taking revenge for the horrors of King Leopold's and later Belgium's exploitation of that colony and its peoples.

Certain women should be struck regularly, like gongs.
                    Noel Coward: *Private Lives* (1930)

Domestic affairs

Turn on the television this evening if you have one and flip the dial – you'll probably hear a woman screaming, see a woman being threatened, grabbed, shaken, slapped, or beaten, or see a woman being chased or terrorized. The second best-kept male secret, after rape, is wife-beating.

Wife- and woman-beating is not confined to any particular race. 'Your average white Anglo-Saxon Canadian male does just as much hitting as any other ethnic group', says David Currie of Metro Family Services Association in Toronto. Most men who batter women, he says, are inflexible or confused about male-female roles. They tend also to be low in self-esteem. They expect a duty-bound wife and yet they cannot separate their personal identity and needs from those of their spouse. In depending for their own sense of identity – and above all for their sense of security as 'real men' among other men – on their relationship to their wives or woman friends, they resent them (Martin Stuart-Harle in the *Toronto Star*, April 4, 1983).

On April 6, 1982, it was reported in the *Vancouver Sun* that more than half of married women in Canada are beaten by their husbands at least once and that half of those are battered regularly. In a paper presented at the annual Conference of the Learned Societies, the three women from Carleton University's School of Social Work responsible for this research added that 80 per cent of first-time beatings occur during pregnancy.

Said Denise Stone:

Violent husbands cut across all socio-economic lines and include police officers, lawyers, doctors and business executives.

Lesley Silver added that a study of 100 assaulted women taken in 1980 indicated that

59 were kicked, 44 were cut with a bottle, razor, or knife, 26 had their noses, ribs or teeth broken, 10 were strangled and 11 were burned or scalded.

It is reported elsewhere that woman beaters who are also Vietnam veterans specialize in inflicting pain in ways that do not show.

As with rape, the basis of woman-beating is rage, fear, hatred, and contempt for women, centered on a colossal insecurity about one's 'masculinity' and capacity to 'perform' as a man (there is here a connection with the 'pride in performance' of the alcoholic, and alcohol is a major factor in woman battering).

Hegel said long ago that the most fundamental of human desires is the desire for recognition as a human being (psychotherapists call it 'confirmation'). The man demands that the woman recognize him as the master of the house. This she is obliged to do by submitting to his control. At the same time he demands that she recognize him as a 'real

FIGURE 5.2   Reprinted from Nicole Hollander: *That Woman Must Be On Drugs* (1981).

man'. But by acting as his slave the woman loses his respect, and to be recognized as a master by a slave is not to be recognized at all.

What he wants is to be recognized as a 'real man' by people he respects, by other masters, that is to say, by other men. But this is precisely the recognition he lacks or believes he lacks. We see that as with rape the pathological relationship with the woman as his victim is in fact a conversation with other men. The woman and her body are the medium of this real and imaginary communication.

He lashes out at the woman for failing to make him feel secure when it is his own behavior that has made it impossible for her to do this. He knows that she cannot possibly respect him because he is a bully; he also knows that as a woman-beater he will not be respected by other men. In the act of beating he knows that by attacking the woman he is putting the relationship in jeopardy. But he depends on the relationship for much of his sense of identity. By beating the woman he is destroying himself as well as her. He is also destroying his respect for himself, which is what he is lacking in the first place.

According to the *Star* article, woman-beaters describe the beating as accompanied by 'out of control feelings', feelings of things 'happening fast', blankness, and even 'self-abuse'. They 'disconnect' with themselves. Afterwards they may feel loss of self-respect, loss of the woman's respect, shame, weakness, fear, crying, remorse, or just silence as they 'reconnect' with themselves.

In its 1980 report 'Wife Battering in Canada', the Canadian Advisory Council on the Status of Women, citing American, Canadian, and British sources, concluded that wife-battering is too widespread to be called a 'mental illness'. That is hardly an adequate definition of either woman-beating or mental illness. The facts seem rather to indicate that there is a new epidemic of violence against women, and that the source of it is massive male paranoia.

The *Star* article on beating women continues, quoting the report:

> It's not related to 'natural male aggressiveness' or male hormones; male role-model lesbian lovers are as likely to beat their 'wives'. It's socially learned 'maleness', not 'biologically learned maleness that precipitates violence'.

Many men who batter were battered children themselves or saw their fathers beat their mothers (not to mention the epidemic of woman-battering on television since the late 1970s).

The batterer may blame alcohol or drugs, besides blaming the victim herself, each of which is an escape from responsibility for the violence by putting it 'outside' the self – as the alcoholic does with his alcoholism. (Responsibility is a function of one's power to be responsible.) Currie says: 'You have to get (wife-batterers) to realize it's them who are doing the hitting.'

Few women lay charges in these cases, and (with some recent exceptions in the U.S.) the police, if called, are not likely to help – most of them hold the same attitudes towards women as most other men. The failure to lay charges leads some men to bring out the old standby, the myth of female 'masochism'. They say that women who get beaten are 'asking for it' – in fact they must like it. The victim of beating is blamed for being beaten in the same way as the victim of rape is blamed for being raped.

The reason for the woman not laying charges may be shame at the man's behavior, a belief that she provoked it, guilt at her failure to please him, or the desire to hide her own shame. Very often, however, the reason is that she will suffer another beating in reprisal if she does.

The woman-batterer makes his victim suffer because he is trapped in at least two double binds:

1(a) My woman will satisfy my desire for recognition as a master by doing what I say.
1(b) By making her do what I say I make it impossible for her to satisfy my desire for recognition as a master.
2(a) By beating her I will make my woman recognize me as a 'real man'. My mastery over women (represented in my relationship to her) will make other men recognize me as a 'real man'.

2(b) By beating her I make it impossible for her – or other men – to recognize me as a 'real man'.

The woman is in the following trap:

If I charge him now, I'll get beaten soon.
If I don't charge him now, I'll get beaten later.

Within this closed and pathological context, it is impossible for the woman to make any decision or take any action that will prevent further beatings. The only solution is to break out of the constraints of the pathology by getting a skilled and well-informed third party involved, getting the man into counselling or hospital, or getting out of the relationship entirely – which may of course be made difficult or practically impossible by lack of money, the needs of children, the problems raised by learned dependency on men (the Cinderella Complex), or any number of other factors.

In times of crisis, the adoption of proper time-perspectives becomes a matter of urgency.
Kresten Bierg: 'The Hollow Men and the Public Speech Act' (1980)

5.2 Civil wars

In *Africa Addio* (1966), a historically backed account of the tour of Africa by Gualtiero Jacopetti, director of *Mondo Cane* (1963), in the making of the film *Africa Addio*, John Cohen writes that during the state of emergency in Kenya (1952-60) – that is to say, during the failed war of independence (1948-60) led by the Kikuyu secret society, the Mau Mau:

Acts of torture and sadism during the British repressive campaign were so frequent that they could never be counted. The government clamped a tight lid of secrecy over any operation that smacked of cruelty, but a few stories leaked out. One teen-aged son of a settler bound suspects together by tying leather thongs round their necks, then shoved burning cigarettes in their ears. This settler's brother flogged another Kikuyu until he was unable to cry out, poured hot paraffin over his body, which was covered with open wounds, and set him afire.

Another settler, backed by a few loyalist Africans, raided a Kikuyu village, bound and flogged several men, and raped the women. There was no specific reason for this attack. It was just a 'reprisal'.

> A British Army captain (who had just ordered an ear sliced off a Kikuyu prisoner) had a hole cut with a bayonet in another prisoner's ear, threaded a wire through the hole, and led the man off by pulling on the wire. Male prisoners were castrated, women were tortured by having beer bottles shoved up their vaginas. It was standard practice to shoot on sight, to kill without asking questions, and Africans were shot on the flimsiest pretexts. Although it was officially illegal, Africans were flogged unmercifully – several were flogged to death. This last, of course, was no great change from pre-emergency practices (pp. 207-8).

The Mau Mau answered in kind by killing a number of whites. The Mau Mau also killed Kikuyu who remained 'loyal' to the colonial government. (Ninety per cent of the Kikuyu remained 'passively loyal' to the Mau Mau, largely because of the British policy of repression and their arbitary confiscations of Kikuyu land.)

At 10 p.m. on March 26, 1953, one thousand Mau Mau in three groups attacked the Kikuyu of Lari. They wired the hut doors shut, set them on fire, while the third group waited with *pangas* for anyone who might escape the flames. This attack, says Cohen, revealed 'the degree of Mau Mau madness'.

> One woman was held from behind while her child's throat was slowly sawed through. Another saw two Mau Mau murder her son and then drink the blood that spouted from his throat. Chief Luka was forced to watch his eight wives mutilated, then he suffered the same fate: his body was chopped in half, and his blood drunk. Women who were pregnant had their bellies slit open before they were killed. This seemed customary. It seemed customary to drink the victim's blood. It seemed customary to mutilate as much as possible before killing (p. 209).

At least 100 Kikuyu died in the Lari massacre. Two hundred homes were burned. One thousand cattle were killed or maimed.

Under colonization the violence of the colonizer against the colonized is translated into violence by the colonized against each other.

As a result of this massacre, Kikuyu enlistments in the Home Guard on the settler's side more than doubled, and from this day forward the Mau Mau were doomed to (military) defeat. Kenya achieved its political victory when it became independent in 1963.

The Mau Mau Land and Freedom Armies totaled about 12,000

men with indifferent or home-made weapons. They were faced by 25,000 Kikuyu in the Home Guard, 450 settlers, and 21,000 police, with British units bringing the total to about 70,000 troops.

(In irregular warfare the counter-insurgency forces usually aim to put into the field ten trained men for every armed guerrilla.)

By the end of 1956, four years after the emergency was first declared in 1952, official figures showed that 10,527 Mau Mau or supposed Mau Mau were dead, 2,633 had been captured, 1,071 had been hanged, and 39,000 members of the 'passive' wing were in detention camps. (At its height there were some 70,000 Africans in detention.)

In the same four years the government forces lost 63 white and 534 African soldiers. In all 32 European civilians were killed, compared with an official figure of 1,926 African civilians.

Algeria

In 1961, in *St Michael and the Dragon*, Pierre Leulliette, a volunteer French paratrooper who had served (1954-57) against the Algerians in their successful war of independence against France (1954-62), wrote of a rebel his unit had captured. The man was left in a cell by the

FIGURE 5.3 The encounter between Barbarella and Diktor in Jean-Claude Forest's cartoon saga *Barbarella* (1964), reprinted in Jasia Reichardt's *Robots* (1978, p. 82). Says Reichardt of the leitmotiv of beauty and the beast, woman and machine: 'In no other literature is the difference between emotion and lust better delineated [than in science fiction], and nowhere is the subject of love and sex treated with greater awkwardness'.

French gendarmes to 'ripen': to allow his untreated wounds to putrefy.

> I watch the man through the peephole in the cell door. All that's left alive of him is his eyes. He is writing slowly on the filthy stone floor.

FIGURE 5.4 Machine Screw: One of the illustrations by Ian Miller for which John Sladek's 'Machine Screw' was written (*Men Only*, October 1975): The ten-foot robot Alpha. Dripping with oil and consuming vast quantities of gasoline, Alpha, or Alf, 'violates with his outsize ramming device all sorts of vehicles including tanks'. To protect the car population from extinction, Alf is supplied with Meg (or Omega), 'a bulbous female'. After their lovemaking amid sparks and detonations, 'Meg takes off like a rocket, with a tremendous explosion, up into the sky. Nothing more is known' (Reichardt, 1978, p. 85).

When the prisoner had refused to respond to the usual slaps and kicks, the gendarmes had used a '394' battery, called in army slang a 'gégenne':

> They had connected the electrodes to the most sensitive parts of the man's body, and then varied the intensity to make him 'come', that is, shriek and talk (p. 93).

For another week the wounded rebel stubbornly refused to talk. After he yielded he was shot.

In Algiers in the 1950s each French army company had its own little torture room. Some of the German torturers from the French Foreign Legion claimed to be ex-SS men. Workbench vises were used to crush the most vulnerable parts of the body, most often the sexual organs. One torturer from Alsace-Lorraine specialized in the 'basic torture', beating, as well as in half-drowning (the technique of the ducking stool). And here of course there was plenty of electric power:

> Torture by electricity, first looked on as useful, then as indispensable, has finally come to be considered matter-of-course, just as normal and proper as any other (p. 288).

The wires are brought into direct contact with the bare skin, generally on the sexual organs.

> They are also moved over the whole body, stopping for a long time on the chest, where the thoracic cavity barely protects the heart, which goes wild, causing the sufferer to bound like a wounded cat . . .
>
> A refinement used by the experts on the more stubborn cases is to hold their noses till they open their mouths, and then push the antennae all the way down their throats. Sometimes, however, the man being questioned reacts to the pain with such a violent closing of his jaws that he severs the wires in one bite. We change to heavier wire (p. 288).

Uruguay and Panama

A United Press International report from Sao Paulo, Brazil (*Vancouver Sun*, January 2, 1981) said that a former navy intelligence officer from Uruguay had charged

> that US manuals were used to train Uruguay's military staff in torture, including electric shock and hot towel interrogations.

This last involves placing a towel soaked in hot water over the prisoner's head and adding more hot water at intervals.

Victor Paulo Laborde Baffico also said that most officers who trained him had attended courses at the School of the Americas run by the US military in Panama.

He said that he had never participated in torture but had seen 'innumerable' torture victims. Departing for political asylum in Denmark, the officer also said: 'Our manuals all came from the United States. They were very modern. They covered physical and psychological torture.'

Afghanistan

The October 1983 issue of *Soldier of Fortune* carries the following report:

> Calling them 'specialists in torture', a former Afghan police colonel accused the Soviets of supervising the torture and execution of thousands of imprisoned Afghan civilians, reported *Christian Science Monitor*.
>
> Colonel Muhammad Ayub Assil, who recently joined the Islamic National Front as security and legal adviser, said that he observed first-hand the Soviet control over the Ministry of the Interior and their active participation in the interrogation and torture of Afghans. 'Soviets are present in every interrogation team', he said.
>
> Soviet torture methods include beatings, sleep deprivation, electric shock, refrigeration of prisoners and hanging prisoners upside down for prolonged periods. Rape was common for female prisoners, according to Assil. At one large prison, Pul-i-Charki, near Kabul, thousands of Afghans have been executed, Assil asserted.

Simon Peter said to [the disciples]: 'Let Mary leave us, for women are not worthy of Life'. Jesus said, 'I myself shall lead her, in order to make her male, so that she too may become a living spirit resembling you males. For every woman who will make herself male will enter the Kingdom of Heaven.'

The Gospel of Thomas (c. 140 CE).
Quoted by Elaine Pagels in *The Gnostic Gospels* (1979)

5.3   Hearts and minds

The 1982 report of the US National Institute of Mental Health (NIMH), *Television and Behavior: Ten Years of Scientific Progress and Implications for the Eighties*, covers many different aspects of the relation between this powerful social medium and individual behavior, including eating, alcohol use, sexual roles, and television's messages about health and medicine, but above all, violence. According to Harry Hendersen's account in *The Press* for December 1982 the 'acid rain' of television images 'pollutes healthy attitudes towards food, alcohol, and sex, and promotes violence as the American way of solving problems, and even of having a good time.'

Of the 2,500 studies on which it was based the report says that 'the great majority . . . demonstrate a positive relationship between televised violence and later aggressive behavior'. Girls as well as boys are influenced. Moreover, says the report,

> the viewer learns more than aggressive behavior from televised violence. The viewer learns to be a victim and to identify with victims. As a result many heavy viewers may exhibit fear and apprehension, while other heavy viewers may be influenced toward aggressive behavior. Thus, the effects of televised violence may be even more extensive than suggested by earlier studies . . . and exhibited in more subtle forms of behavior than aggression.

Many children will learn from television 'to accept violence as normal behavior'. The Saturday morning cartoon shows are among the most violent programs on North American TV.

According to the study most families spend about half their waking hours at home watching television.

Families

The men are portrayed as mostly 'physically strong and virile', the women 'usually passive and feminine', and 'even more stereotyped than the males'. More recently, the report notes an increase in references to sex, in sexual innuendo, and in seductive actions and dress. The report also says:

> Both parents and behavioral scientists consider television to be an important sex educator not only in depictions specifically related to sex, but in the relationships between men and women throughout all programs.

About fifty different families are presented weekly on North

American television. In some instances watching television families deal with problems helps real families deal with their own. And when the television teenage character 'Fonzie' in a 1980 *Happy Days* episode took out a library card, the attendance of 8- to 14-year-olds in libraries reportedly increased by 500 per cent.

A major study of 600 urban children from the fourth, sixth, and eighth grades revealed that *The Waltons* and other 'idealized' families led the children to believe that real-life families are co-operative and helpful. Programs showing broken families with or without teenagers led the children to believe that real families are antagonistic, verbally aggressive, and punitive.

The television programs children watch change their behavior. After watching violent or aggressive programs, children tend to become 'aggressive and disobedient'. But if they see more positive programs 'they will more likely become more generous, friendly, and self-controlled'. Thus the report emphasizes that television can have beneficial affects and is a potential influence for good.

Violence

Box-office films rerun on television lead in dramatizing violence and sex. As with other violent programs viewers become habituated to what they see: with repeated exposure strong reactions to violence grow weaker and even vanish. The report considers this a danger to real-life behavior: 'If people become inured to violence from seeing much of it, they may be less likely to respond to real violence by, for example, helping the victims.'

'Television remains a form of violent entertainment.'

The report indicates that parents underestimate the amount of violence their children see, do not fully recognize what children regard as violent, and may not recognize how much children respond to what they see.

About half the adult audience considers some television programs unsuitable for children, notably those with violence. There is also concern about vulgar language, sexual behavior, drinking, smoking, lying, and the exploitation of children in commercials.

How many people consider the programs unsuitable for adults is not reported.

The NIMH report draws attention to the unconscious syntax of the video medium: 'The signaling of content changes by camera cuts, music, and rhythm changes . . . to reinforce attention and emotional arousal'. It expresses the hope that the schools will develop ways to teach children 'how to watch television', remarking however that the field of critical television viewing is in its infancy. The report also sees a trend toward 'setting television in its place as part of the overall system of cognitive and emotional development'.

Sex and violence

By stimulating 'residual feelings', explains Henderson, excitation can be transferred from the screen to real life. According to the NIMH report, the one kind of content that consistently produces high levels of arousal in both men and women is 'explicit erotica'.

The aggressive behavior that can be correlated with violent scenes on television may be the result of 'arousal or excitatory features of the violent scenes rather than the violence as such'.

In one investigation adult males were first provoked, then after seeing a 'neutral', an 'aggressive', or an 'erotic' film, they had the opportunity to retaliate against the person who provoked them. As predicted: 'The erotic film – the most arousing – produced the most retaliation.'

It is not clear, however, what this particular study means by 'erotic'. Eroticism – egalitarian, caring, loving – is to be distinguished from pornography – dominating, humiliating, hating.

Sexual violence

In September 1982, United Press International reported from Decatur, Illinois:

> Sexually violent movies on TV and in theatres – now at an all-time high – increase men's willingness to inflict violence on women, including wife-beating, random rape, and forced sex in dating . . .

A survey by Edward Donnerstein at the University of Wisconsin and Neil Malamuth of the University of California in Los Angeles, released by the National Coalition on Television Violence on September 14, 1982, and presented at the annual convention of the American Psychological Association the week before, reveals that 35 per cent of American and Canadian men 'admitted there was some chance they would rape a woman if they could be sure they would not be caught'.

Donnerstein and Malamuth found that

> a significant minority of adult men had attitudes very similar to convicted rapists in accepting the myth that women enjoyed being raped and that force in sexual relations was normal.

The studies used four types of films:

1 sexually violent
2 violent but not sexual
3 explicitly sexual but not violent
4 neutral (a David Susskind interview).

The researchers found that

only films exhibiting violence and sexual violence resulted in major increases in the willingness to 'administer pain to women'.

Donnerstein said that

Violent pornography is a common instigator of aggression against women, including wife-beating, rape and forced sex during dating relationships . . .

He noted also that

erotic material alone did not increase violent attitudes to women (emphasis added).

As already remarked on, the 1982 report by the National Institute of Mental Health cites a study with a different finding. But the NIMH study did not distinguish between human sexuality – eroticism – and perverted sexuality – pornography.

(Pornography involves physical, mental, or emotional violence, dominant-subordinate relations, the objectification of the subordinate partner, and real or fantasized humiliation or degradation. The pornographic ideology is nowhere more evident than in the style and content of men's 'jokes' about women.)

Teenagers

Linda Hossie reports in the *Toronto Globe and Mail* for March 11, 1986, that research by James Check of York University in Toronto suggests that

young people between the ages of 12 and 17 are the primary consumers of pornography in Canada and that 37 per cent of them watch sexually explicit videos at least once a month.

Check's material was assembled for the first time in February 1986 for the Metro Toronto Action Committee on Public Violence Against Women and Children.

Check also found that college students display an 'unbelievable' acceptance of rape myths and violence against women. 'It may very well be . . . that students learn about the social and behavioral aspects of human sexuality from pornography', he said.

In other words, pornography is sex education for young people, and often their first exposure to highly intimate sexual behavior.

He added that US studies have shown that 40 per cent of Los Angeles high school students, both male and female, showed some acceptance 'for forcing a woman to have intercourse if she gets the man sexually excited, is stoned or drunk, or has had intercourse with other men'.

York University students (107 male and 197 females) were asked whether when a girl engages in necking and petting and 'she lets things get out of hand', it is her own fault if her partner forces sex on her. Thirty-one per cent of the men and 22 per cent of the women said yes. Asked whether women pretend reluctance, really hoping that men will force them, 32 per cent of the men and 20 per cent of the women agreed.

Noting that perhaps only 5 to 10 per cent of US and Canadian rape victims report the crime to police, Professor Check ended by saying:

There is ample evidence to indicate that rape myths and sexual coercion are accepted to a surprising degree in our society, and that many victims of sexual aggression simply go undetected.

Attacks

In Timothy Beneke's *Men on Rape* (1982, p.73), Chuck, convicted of one rape and three attempted rapes, explains his motivations:

I started hating all women. I started seein' all women the same way, as users. I couldn't express my feelings to nobody . . . I'd thought about murder and other ways of getting even with women and everyone who'd hurt me. I was just waiting to explode.
   Then one night about a year after I split from my wife, I was out partyin' and drinkin' and smokin' pot. I'd shot up some heroin and done some downers and I went to the porno bookstore. Put a quarter in a slot, and saw this porn movie. It was just a guy coming up from behind a girl and attacking her and raping her. That's when I started having rape fantasies. When I seen that movie, it was like somebody lit a fuse from my childhood on up. When that fuse got to the porn movie, I exploded. I just went for it, went out and raped. It was like a little voice saying, revenge: 'You'll never get caught. Go

out and rip off some girls. It's all right; they even make movies of it.' The movie was just like a big picture stand with words on it saying go out and do it, everybody's doin' it, even the movies. So I just went out that night and started lookin'. I went up to this woman and grabbed her breast; then I got scared and ran. I went home and had the shakes real bad, and then I started likin' the feeling of getting even with all women.

Victims

Thomas Radecki, chairman of the National Coalition on Television Violence (NCTV), which maintains offices in Illinois and Washington, said that monitoring by NCTV has found movie violence at an all-time high, with rape scenes quite common.

Radecki noted a *Chicago Tribune* report that one in every 34 Chicago women were sexually assaulted in 1981.

He concluded:

> For many viewers sexually violent entertainment is like a nicotine habit. The viewer needs stronger doses to keep getting the excitement and that's where the problem lies.

Recall now the fact announced by the NIMH report: that television not only trains and encourages the aggressors to be aggressors, but also trains the victims to be victims. It is not necessary to suppose that this process is consciously intended by the opinion-making class in charge of the social media, although in some cases no doubt it is. What must be understood about the social media – and eventually countered – is not the supposed intent of those responsible for the media's style and content, but rather the actual effects of what the media communicate, consciously or not.

The dominant effect of the social media at present is to create and recreate the dominant-subordinate relationships – primarily relations of race, class, and sex – that modern society obliges its victims to accept. This 'lose-lose' strategy teaches women and other oppressed individuals and groups how to feel inferior, how to feel powerless, and how to fail (5.5 below). It not only attacks the victim but also creates the victims to be attacked.

This male strategy is counter-adaptive. It is adapting us to destruction and the planet is finite even in that.

Oppression in any form requires the complicity of the oppressed. To come out is to refuse to oppress one's self, to refuse to play the game. To come out is to assert one's validity and equality, and to declare that one will defend them. It is the only real form of self-respect.

Peter Fisher: *The Gay Mystique* (1972)

5.4   The origins of war

Theories of the origins of war are ultimately theories about every other aspect of human life in society. The prevailing ideology in our society tends to blame war on the individual, on the supposedly biological or 'innate violence' of 'human nature' (original sin). That, of course, is the easy view, for it absolves us from responsibility for our behavior towards other people. It is a male view also. If everyone is believed to be innately violent then force and force alone rules the world.

The cultural anthropologist Marvin Harris of Columbia University has developed a persuasive theory of the origins of warfare in non-state societies (band and village societies). Writing in 1977 in *Cannibals and Kings: The Origins of Culture* (pp. 47-64), Harris begins by reviewing four common theories of the origin of war: *war as solidarity, war as play, war as human nature,* and *war as politics.*

War as solidarity According to this view people go to war to maintain 'group togetherness'. Harris does not deny the role of solidarity in war (as anyone who has experienced it is unlikely to forget), but he does deny that it is the origin of war. He argues that there are many other ways of maintaining solidarity, including myth, ritual, dance, games, and the mock warfare of competitive sports.

Approaching the question from a qualitative assessment of costs and benefits, he notes that the solidarity argument fails to show how and why the deadly recourse to war functions to prevent an even more deadly consequence than war. 'No one has ever shown or will be able to show that the consequences of less solidarity would be worse than deaths in combat.'

War as play Harris agrees that people, 'especially men, are frequently brought up to believe that warfare is a zestful or ennobling activity', the ultimate competitive team sport. But different societies show that one can be brought up to enjoy stalking and killing other human beings or to hate and fear war and be revolted by its results. If warlike values are believed to cause wars, the crucial problem becomes that of specifying the conditions under which people will or will not be taught to value and revere war. This the theory of *war as play* cannot do.

War as human nature In this view 'human nature' is said to include an inherent or biological or genetic 'urge to kill'. But the notion of an innate 'death instinct' assumes what it is supposed to prove: that humans are 'programmed' to kill. (An 'instinct' is a name for a process we do not understand.)

The death instinct theory ignores the ecological, historical, and social environments in which wars and killing do or do not take place. This 'human nature' argument (its latest incarnation is the 'genetic determinism' of sociobiology, which goes so far as to call rape a logical action in the interests of the 'reproductive success' of the rapist) contradicts itself the moment one notes that war and killing are neither universally admired nor universally practiced. There are moreover such vast distinctions between the accepted 'rules of war' at different times and in different societies, and such great differences in the amount and type of violence used, that the 'killer instinct' theory is untenable even when a society does go to war.

Human beings are of course capable of becoming dangerously aggressive and learning to enjoy war and the exercise of cruelty. But 'how and when we become aggressive', says Harris, 'is controlled by our cultures rather than by our genes' (p. 54).

(Harris calls this aspect of his perspective 'cultural determinism' – as distinct from the 'genetic determinism' of sociobiologists such as E.O. Wilson, the Harvard entomologist. But it is not necessary to accept Harris's deterministic causal model and its matter-energy metaphors to be persuaded by his arguments about non-state warfare.)

War as politics This theory claims that armed conflict is 'the logical outcome of an attempt of one group to protect or increase its political, social, and economic welfare at the expense of another group' (p. 54). This is of course a definition of imperial war, of war between states, where one state fights to raise its standard of living at the expense of others (the underlying economic interests may of course be overlain by political, racial, and religious themes). In fact the state came into existence precisely because it was a type of political organization – imperialist within and without – able to carry out wars of territorial conquest, economic plunder, and colonization. *War as politics* still fails to explain the origin of non-state warfare.

Moreover, with the exception of 'primitive states' such as the nineteenth-century Zulu Empire (organized on Portuguese lines), band and village societies do not generally conquer territories or subjugate their enemies.

Political expansion cannot explain warfare among band and village societies because most such societies do not engage in political expansion. Their entire mode of existence is dominated by the need *not to expand* in order to preserve the favorable ratio of people to resources (emphasis added).

The ecology of war

Only a handful of known 'primitive' societies never wage war. Harris's list includes the Andaman Islanders, who live off the east coast of India south of the border with Burma, the California-Nevada Shoshoni, the Yahgan of Patagonia in southern Argentina, the California Mission Indians, and the Semai of Malaysia.

Warfare is thus not universal, even though the exceptions are few. Nor is warfare everywhere identical in motivation, character, or effects. Warfare between hunter-gatherer societies in the late stone age (before about 10,000 BCE) must have been moderated by the fact that although such societies inhabit and use a territory, they do not regard it as a possession, and do not have to defend it in order to earn their living. Combat between such groups is usually the result of personal grievances between influential individuals, not of political or other collective factors. The first definite archeological evidence of warfare is associated with fortified villages and towns practising agriculture, where there is a territory that must be defended. The oldest of these is pre-Biblical Jericho, which by 7500 BCE was an elaborately fortified town.

Following the collapse of the 'prehistoric' big game hunting cultures in about 13,000 BCE, warfare between hunter-gatherers probably became more severe. Climatic changes at the end of the last ice age permitted forest ecosystems to invade the grassland ecosystems that had supported the great abundance of game in the old stone age. The result was the massive and sudden extinction of many species of big game mammals at various times all over the world, including the woolly mammoth, the woolly rhinoceros, the steppe bison, the wild elk, the European wild ass, and a whole genus of goats (sharply decreased numbers of horses and cattle survived). The result was an equally sudden decrease in the high standard of living enjoyed by earlier peoples, and an intensification of production to try to reverse it.

Harris goes on to argue that behind non-state warfare lies the ecology of population, production, and resources. Warfare, he says, is the result of feedback (as we would say) between the following systemically and cybernetically related factors (as we would say):

increases in population
resulting in intensified economic production
leading to environmental depletion
lowering the standard of living
requiring population control.

(The best way to adapt to straitened circumstances and maintain one's standard of living is not to increase production but to reduce population.)

'Primitive' war thus stems from

the inability of preindustrial peoples to develop a less costly or more benign means of achieving low population densities and low rates of population growth (p. 51).

Infanticide

Harris is not arguing that population control is achieved by deaths in war: the huge death toll of soldiers and civilians in World War One had little effect on population growth, and three hundred years of increasingly destructive warfare did not prevent the world population from increasing from about 103 million in 1650 to some 594 million in 1950. Nor is Harris providing a theory of state warfare, which is far more a consequence of economic and political factors than of ecological and demographic factors.

What he is arguing is that population control in the so-called primitive societies is the result of male supremacy.

A society's birth rate depends on the number of women able to bear children, and not on the number of men able to impregnate them. Thus in the absence of contraception or abortion the only way to control population is to control the number of women. This is achieved in the other societies by preferential female infanticide – killing more girl babies than boy babies – a practice justified by the ideology of male supremacy, itself predicated on the apparent need to favor the upbringing of men to protect the society by waging war.

These systemic relationships are not particularly complicated, but they are very harsh. War requires warriors; male domination decrees that warriors shall be men; boy babies are thus valued over girls; more girl babies than boy babies are killed by their parents or allowed to die of neglect; fewer girl babies survive to bear children; the population remains well below the carrying capacity of its territory; increased economic production is not necessary; the natural environment is protected; and the whole survives in the long range at the expense of a proportion of its female children killed at birth and a proportion of its male warriors (and probably some women and children) killed in war.

At age 10 in such societies there may typically be 110 boys for every 100 girls. At age 30 the ratio will be practically equal.

Harris emphasizes that to regulate population growth by the preferential treatment of male babies is a decisive example of the power of culture (society) over nature (genetic potential). A very powerful cultural influence was needed to motivate parents to neglect or kill their own children, and an even more powerful cultural influence was needed to get parents – mainly mothers – to kill more girls than boys (p. 60).

(Preferential killing of girl babies sometimes occurs in societies that do not make war, notably many Eskimo groups. The reason is said to be that the Arctic environment demands maximum muscle and brawn for ordinary hunting activities and that Eskimo women are not involved in economic production through collecting plant and insect foods.)

Martial and other arts

Women have of course always been more valuable to society than men – not only by their reproductive labor in bearing and nursing children, not only by their sexual labor in pleasing men, and not only by their emotional labor supporting male morale, but also by their day-to-day physical labor in the production of social necessities and caring for their families.

Harris points out elsewhere that there is no individual biological reason for the subordination of women to men. Today, with the decline of brute-force hand-to-hand combat in modern warfare and with the vast array of ordinary and extraordinary 'equalizers' available to combatants, including Special Forces training in close-in killing, women armed with discipline, the right weapons, and a strategic understanding of male strategy and tactics are certainly a match for men.

Physical size is not a decisive factor in modern war: Most Vietnamese men, for example, are no bigger than most French, American, or Australian women.

There is no necessary or genetic reason why women could not engage in hunting. It is the co-operation between individuals with diverse skills, and not individual physical strength, that makes hunting successful, whether by men or women or both. Moreover, says Harris, in temperate or tropical zones, 'the rate of the production of meat is limited by the rate of reproduction of the prey species rather than by the skills of the hunters' (p. 62).

Nor does the need for women to nurse babies bar them from hunting. Hunting is an intermittent activity, and the extended families of band and village societies provide any number of substitute parents – this is the major source of their great superiority over us in raising children – certainly enough to look after the infants and others while the young women hunt.

The reason women are excluded from hunting must lie in the practice of warfare and the male supremacist sex roles that arise from it. In practically all societies men and boys are the only ones to be taught proficiency in weapons (besides proficiency in strategy), and women are often forbidden even to touch such things.

Band and village societies train males physically and mentally for hunting and warfare through competitive sports such as wrestling, racing, and duelling. But women seldom participate in such events – and above all, they never compete with men (p. 63).

Some women are of course physically stronger than some men, but they are still excluded from sports, hunting, and war. The reason for this, argues Harris, is that 'the occasional military success of well-trained, large and powerful females against smaller males would conflict with the sex hierarchy upon which preferential female infanticide is predicated'.

The primary reward for the 'successful' male supremacist warrior is in any case increased access to more women. Such men may take several wives, and they enjoy 'sexual privileges that depend on women being reared to accept male supremacy' (p. 64). Thus,

> if the whole system is to function smoothly, no woman can be permitted to get the idea that she is as worthy and powerful as any man (p. 63).

'Internal' and 'external' warfare

A major stumbling block to this interpretation of the mutual causal processes linking male supremacy, female infanticide, sexual rewards for aggression, non-state warfare, and population control has been that many extremely warlike societies, such as the Iroquois, have relatively weak 'male supremacist complexes' and often matrilineal descent as well.

('Matrilineal descent' means descent through the female line. The term refers only to the pathways of inheritance, and not to female control, as the term 'matriarchy' does. Among known societies, descent in the male line – patrilineality – is five times as common as matrilineality.)

The solution to the problem is that matrilineal village societies tend to practice a different kind of warfare from patrilineal societies (pp. 86-7). William Divale has shown that matrilineal societies typically engage in 'external warfare' – large raiding parties penetrating deep into the territory of linguistically and ethnically distinct enemies (as in the case of the Iroquois) – rather than in what he calls 'internal warfare' – set-piece battles between villages of the same ethnic group, attacks by small groups of raiders on nearby villages in which the enemies share the same language and probably a fairly recent common ancestry – as in the case of the Tsembaga.

The relationship between 'external warfare' and descent in the female line – where the mother's brother is more important to the upbringing of her children than their biological father – is that men who go off on lengthy expeditions must rely on the women to supervise economic

THE SUFFRAGETTE THAT KNEW JIU-JITSU
The Arrest.

(*July 6, 1910*)

FIGURE 5.5 The suffragette who knew jiu-jitsu: A *Punch* cartoon from 1910 that gives some indication of the power behind women's struggle for the vote in Britain in the hey-day fever of the years preceding World War One. [Reprinted from *Mr Punch's Cavalcade: A Review of Thirty Years*, edited by J. Hammerton. London: Educational Book Co., c.1935.]

production and protect the men's interests while they are away.

The result of this increased female responsibility is increased female power – but the increased freedom and independence of privileged women in these societies is not the result of ethics, civil rights, or 'social progress'; it is the result of male supremacy and war.

Women on war work

In our own society the status of women – as well as that of ethnic minorities – increases markedly in every major war, only to decline again soon after the men come home. Figure 5.6 indicates something of the increased acceptance of women's strengths and skills in the First World War, condescending as it was, even at the time.

During and after the Second World War (before the McCarthy years), similar apparent increases in the status of women and blacks are evident in such films as *His Girl Friday* (Rosalind Russell, 1939), *Ninotchka* (Greta Garbo, 1939), *Ball of Fire* (Barbara Stanwyck, 1941), *Mrs Miniver* (Greer Garson, 1941), *Cry Havoc* (nurses on Bataan, Margaret Sullavan, Ann Sothern, Joan Blondell, Fay Bainter, and others, 1943), *Edge of Darkness* (Ann Sheridan, 1943), *Cabin in

FIGURE 5.6   *Women on War Work* (1916): Twelve cigarette cards from a set of 50 issued in color by Carreras of London and Montreal. Millions of these cards on thousands of subjects were enclosed with cigarettes in the United States and Britain between 1880 and 1939. Of the women harrowing wheat the caption on the back of the card says that the 'feminine farm labourer' can 'undertake all the work an ordinary farm labourer used to do'. In the heavy work of driving steam rollers 'women have done wonderfully well, showing

both nerve and capacity which has surprised a good many people'. 'Sportswomen' who have taken up gamekeeping 'are proving themselves thoroughly capable and efficient'. Women sheet iron workers have proved themselves capable of tasks that before the war were not considered to be 'women's work'. Another card 'Carriage Repairs' declares that in upholstering, joinery, and carpentry 'women have demonstrated that they can more than hold their own in competition with male labour.'

the Sky (Ethel Waters, Eddie 'Rochester' Anderson, 1943), *Spellbound* (Ingrid Bergman, 1945), *Home of the Brave* (James Edwards, 1949), *Pinky* (Jeanne Crain, 1949), and *No Way Out* (Sidney Poitier, 1950). Recognition of American blacks as fighting men in World War Two led to the integration of the US Army by President Truman. With black service in Korea (1950-53), this was the most important single factor leading to the school desegregation decision – 'separate is not equal' – by the US Supreme Court in 1954.

George Thomson showed in 1941 in *Aeschylus and Athens* (pp. 188-92), that women enjoyed an unusually elevated status in Sparta in the fourth century BCE. Sparta was a military (and fascist) state supported by serfs and slaves, an entire society organized for war. The Spartans defeated the Athenian Empire in the Peloponnesian War (431-404 BCE), but losses in later wars and other factors led to its decline from a population of 8000 citizens in 480 BCE to some 2000 a century later, and to about 1000 by the time of Aristotle (384-22 BCE).

Discussing the Spartan constitution in his *Politics* (II, vi), Aristotle said of the Spartan women that their 'freedom is detrimental' to the constitution and 'the happiness of the state'. Their position was 'badly regulated', he wrote, accusing them of 'luxurious and dissolute behavior'. The Spartan men he accused of being controlled by their women, who had behaved in a 'harmful' fashion in war (an outright lie), and who, he said, were largely to blame for Sparta's fall. The 'errors in the status of women' in Sparta, he wrote, 'seem not only to cause a certain unseemliness in the actual conduct of the state but to contribute in some degree to the undue love of money.' (Nearly two-fifths of Spartan territory was owned by women.)

That a reactionary and unimaginative male autocracy like Sparta could allow its upper-class women to enjoy greater powers, privileges, and personal freedom than the women of 'enlightened' Athens (where women were particularly despised) is the result of 'external' war against surrounding hostile states (besides their suppression of the Helot population that bore the Spartan state on their backs). Leaving the administration of their estates to their wives, the Spartan nobles had to teach them the strategy of management. The result was that although upper-class women were excluded from political power in Sparta, they nevertheless exerted great economic influence.

Literacy is power. In teaching their wives the strategy of management, the Spartan nobles were sharing with them many of the male secrets about the exercise of power. Information of any kind may confer power on those whose literacy enables them to control it, and in this case the information being shared was not simply tactical information (how to give the right orders), but also strategic information (how to know what orders to give).

(The same was true of many upper-class women during the 'age of chivalry' in Europe (c. 1000 CE to 1250 CE), when the virtues of women and 'courtly love' were celebrated by the troubadours, at a time when most feudal lords were away on crusades and other piratical adventures.)

Matrilineality

Inheritance and descent in the female line is not invariably related to the practise of 'external war'. Hunting and fishing expeditions and long-distance trading are two other male-centered activities associated with matrilineality.

Another objection to the association of matrilineality and 'external war', adds Harris, is that not all non-state societies practising this kind of warfare are matrilineally organized (1977, p. 90). The significant examples in Africa are patrilineal pastoral nomads such as the Nuer and the Maasai. But nomads such as these do not launch expeditions from a 'home base' that they leave behind them in the care of others. They take their base – livestock, women, men, and children – with them to the war.

The development of matrilineal institutions seems however to have exerted a moderating influence on the severity of the male supremacist complex lying behind them. Because of the importance of women in descent, matrilineality tends to lead to a decline in female infanticide, and may even lead to a preference for girls over boys (p. 92).

The sexual hierarchy is modified by the fact that marriages in matrilineal societies are easily broken by the women. Among the Pueblo Indians of Arizona and New Mexico, for example, where husbands live with the family of their wives, an inconvenient husband was ejected simply by putting his moccasins outside the door.

This is not to deny the power exerted by women even in highly oppressive patriarchies, such as those of Islamic societies. During the Algerian War of Independence (1954-62), French anthropologists whose studies of Algerian society were used by French counter-insurgency forces (like CIA anthropology in Indochina) discovered that behind the moderately severe Algerian patriarchy (less severe than Saudia Arabia or Iran, for example), Algerian women exerted a great deal of influence through complex networks of interpersonal relations inside and outside the family. And as Gillo Pontecorvo showed in *The Battle of Algiers* (1967), Algerian women played important and dangerous roles as urban guerrillas for the Front de Libération Nationale.

The Iroquois

Of all peoples, probably no other was as preoccupied with war, slavery, sorcery, torture, and cannibalism as the matrilineal Iroquois of the lower Great Lakes region. But an Iroquois woman might at any time tell a man to pick up his blanket and go elsewhere, and Iroquois women had far more political power than most women in most non-state societies.

It is true, as Lewis Henry Morgan wrote in the nineteenth century, that the Iroquois male

> regarded women as the inferior, the dependent, and the servant of man, and from nurture and habit, she actually considered herself so (quoted by Harris, 1977, p. 92).

But Iroquois matrons had the power to raise and depose the male elders elected to the highest ruling body, the council. Through a male representative the older women could influence its decisions, including decisions about war, peace, and alliances with other tribes. Eligibility for office passed through the female line, and it was the duty of the women to nominate the men to the council. But Iroquois women could not themselves serve on the council, and the men who did had a veto power over the women's nominations.

> The receptive ability of the great masses is very limited, their understanding is small. On the other hand their forgetfulness is great. All propaganda should be limited to a very few points. It has to confine itself to little and repeat this eternally. . . .
> People in the overwhelming majority are so feminine in nature and attitude that their activities and thoughts are motivated less by sober considerations than by feeling and sentiment.
> > Adolf Hitler: *Mein Kampf* (1924-26).
> > Quoted by Harold Ettlinger in *The Axis on the Air* (1943)

5.5   Pacification

In another of his cross-cultural studies, *Cows, Pigs, Wars and Witches*, published in 1974, Marvin Harris analyzes the dominant social relations of the Yanomamo, a South American Indian tribe of brutal and treacherous men who beat, torment, wound, mutilate (and sometimes) kill their several wives; who gang-rape women captured from other Yanomamo villages in their constant 'internal' wars; and who spend most of their waking hours either arguing or fighting (usually over women), or lying about dripping snot in a men-only hallucinogenic haze (Chagnon, 1968).

A Yanomamo woman with a 'kind' husband will judge the strength of her husband's love for her by the frequency and intensity of the beatings she receives.

(Note that, as unpleasant as they may be, Yanomamo warriors treat women no worse than English, French, American, Russian, German, Italian, Japanese, and other soldiers and bandits have done in this century.)

In the most violent of the villages Yanomamo men compete with each other in chest-pounding, side-slapping, rock-pounding, machete-slapping, and club-fighting duels of increasing violence, where first one and then the other waits to receive the full force of his adversary's blow, and then returns it. A quarter to a third of Yanomamo men die in war.

Harris concludes that *if* sex is to be used to energize, control, and reward aggressive, vicious, and warlike behavior, then both sexes cannot be equally brutalized to behave this way (1974, p. 106):

> One or the other must be trained to be dominant. It cannot be both. To brutalize both is to invite a literal war of the sexes. Among the Yanomamo this would mean armed struggle between men and women for control over each other as a reward for their battlefield exploits. In other words, to make sex a reward for bravery, one of the sexes has to be taught cowardice.

That's a very harsh judgment indeed. It takes far more than ordinary courage to live the life of a scapegoat and a victim day by day. It would be more reasonable and less unjust to say that if female infanticide, war, and male supremacy are to exist as a system of population control, then the women must be trained to accept their victimization by men as a status that is inevitable, natural, deserved, and even desired.

Victimization of this sort has another name: colonization. Male control over women and their bodies is the oldest form of private property; the division of productive labor by sex is the oldest form of class distinction; male monopolies of myth, ritual, and religion are the oldest forms of ideology; male supremacy is the oldest form of imperialism.

We know from the experience of millions upon millions of subjugated peoples – untouchables, Africans, blacks, Hispanics, Jamaicans, Filipinos, Catholic Irish, Indians, Chicanos, and others – that colonization cannot exist without the active (if only partly conscious) support of most of the colonized who suffer under it.

Similarly, male supremacy cannot exist without the active (if only partly conscious) support of most of the women it oppresses.

Although the role of armed force and physical fear in colonization is not to be neglected, the secret of colonization does not lie simply in the physical power of the colonizer to force the colonized to accept the pain, humiliation, and degradation of their inferior position. Force alone is not enough; it must be supported by an ideology that proclaims the superiority of the colonizer over the colonized.

But again it is not enough for the colonizers alone to believe the myth of their God-given, 'natural', innate, and hereditary superiority; the colonized must be taught to believe it too, and just as fervently, if not more so.

The reason is that if the colonized were not taught from birth to death to collaborate in their own oppression, physical force alone could not be guaranteed to quell the mutinies, revolts, and rebellions that would result.

The colonizer must control and conceal the strategy of colonization. The colonized must be taught to respond to this strategy, not by a countervailing strategy, but by a variety of tactical behavior that serves to maintain and reinforce it.

The colonized must come to believe that they are with few exceptions exactly what their colonizers say they are: stupid, lazy, inferior, deceitful, promiscuous, unfaithful, selfish, ignorant, greedy, dirty, 'uncivilized', savage, barbaric, violent, 'primitive', 'animalistic', and even the essence of evil itself.

In this way the colonizer not only controls the economic, social, and political life of the colonized, but he also controls their sense of identity as well – and with that, their self-esteem, the most important of personal values. The colonizer so convinces the colonized of their inferiority that they come to think, act, and live out their lives as if they really were inferior.

In *Damned Whores and God's Police: The Colonization of Women in Australia* (1975, p. 247), Anne Summers writes:

> Divide and rule is the technique employed by the colonizing powers to ensure the allegiance of a strategic majority of the colonized, to convince them that colonization is beneficial to them, and to persuade them to collaborate in the task of pacifying or punishing the more recalcitrant of their sex who refuse to accede to the demands of the invaders.

By encouraging divisions among the colonized, and by allowing privileges to the favored group of hated collaborators,

the colonizing power is able to prevent the colonized from forming a united opposition and from refusing to perform the labour required of them by the invaders.

The respective roles of the Damned Whores and God's Police in Australian history are summed up in two quotations at the beginning of Summers' book.

On sighting the *Lady Juliana* coming into Sydney Harbour in June 1790 with over two hundred female convicts aboard, Lt Ralph Clark exclaimed:

No, no – surely not! My God – not more of those damned whores! Never have I known worse women.

In 1847, in *Emigration and Transporation Relatively Considered*, Caroline Chisholm wrote:

If Her Majesty's Government be really desirous of seeing a well-conducted community spring up in these Colonies, the social wants of the people must be considered. . . . For all the clergy you can despatch, all the schoolmasters you can appoint, all the churches you can build, and all the books you can export, will never do much good, without what a gentleman in that Colony very appropriately called 'God's police' – wives and little children – good and virtuous women.

Once again the women's choice is either wickedness or virtue.

I argued in *The Imaginary Canadian* in 1980 that colonization is the common principle underlying most if not all kinds of oppression, and especially oppression by class, race, and sex. Summers, whose book I came across more recently, shows why colonization is such a useful explanatory principle in the case of the oppression and exploitation of women. She summarizes the 'classic colonial situation' (p. 198) as follows:

1 the invasion and conquest of a territory
2 the cultural domination of its inhabitants
3 the control of the territory's inhabitants by setting them at each others' throats (divide and rule)
4 the extraction of profits from the colonized territory.

Colonization also requires the more or less violent destruction of the original inhabitants' culture and way of life, damping potential revolt and forcing or persuading them to believe that their culture is inferior and that they should adopt that of the colonizing power. Every ideological weapon is brought into play, whether it be associated with religion, health care, philanthropy, treaties, commercial exchanges, or the 'civilizing mission' of the invaders as they seek to pacify the colonized and convince them that their colonization is for their own good.

Using the term 'colonization' to describe the situation of women ceases to be a metaphor, says Summers (p. 200), once it is recognized that in the case of women the conquered colonial territory is the body:

Women are colonized by being denied control over their own bodies.

We have already seen from Susan Brownmiller's *Against Our Will* (1975) that over and over again in cases of rape – notably in the rape, mutilation, and murder of captured enemy women, but also in the assault and humiliation of women by the typical police blotter rapist – the woman's body is being used as a message in the discourse of the Other.

We saw also from the young paratrooper's account in *St Michael and the Dragon* (1961) that electric torture by the French in Algeria became the ultimate invasion of the body, the universal act of rape, the forcible entry of agony at every bodily orifice, at every nerve.

Looking now at Frantz Fanon's *Wretched of the Earth* (1961), p. 268 of the Grove Press translation by Constance Farrington, where Fanon (1925-1961), the black psychoanalyst and radical political philosopher from Martinique, recounts his obligation as a therapist to treat not only Algerians surviving torture during the war of independence (1954-62) he supported, but also the mental and emotional problems of the Frenchmen doing the torturing, we find the following account by a 30-year-old European police inspector who had begun to threaten people who crossed him and cruelly assault his wife and children in 'fits of madness':

The fact is that nowadays we have to work like troopers. . . . The thing that kills me most is the torture. You don't know what that is, do you? Sometimes I torture people for ten hours at a stretch. . . . You may not realize, but it's very tiring.

It is true, continues the inspector, that he and the others take turns, but the question is to know when to let the next man have a go. No one wants to go to all the trouble of softening up a subject and then have him 'come' in the hands of someone else, who would then get all the glory.

Our problem is as follows: are you able to make this fellow talk? It's a question of personal success. You see, we're competing with the others. In the end your fists are ruined. So you call in the Senegalese. But either they hit too hard and destroy the creature or else they don't hit hard enough and it's no good (p. 269).

Torture is gang rape taken to its pathological conclusion. The torturers are competing with each other over who has control of the victims' bodies and what they do to them. Here again someone's body

From The Crisis

THE WAR FOR HUMAN RIGHTS WILL FREE THE NEGRO.

FIGURE 5.7 This cartoon from World War One is reprinted from *The World War for Human Rights . . . and the Important Part Taken by the Negro* by Kelly Miller, Dean of the College of Arts and Sciences, Howard University, Washington, D.C. (Austin Jenkins Co., 1919). Miller devotes a chapter apiece to the Canadians, the Anzacs, and the relation between war work and the emancipation of women. The American Army' first integrated units (and not simply black units with white officers) appeared late in World War Two – the major reason for their creation being the high morale and unusual 'combat efficiency' of black and white troops working together. In Vietnam a greater proportion of blacks fought and died in the front line than their share of the US population.

FIGURE 5.8　Self-satisfaction and good humor at a Nebraska lynching in 1919 – one more victim's body being used as a message in the discourse of the Other. Reprinted from a chapter by A. Sivanandan in Parnell's *20th Century* (1973), edited by A.J.P. Taylor and J.M. Roberts.

FIGURE 5.9   'This is her first lynching!' Here the body of the victim is a means of communication between whites. The cartoon appeared in *The New Yorker* in the early 1930s; it was reprinted in *The New Yorker Album 1925-1950*.

is being used as a medium of communication between men, as a channel of the discourse of the Other.

You have to be 'intelligent' to make a success of this kind of work, explains the inspector, you have to have a flair for it. Above all, he explains,

> what you mustn't do is to give the chap the impression that he won't get away alive from you. Because then he wonders what's the use of talking if it won't save his life. . . . He must go on hoping; hope's the thing that'll make him talk.

Once he talks, however, the French have no more use for him and usually kill him anyway.

The inspector could not see his way to stop torturing people – he would have to resign. So he asked Fanon straight out 'to help him go on torturing Algerian patriots without any prickings of conscience, without any behavior problems, and with complete equanimity' (pp. 269-70).

It suddenly dawns on me, long after the event, that the theme of the body as the discourse of the Other is the theme of Franz Kafka's parable *In the Penal Colony*, written in 1914 and published in 1919. Prisoners in the colony are slowly put to death by an apparatus whose vibrating needles write their sentence in their flesh over and over again and ever deeper: 'Whatever commandment the prisoner has disobeyed is written upon his body by the Harrow. This prisoner, for instance' – the officer indicated the man – 'will have written on his body: HONOR THY SUPERIORS!'

> A gun is power. To some people carrying a gun constantly was like having a permanent hard on. It was a pure sexual trip every time you got to pull the trigger.
> Vietnam veteran quoted by Mark Baker in *Nam* (1981)

Baby-san

'What you got there?', said the soldier. 'Hey, you VC? What do you got?' It was a 'baby-san' and a 'papa-san', a teenager of about fifteen or sixteen and her father, about forty, he told Mark Baker in *Nam* (1981, pp. 169-70):

They had a can of pears! American pears in a big green can marked with a big U.S. on it in large print. We say, 'Isn't this some shit. Here we are in the field, we don't know what pears is. They got pears! And *we* don't have pears'. I'll never forget the guys' faces in the unit from the GIs up to the captain. We are shit in the field, and the guys in the rear have given these gooks pears, man.

'The GIs gave you pears? Oh, yeah? For that, we're going to screw your daughter'. So we went running, taking the daughter. She was crying. I think she was a virgin. We pulled her pants down and put a gun to her head.

Guys are taking turns screwing her. It was like an animal pack. 'Hey, he's taking too long to screw her'. Nobody was turning their back or nothing. We just stood on line and we screwed her.

I was taking her body by force. Guys were standing over her with rifles, while I was screwing her. She says, 'why are you doing this to me? Why?' Some of the gooks could talk very good. 'Hey, you're black, why are you doing this to me?'

Baby-san, she was crying. So a guy just put a rifle to her head and pulled the trigger just to put her out of the picture. Then we start pumping her with rounds. After we got finished shooting her, we start kicking them and stomping on them. That's what the hatred, the frustration was. After we raped her, took her cherry from her, after we shot her in the head, you understand what I'm saying, we literally start stomping her body.

And everybody was laughing about it. It's like seeing the lions around a just-killed zebra. You see them in these animal pictures, *Wild Kingdom* or something. The whole pride comes around and they start feasting on the body. We kicked the face in, kicked in the ribs and everything else.

Then we start cutting ears off. We cut her nose off. The captain says, 'Who's going to get the ears? Who's going to get the nose? So-and-so's turn to get the ears'. A good friend of mine – a white guy from California – he flipped out in the Nam. The dude would fall down and cry, fall down and beg somebody to let him have the ears. Captain says, 'Well, let So-and-so get the ears this time. You had the last kill. Let him get it this time'. So we let this guy get the ears. We cut off one of her breasts and one guy got the breast. But the trophy was the ears. I had got a finger from the papa-san. That was about it, what I got from the incident. We let the bodies stay there mutilated.

It is by study of the many variations of bush warfare in different parts of the world that British officers, who are by nature endowed

with jungle instincts beyond other European races, can ensure
success.
'Warfare Against an Uncivilized Enemy': *Field Service Regulations*,
Part I, Operations, 1912

5.6   Basic training

According to research principally by Eleanor Maccoby of Stanford
University, Lisa Serbin of Concordia, and Jeanne Block of the
University of California at Berkeley, summarized in the 1980 *Nova*
television program, *The Pinks and the Blues* (WGBH, Boston), girls
and boys are brought up from birth onwards in fundamentally
different ways with fundamentally different results,

Mothers and fathers expect boys to be strong-willed, hard-working,
intelligent, ambitious, and aggressive. Mothers and fathers expect girls
to be kind, loving, well-mannered, obedient, attractive, unselfish, lady-
like, not aggressive, and not assertive. Boys are expected to be noisy,
rambunctious, and self-reliant; girls are expected to be quiet, polite,
and dependent.

The education and training of the growing girl is likely to be more
structured, supervised, circumscribed, restricted, and protected than
that of the growing boy. The young girl tends to be imbedded in the
family network and insulated from experience.

In contrast, the growing boy is less supervised, encouraged to be
more spontaneous, given more freedom to explore, taught to
improvise when faced with the unexpected, encouraged to solve
problems on the spot, taught to develop an active understanding of
experience and an ability to take advantage of opportunity.

Girls' games tend to be 'rule bound' so that deviations from the
rules are really not permitted or expected. When a dispute arises girls
are often unable to negotiate their differences. Rather than agreeing to
modify the rules, they will stop playing altogether, or start another
game.

Boys in contrast play more complex games which require more
refereeing and negotiation about rules. Boys become more experienced
in negotiating disputes than do girls.

Girls are generally provided with far fewer opportunities for
spontaneous engagement, trial and error learning, or active experi-
mentation.

When fathers help their sons with tasks they tend to emphasize
cognitive principles, do's and don't's, and intellectual achievement.
When fathers help their daughters, however, they tend to emphasize
the affective relation of simply being together, rather than performance or achievement.

When mothers help their daughters with a task they tend to inject unnecessary and interfering aid, even when their daughter is doing well. Such oversolicitous aid tends to devalue the capabilities of the child, makes her doubt herself, and encourages her to believe that she could not have accomplished the task on her own.

In school boys will tend to attribute their successes to their own capacities; girls tend to attribute theirs to luck or some other impersonal factor. Conversely, boys tend to blame their failures on external circumstances ('the test was too hard', 'the questions were tricky'), whereas girls tend to blame their failures on themselves, besides underestimating their actual successes.

Boys are taught to seek to master the external world, to take an instrumental approach to objects, and to see themselves as people with the power to make things happen, to make a difference. Girls are not.

It should be emphasized that these differences are the result of persuasion, guiding, training, teaching, socialization, adult expectations, and conformity to social norms, much of it unconscious and unrecognized whether by the adult or the child. They are not the result of genes, innate tendencies, hormone balances, anatomy, brain differences, or 'masculinity' or 'femininity'.

The results of these radically different experiences of childhood can be summarized under several headings.

Aggression or assertiveness: Boys are more adventurous, more competitive, more likely to be anti-social or engage in violence than girls.

Activity: Boys 'can't sit still': they are more active and more interested in the outside world, engage in more activities and change them more often than girls.

Curiosity, exploration: Boys are more curious about 'how things work', take more chances, and are more likely to explore on their own than girls.

Impulsivity: Boys are more easily distracted, less successful in resisting temptation, and more likely to run into trouble or danger than girls.

Accident rate: At every age level, boys have more accidents and suffer more injuries than girls.

Anxiety: Girls tend to be more fearful and anxious than boys; they are more afraid of more things than boys.

Social relationships: Girls are more compliant and obedient than boys, and much more concerned with 'doing the right thing'. Girls are more nurturing, more concerned with group welfare, more ready to co-operate and compromise, better able to put themselves in other people's shoes, and more empathetic than boys.

Friendships: Boys tend to have more extensive networks of friends, but less intimate friendships, than girls. Girls tend to share their hopes and despairs more intensely with their friends than do boys.

FIGURE 5.10   A detail from *Hell* by Hieronymus Bosch (?1450-1516). As de
Tolnay says, the means of earthly pleasure have been turned into 'an orchestra
of instruments of vengeance that draw their harmonies from [human]
suffering'. Reprinted from: Charles de Tolnay: *Hieronymus Bosch* (1965), p.
32 and plate 244.

FIGURE 5.11 *Fashions of 1934*, starring William Powell and Bette Davis: A 'hallucinatory moment' from the musical number 'Spin a Little Web of Dreams'. This is the 'Hall of Harps', one of several tableaux by Busby Berkeley (1895-1976) in this film, directed by William Dietele. Reprinted from: Ted Sennett: *Hollywood Musicals* (1981), p. 74.

Interpersonal relationships remain more important to women throughout life than they do to men.

Self-esteem: Boys seem to view themselves as more powerful, with more control over events in the world, than girls. Boys act as more instrumental and more effective agents, they are more assertive, more confident that they will achieve their ambitions, and see themselves as able to 'make things happen'. Girls do not appear to share these qualities to any similar degree.

Achievement: Boys expect to do better and entertain higher levels of aspiration for themselves than do girls. Girls are less confident and more likely to underestimate their performance even when they do well.

Or as Colette Dowling puts it in *The Cinderella Complex* (1981): 'Women are not trained for freedom at all, but for its categorical opposite, dependency. Males, however, are educated for independence from the day they are born' (pp. 15–16).

Two remarks from the nineteenth century will put the foregoing into a representative context. The first is taken from the zoologist Carl Vogt's *Lectures on Man* (1864), quoted by Stephen Jay Gould in *The Mismeasure of Man* (1981, p. 103):

> The grown-up Negro partakes, as regards his intellectual faculties, of the nature of the child, the female, and the senile white. . . . Some tribes have founded states, possessing a peculiar organization, but as to the rest, we may boldly assert that the whole race has, neither in the past nor the present, performed anything tending to the progress of humanity or worthy of preservation.

The second is from an article by the noted psychologist and student of mass behavior Gustave Le Bon, published in the *Revue d'anthropologie* in 1879, also from Gould (p. 105):

> All psychologists who have studied the intelligence of women, as well as poets and novelists, recognize today that [women] represent the most inferior forms of human evolution and that they are closer to children and savages than to an adult, civilized man. They excel in fickleness, inconstancy, absence of thought and logic, and incapacity to reason.

I am talking of millions of men who have been skilfully injected with fear, inferiority complexes, trepidation, servility, despair, abasement.

Aimé Césaire: *Discours sur le colonialisme*. Quoted by Frantz Fanon in *Black Skin, White Masks* (1952)

5.7   Who is speaking and to whom?

Colette Dowling asked three men, a financial reporter, a stockbroker, and an advertising executive, to give her their impressions of the way women look and act and sound when they do business:

Reporter: A few months ago I interviewed a woman with a big position on the New York Stock exchange. . . . As she talked she would switch into and out of different styles. For a while she'd be very serious and confident-sounding. Then she'd back off for a second and kind of giggle, and give a little shoulder, or a little nod (pp. 52-3).

The broker had also remarked on this kind of communication by women (without using these terms): the communication of 'status-markers' where communication about relationship temporarily or erratically dominates the communication of content. The result is ambiguity, he said:

You get this schizy feeling, as if you don't know what person they're going to slip into next.

The reporter went on to say about the woman he had interviewed:

This woman's diction was super slow. She was very careful with her words, hyperconscious of how she was speaking, how she was coming across. Then she did this thing I've seen a lot of women in good jobs do. They finish their sentences by softening their words and nodding a little as they soften.

The broker and the adman agreed, the latter remarking that the nod is intended to get you to agree.

(Dominated by American capital and British traditions, English-speaking Canadians – noted for their lack of a sense of cultural or national identity and their 'inferiority complex' vis-à-vis other nationals – show the same kind of diffidence in ending their sentences with the distinctively Canadian 'eh?'.)

The advertising man added:

I've noticed in business that women never really swing, conversationally. You'll never hear them say, 'Are you *crazy?*' or something like that. Very often you'll find that men in business really let their personalities fly and soar. That's how they *do* business. . . . They get *into* it. Women are polite and formalistic. They want the rules right out there in front.

The reporter said:

It's as if women are afraid to actually get behind the *force* of a statement. They'll be talking and talking and really working up some force, and then suddenly it's as if they *see* themselves getting forceful and they have to back off. I think they're afraid of power.

We can translate these passages into Hegel's theory of human desire (as distinct from animal or biological need, such as hunger). 'Human desire', he says, 'is the desire of the Other.' We desire recognition by the Other (the master or the ideal or the model) already mentioned (5.1 above); our desires are mediated by the Other. (They are thus relations rather than forces or things.) The mediation of desire by the Other may or may not involve its alienation (literally 'othering').

In alienated desire one desires to be the desire of the Other, one desires to be what (one imagines) the Other desires. It is precisely this alienated form of mediation that is manifest in the diction and body communication of the women being discussed.

Rather than speaking, they are being spoken.

Robin Lakoff finds the following characteristics to be consistent in women's speech:

the use of empty, fluffy adjectives (marvelous, divine, terribly, etc.), which makes people take them less seriously
the use of tag sentences after a declarative statement ('It's really hot today, don't you think?')
the use of dipping or questioning intonation at the end of a statement, rendering it less forceful
the use of hedging or modifying phrases giving their words a tentative, uncommitted quality
the use of 'hypercorrect' and excessively polite speech (p. 55).

Sally Genet of Cornell calls these distinguishing marks the 'diffident declarative'. Mary Brown Parlee of *Psychology Today* notes that 'speech may not only *reflect* power differences. It may help to *create* them.'

Dowling quotes the psychologist Phyllis Chesler, author of *Women and Madness* (1974), who argues that women communicate these messages deliberately (if not always consciously). In *Women, Money and Power* (1976) Chesler says:

> Women of all classes, within the home and in public, use a basic
> body language to communicate deference, inconsequentiality, help-
> lessness . . . a stance which is supposed to put others at their ease,
> and men 'on top'.

This self-subordination to the discourse of the Other is the result of a learned dependency on other people, and notably on men – a deeply felt desire to be taken care of by others through which women come to sabotage their own creativity and individuality.

Studying adolescents at the University of Michigan, for example, the psychologist Elizabeth Douvan finds that

> up until the age of eighteen (and sometimes past that) girls show
> virtually no thrust toward independence, aren't interested in
> confronting authority with rebellion, and don't insist 'on their rights
> to form and hold independent beliefs and controls'.

In all these respects girls differ from boys. Girls are trained into dependency: boys are trained out of it. The evidence indicates that dependency in women increases as they grow older (p. 101).

Independence does not of course mean 'autonomy'. Independence, like identity and like self-esteem, is a relationship to others.

The process of switching over to a more independent relationship to others and the world begins, in boys, at the age of 2. Most boys have developed their sense of distinction from others and their sense of self-esteem by the time they are 6. With girls, however, both passivity and a dependent orientation towards adults appears consistently all the way into adulthood. These two personality factors are the most stable and predictable of all female character traits (p. 103).

Dowling asks:

> Why, when we have the chance to move ahead, do we [women]
> tend to retreat? Because women are not used to confronting fear
> and going beyond it. We've been encouraged to avoid anything that
> scares us, taught from the time we were very young to do only those
> things which allow us to feel comfortable and secure (p. 15).

Men and boys in contrast are taught to experience and master fear and even to enjoy it. But for women, at least for white middle- and upper-class women:

> fear, irrational and capricious – fear that has no relation to

capabilities or even to reality – is epidemic among women today (p. 58).

The fear of independence and individuality differs greatly in its intensity and effects, of course, depending on individual experience, and it is expressed in many different ways: in low self-esteem, lack of self-confidence, underestimation of one's actual abilities and achievements, a narrowed stretch of the imagination, a choice of goals far below one's capacities, antagonistic competition with other women (producing and reproducing insecurity), prejudice against them (and often against oneself), self-deprecation and sometimes self-hatred, attraction to the source of one's fears (dominating and alienating Others), ignorance of one's own culture, history, and traditions (often coupled with a lack of respect for them), fear of being too competent (for a man), fear of not being competent enough (with a man), fear of being subordinate, fear of being dominant, fear of being the same, fear of being different, fear of being with a man, fear of being without one, fear of failure, fear of success – and at its worst fear of movement, discovery, change, innovation, imagination, the unfamiliar, the unknown, and above all, normal aggressivity and assertiveness.

The result is an unwillingness to take charge of one's own life accompanied by a real inability to do so.

'Men are active', says Dowling, 'women are reactive.' 'Men are stretchers, women are shrinkers.'

The Cinderella Complex teaches one to act inferior and believe it to be true. It is not simply a mistaken view of this or that aspect of reality. It is rather a strategic disability that, like a self-fulfilling prophecy, ensures that so long as it remains unrecognized most women will continue to accept and support the domination of men, and teach male supremacy to their children as well.

The result of this strategic disability is the loss to a world society in crisis of most of the diversity and creative capacity of over half the world population. Here too male supremacy is a counter-adaptive response to the need for adaptive change. If our society is to survive in a human form – if it is successfully to undergo the necessary adaptation of a revolution in structure, values, and goals – we all need all the help we can get.

In this disability however women are not alone, for the Cinderella Complex is the psychological paradigm of every other kind of colonization.

> It is not easy to escape mentally from a concrete situation, to refuse
> its ideology while continuing to live with its actual relationships.
> > Albert Memmi: *The Colonizer and the Colonized* (1957)

5.8 And babies?

Ellen Hale shows in a recent article that there is a relation between
cases of multiple personality and violence. Multiple personalities are
now believed to be much more common than previously supposed,
many perhaps being wrongly diagnosed as 'hysterical, depressed,
neurotic, borderline schizophrenic, epileptic or as abusers of drugs or
alcohol' (*Vancouver Sun*, April 23, 1983). Dr Frank Putname Jr of the
National Institute of Mental Health in Bethesda, Maryland, is one of
several psychiatrists researching the subject.

Natasha is one of his patients.

> From the time she was two until she turned sixteen, she said, she
> was continually raped by her father, a well-known Oklahoma
> banker and farmer. Until she was twelve the rapes took place with
> her mother's passive compliance and often with her active
> participation.

At 12 when Natasha began to develop physically, her mother ordered
a stop to the abuse. But, under the guise of teaching his daughter the
banking business, this man took her to his office on Saturday
mornings and raped her on his desk. At 16 she became pregnant by
her father. For sixteen years her father controlled her body; for sixteen
years Natasha managed to control her mind. She claims to have 127
different personalities or personality fragments.

The work of family therapists like R.D. Laing and colleagues in
Britain and Gregory Bateson and colleagues in the United States
taught us that madness is very often an adaptive response to a
pathological situation, a response with survival value for the victim.
Or as Harry Stack Sullivan said many years before, the process of
going mad is the beginning of the cure.

Multiple personalities fit this pattern. As Putnam explains, they are
one of the most ingenious and intricate processes of psychological self-
defense. 'It develops, apparently, in early childhood, as a result of
brutal and continual physical and mental abuse by parents, relatives or
close friends.' Some 100 psychiatrists surveyed by Putnam reported
that more than 90 per cent of the patients they had treated for
multiple personality had been severely abused physically or sexually
for long periods in childhood.

Child-abuse is a great deal more common than generally realized.
But since only a few of the abused children develop multiple

personalities, it appears that those that manage to do so have an unusual capacity to disassociate or hypnotize themselves in self-defense. They learn to escape mentally and emotionally from the inexplicable brutality of those who supposedly love them by developing separate personalities to deal with the torments they suffer.

Eighty-five per cent of the patients with multiple personalities are women.

Human nature has been conditioned very largely by those who said it could never be changed.

M.J. Bernard Davy: *Air Power and Civilization* (1941)

5.9   Male supremacy: The struggle for extinction

In *Making of Mankind* (1981) – humankind – Richard Leakey remarks that the common idea that violence is innate in human beings is 'one of the most dangerous and destructive ideas that mankind has ever had' (p. 21). It is dangerous precisely because of the decisive influence of culture and learning on human values and behavior. Unlike animals, what we do or do not do is never independent of what we have learned to believe is possible or impossible, right or wrong, pleasurable or offensive, useful or useless, good or bad – alternatives that are arrayed in level upon level in the complexity of the human world.

The 'death instinct' view of warfare is dangerous also because it denies our responsibility to others for our words and deeds. It is dangerous because by making violence appear genetic and thus inevitable, it replaces ethics by defeatism, and reinforces the ideology of genetic determinism: the social darwinism of the 'survival of the fittest' that explains away oppression on the grounds that the oppressed are oppressed because they don't have what it takes to do better. It is dangerous above all because it masks the fundamental counter-adaptivity of the beliefs and behavior of men.

Against the idea of a genetic 'killer instinct' Leakey quotes the prehistorian Bernard Campbell (p. 242):

Anthropology teaches us clearly that Man lived at one with nature until, with the beginnings of agriculture [about 12,000 years ago], he began to tamper with the ecosystem: and expansion of his population followed.

It was not until about 5000 years ago, says Campbell, with the development of the temple towns, that 'we find evidence of inflicted death and warfare':

> This is too recent an event to have had any influence on the evolution of human nature. . . . Man is not programmed to kill and make war, nor even to hunt: his ability to do so is learned from his elders and his peers when his society demands it.

Warfare, in other words, is learned, and not genetically programmed, behavior.

Speaking of the Yanomamo in *Cows, Pigs, Wars and Witches* (1974, p. 87), Harris argues that male supremacy depends on the self-reinforcement and self-amplification of positive feedback:

> The fiercer the males, the greater the amount of warfare, the more such males are needed. Also, the fiercer the males, the more sexually aggressive they become, the more exploited are the females, and the higher the incidence of polygyny – control over several wives by one man. Polygyny in turn intensifies the shortage of women, raises the level of frustration among junior males, and increases the motivation for going to war. The amplification builds to an excruciating climax: females are held in contempt and killed in infancy, making it necessary for men to go to war to capture wives in order to rear additional numbers of aggressive men.

This relationship of competitive symmetry is no different from the positive feedback – the mutual amplification – of the arms race between the superpowers, with no negative feedback – the control of escalation – in sight.

There have been three major escalations of the arms race since 1945: that initiated by Democratic President Truman after the United States blundered into the Korean War in 1950; that initiated by Democratic President Kennedy after the Cuban Missile Crisis in 1961; and that initiated by Republican President Reagan in 1980.

The arms race has taken a new turn. If we are to judge from Defense Secretary Caspar Weinberger's annual report to Congress for the 1984 fiscal year, American strategic superiority is no longer enough. Superiority must be absolute, the technology invulnerable, the defense impregnable, and the system of strategic communications and electronic countermeasures (C^3ECM) immune from attack.

The desire for the possible and the probable has been replaced by the desire for the absolute.

America, President Reagan told the National Association of Evangelicals in 1983, is engaged in a 'struggle between right and wrong' against the 'aggressive impulses of an evil empire'. The source of America's strength, he said, 'is not material but spiritual, and because it knows no limitation, it must terrify and ultimately triumph'. Absolute good thus faces absolute evil, and paranoia replaces politics.

If we look back to the beginnings of warfare thousands of years ago, and follow its increasing severity, brutality, and destructiveness as it became the monopoly of the state, and later the instrument of empire, the pattern we see is that of a continually escalating symmetrical competition between men – an arms race stretching backward to the beginning of history and forward to the end of the world.

The whole ghastly pathology brings us right back to the relations between women and men. For as long as we are unable to recognize the simple truth that men and women are above all brothers and sisters, and as long as we are unable to put an end to male supremacy – the most massive system of organized bullying ever to arise on earth – and thus end the war between the sexes, then it is certain we will never be able to put an end to the wars between the nations, much less end the wars between people divided by race and class.

And without an end to war the radical and democratic dream of the right to life, liberty, equality, and the pursuit of happiness must ever remain beyond our reach.

CHAPTER 6

Strategy and tactics, discipline and character

To have the arts of peace, but not the arts of war, is
to lack courage. To have the arts of war, but not the
arts of peace, is to lack wisdom.
                    Hayashi Razan (1583-1657): *Sonshi Genkai:*
                                          An Explanation of
                              Sun Tzu's Maxims (c. 1626).

6.1   Zenobia, Queen of Palmyra

Even in the days of Solomon, says Anna Jameson, writing in 1894 in
Great Men and Famous Women, in the volume devoted to 'Workmen
and Heroes', the Syrian city of Palmyra was the emporium for the
gems and gold, the ivory, gums, spices, and silks of the far Eastern
countries, which from the confluence of trade routes meeting at this
city, 150 miles northeast of Damascus, found their way to the
remotest parts of Europe (Map 7.1, p. 260).

In origin the citizens of Palymra were Egyptian: their love of luxury
and their manners were Persian: their language, literature, and
architecture were Greek.

Palmyra owed its splendor to the opulence of its merchants, but its
chief fame and historical interest it owes to the genius and heroism of
a woman: Zenobia, Queen of Palmyra, who reigned 267-73 CE.

Zenobia was the daughter of a nomadic Arab chieftain. She married
Odenanthus, chief of several desert tribes near the city, who held the
Roman colony of Palmyra as a client-king, subordinate to the Empire.

Jameson explains Zenobia's unusual education:

Odenanthus was as fond of the chase as of war, and in all his
military and hunting expeditions he was accompanied by his wife
Zenobia – a circumstance which the Roman historians record with
astonishment and admiration, as contrary to their manners, but
which was the general custom of the Arab women of that time.

(This was of course four centuries before the mission of Mahomet and the victorious spread of the Islamic religion in the seventh century of our era, a creed that relegates women to a status if anything lower than their status in Christianity.)

> Zenobia not only excelled her countrywomen in the qualities for which they are all remarkable – in courage, prudence, and fortitude, in patience of fatigue, and activity of mind and body – she also possessed a more enlarged understanding; her views were more enlightened, her habits more intellectual.

As a reward for reconquering the Persian provinces on behalf of Rome (which Jameson says was in many respects due to the assistance of his queen), Odenanthus obtained from Rome the title of 'Augustus' and 'Governor of the East'. There ensued, however, a domestic conspiracy in which Zenobia may or may not have been involved. In 267 or 268 Odenanthus was assassinated while hunting.

The Roman emperor Gallienus refused to recognize Zenobia's claim to sovereignty over her husband's dominions, and dispatched a large army against her. But she took the field against the Roman general, Heraclianus, and defeated him in a pitched battle. Not content with taking over her husband's inferior status as a Roman client, in 269 she sent her army under general Zabdas to seize the Roman province of Egypt, took control of the Roman colony of Palestine, conquered part of Armenia, and in 270 won control of most of Asia Minor. Ruling now from the river Euphrates in Mesopotamia to the shores of the Mediterranean, with Jerusalem, Antioch, Damascus, and other great cities among her dominions, Zenobia took the final step: she declared her independence of Rome.

Historians relate that she restored and embellished the already magnificent buildings of Palmyra, whose forgotten ruins were discovered by accident by English travellers in the late eighteenth century.

What we have most difficulty in reconciling with the manners of her age and country, writes Anna Jameson, is Zenobia's passion for learning, and her taste for Greek and Latin literature. She is said to have drawn up an epitome of world history for her own use; she was familiar with the Greek historians, poets, and philosophers; and she invited Cassius Longinus, one of the most elegant writers of antiquity, to her court as her secretary and minister. For her he composed his celebrated 'Treatise on the Sublime', which, besides its own esthetic virtues, preserved for posterity many beautiful fragments of poets whose works are now lost, notably the love poems of Sappho of Lesbos, written in the sixth century BCE.

In female dignity and discretion, as well as beauty, it is said that Zenobia far surpassed Cleopatra, the luckless consort of Julius Caesar and Mark Antony in the first century BCE.

She administered the government of her empire with such admirable prudence and policy, and in particular with such strict justice to all classes of her subjects, that she was beloved by her own people, and respected and feared by the neighboring nations.

But she also took on Greek and Roman manners, and affected to despise her Arab ancestry, which alienated the fighting men of the Arab desert tribes, unequalled as irregular cavalry, who ceased to form the backbone of her army and whose disaffection seems to have cost her dearly in her war with Rome.

Aurelian, the new Roman emperor, a fierce and active man (reigned 270-275 CE), determined to put an end to Zenobia's defiance. Backed by the skill, discipline, determination, and ingenuity of the Roman legions, still the finest troops in the ancient world, he mounted an expedition against her, defeating her first at Antioch and then at Emessa. She retired to Palmyra, rallied the citizens, strengthened the fortifications, and made ready for a long siege (271-272 CE).

At first Aurelian could gain no advantage. In one of his letters he wrote:

> Those who speak with contempt of the war I am waging against a woman, are ignorant both of the character and power of Zenobia. It is impossible to enumerate her warlike preparations of stones, of arrows, and of every species of missile weapons and military engines.

Later however, with the city close to defeat, Zenobia set out on a racing camel to seek aid among the desert tribes (so it is said). She was captured by the Roman cavalry and made Aurelian's prisoner. She was at this time the proximate cause of the death of Longinus at the hands of the Romans, an event that does her little credit.

When she graced Aurelian's triumph on his return to Rome in 272,

> every eye was fixed on the beautiful and majestic figure of the Syrian queen, who walked in the procession before her own sumptuous chariot, attired in her diadem and royal robes, blazing with jewels, her eyes fixed on the ground, and her delicate form drooping under the weight of her golden fetters . . . while the Roman populace, at that time the most brutal and degraded in the whole world, gaped and stared upon her misery, and shouted in exultation over her fall.

The Palmyrenes rose in revolt again in 273, and put the Roman garrison and governor to death. Aurelian's vengeance was swift and sure. He seized the city, ordered the massacre of every woman, man, and child, put its buildings to the torch, and razed it to the ground.

Palmyra disappeared from history for sixteen hundred years.

In Rome Aurelian not only pardoned Zenobia but also granted her a fine villa at Tivoli, where she resided in great honor. Little is known of her life in Italy, and some sources suggest that she committed suicide. But it is generally accepted that she later married a Roman senator with whom she passed her declining years. Her daughters married Romans, and as late as the fifteenth century there existed Italian families who claimed to be descended from Palmyra's famous queen.

The moral of the story of Zenobia, in spite of her final defeat, is that only because she was educated as a man by her husband, and only because she was taught the male strategy of command, communication, and control as it existed in her time, was she able to take up the strategy of her husband and go beyond it to define her own – defying the most powerful nation on earth, living the life of a completely independent woman, and ruling her territories as an independent queen.

This is not to suggest that learning the practice of imperialism by following the strategy of male supremacy is in itself a good idea, but it is to insist that without command of that ever-dominant strategy, women can neither defeat it, control it, nor go beyond it – and thus never successfully declare their independence of men.

Theory is instituted so that each person in succession may not have to go through the same labor of clearing the ground and toiling through his subject, but may find the thing in order, and a light admitted on it.

Carl von Clausewitz: *On War* (1832)

6.2   Levels of strategy

Banish from your world view the idea that strategy and tactics are (a) strictly military, (b) bad manners, (c) deceitful, or (d) the last refuge of scoundrels. Every living creature has at least one strategy – to reproduce its kind – and at least one tactic – a means of reproduction – to make the strategy real.

Strategy and tactics are characteristic of all goal-seeking, adaptive, open systems – systems involving or simulating life or mind, dependent on their environments, and organized by information. Complex open systems may contain hundreds or thousands of levels of goal-seeking: the more complex are capable of changing goals, the most complex, of imagining new ones. Such systems may pursue many goals in many ways at many levels.

Carl von Clausewitz (1780-1831), disciple of Napoleon and modern apostle of 'absolute war', defined the generality of strategy and tactics in defining the place of war in human affairs. In Book 2, Chapter 3 of *On War* (1832), he wrote:

> We say therefore that War belongs not to the province of Arts and Sciences, but to the province of social life. It is a conflict of interests which is settled by bloodshed, and only in that is it different from others. It would be better . . . to liken it to business competition, which is also a conflict of human interests and activities; and it is still more like State policy, which again, on its part, may be looked upon as a kind of business competition on a great scale.

(It was in Clausewitz's lifetime that England emerged as the first modern capitalist system, based on a distinctly increased extent and intensity of competition, both between capitalist and capitalist and, in the newly emerged labor market, between wage laborer and wage laborer.)

Figure 6.1 offers a simple model of the four-level structure of general strategy. The major distinction is of course that between strategy and tactics. In the simplest sense, strategy is what we want to do and tactics are how we go about it. In the military sense tactics is the art of fighting battles; strategy, the art of fighting wars.

As Antoine Henri Jomini explained in 1837, in his *Précis de l'art de la guerre*, under 'Strategy':

> To learn tactics, one must first study in the school of the platoon, then in that of the battalion, and finally manoeuvres in line; then one passes from minor operations to those of a full campaign, then to the art of encampment (*castramétation*), and finally to the formation of armies. But in strategy, the beginning is at the summit, that is to say the entire plan of campaign.

Tactics is thus learned 'bottom-up', an operation typical of the left hemisphere of the brain, whereas strategy is learned 'top-down', in a manner of the right hemisphere, the domain of what Clausewitz calls the *coup d'oeil*.

Grand strategy corresponds to the setting of general goals; *strategy*, to the orientation of means to reach those ends; *grand tactics*, to the framing of operations within those means; and *tactics*, to the punctuation of action within the frame of operations.

(By calling this structure a 'semi-dependent hierarchy', I mean that although under normal circumstances each higher level constrains the

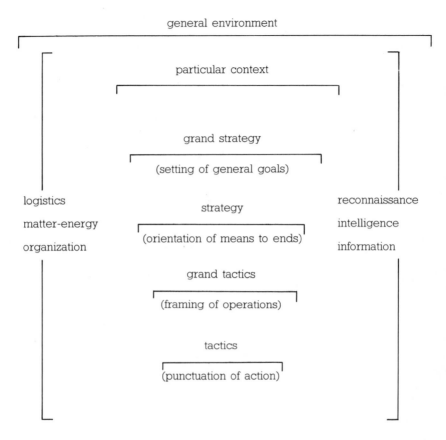

FIGURE 6.1   The structure of general strategy, a semi-dependent hierarchy. The precise definition of the four levels depends on the context. In the simple military sense, grand strategy concerns the overall goals for which wars are fought and the organization of resources to attain them (national policy); strategy is the art of fighting wars; grand tactics is the art of planning major operations and the course of campaigns (and thus merges closely with strategy); and tactics is the art of fighting battles. The position of logistics, reconnaissance, and intelligence in the diagram indicates that they are all required at every level. The hierarchy is called 'semi-dependent' because under given conditions changes at the higher levels can become dependent on the results of novel events at the lower levels. Tactical innovations, for example (6.3), can restructure the constraints of strategy, after which the hierarchy assumes once again its normally dependent form. The hierarchy is also a hierarchy of levels (or orders) of communication and reality, including levels of organization, levels of responsibility, levels of decision, and levels of goal-seeking. (An order of organization, responsibility, decision, and so forth, consists of more than one level.)

levels below it, and the lower levels depend on the higher levels, under other conditions constraints can be restructured by innovation from below. The higher levels then become dependent on the outcome of events at the lower levels. In other words, innovations at the level of the messages (tactics) can be projected into the level of the code (strategy), as happens with a surviving mutation in natural evolution, a new paradigm in science, a major invention in technology, a novel event in cultural evolution, or a political or economic revolution in history. The innovation breaks through the constraints of the existing code (or codes) and restructures it, making radically new messages possible. The hierarchy then re-assumes its normally dependent character.)

Strategy means literally 'the art of the general' (Greek *stratēgos*); tactics, 'the art of arrangement'. In his *Stratagems* (84-96 CE) the Roman military and civil engineer Frontinus says that

> everything achieved by a commander, be it characterized by foresight, advantage, enterprise, or resolution, will belong under the head of 'strategy'.

The term strategy came into general use in Europe just as the revolutionary 'total war' waged by Napoleon between 1793 and 1815 was replacing the formalized, geometric, and limited warfare of eighteenth-century Europe – summed up by the Marshal de Saxe (1696-1750) when he said in his posthumous *Reveries on the Art of War* (1757):

> I am not in favor of giving battle, especially at the outset of a war. I am even convinced that a clever general can wage war all his life without being compelled to do so.

Grand strategy in the usual sense is the level of overall national policy, decided on by those who command the generals, combining political, social, and economic objectives with military priorities. It includes the creation and maintenance of alliances and the organization and protection of the natural resources, the technology, the productive capacity, and the personnel required to fight the war.

Strategy is the art of applying military and other means to fulfil the ends of policy. It is the domain of planning the military war, mapping out the course of campaigns, and regulating the battles to be fought in each (Montross, quoting Clausewitz, 1974). Manoeuvering armies before battle is usually called strategic, as distinct from the tactics of manoeuvering within battles (7.2). In *On War*, largely composed by 1827 but not published until 1832, Clausewitz writes:

> By the strategic plan is settled *when, where*, and *with what forces* a battle is to be delivered (Book 2, Chapter 1).

The Confederate general Nathan Bedford Forrest (1821-77) – whose formula for victory was 'get there first with the most men' – put it more simply:

Strategy is horse sense; when practised by Indians it is called treachery.

Grand tactics, another term that came into use during the Napoleonic period, is often identical with strategy. (Some twentieth-century commanders have called it 'operational strategy'.) It concerns the planning, organization, and execution of major operations, such as the North African campaign or the D-day landings in World War Two.

Tactics is the expression of strategy. It deals with the immediate approach to the field of combat, the disposition of troops on the field, the use made of the various arms (infantry, artillery, armor, tactical air support, and so on), and the manoeuvres employed in battle (7.2). Tactics concerns the *form* of a particular engagement; strategy its *use* and its *signification* (Clausewitz).

A simpler definition, source unknown:

Tactics is merely common sense applied with imagination.

For Saul Alinsky in *Rules for Radicals* (1971, p. 126), tactics means 'doing what you can with what you have'.

The components of tactics in the military sense are attack and defense, cohesion and dispersion, protection and mobility, missile and shock effect, and moral and material values (Montross, 1974). Moral or psychological factors generally play a more important part than material means, but where morale, discipline, and technology are equivalent God remains on the side of the big battalions.

Logistics is the domain of resources: food and arms production, general supplies, transportation, bases and depots, communications and other facilities, and hospitals and other services required by troops.

Reconnaissance involves the gathering, evaluation, and use of intelligence, both strategic and tactical. Intelligence is so vital that a good spy may be worth more to an army than a good general (Montross, 1974).

What is at the level of grand strategy for a goal-seeking system in one environment will not necessarily have the same strategic significance if the boundaries of the system-environment relation are changed in space or time. Similarly, what may be strategy in one system-environment relation may be tactics in another. The critical strategic decision for any situation at any level is therefore the correct designation of the boundary or boundaries between system(s) and environment(s).

Strategy and tactics are actions at different levels, but as Clausewitz says, they 'mutually permeate each other' in space and time. The same action may be both strategical and tactical. The march to battle is an instrument of strategy, but since it involves readiness for combat at any moment, including protection against surprise, it stands also under tactical rules. Other relations on the march, such as building bridges or roads, are neither strategic nor tactical, but logistical (Clausewitz, Book 2, Chapter 1).

Underlying the successful use of any strategy or tactic are a number of basic principles of action (7.4). These include the seizure of the initiative, speed in decision, rapidity in movement, requisite mobility, the concentration of strength at the point of decision, the coordination of the requisite diversity of forces, and the selection of intermediate objectives and stages of deployment, as well as the maintenance of a reserve adequate to exploit success and remedy unforeseen difficulties. They also include security against surprise, the maintenance of protected lines of communication and supply, a safe base of retreat, and, last but not least, the means of getting there (adapted from Chandler, 1974).

The four orders of general strategy are implicit in every kind of communication, organization, and action. The hierarchy is also the basic model of the relation between theory and practice. One can create a theory without a practice, but one cannot act in practice (tactics) without a corresponding theory (strategy).

In Clausewitz's words: 'we fall into error . . . if we attribute to strategical combinations a power independent of tactical results' (Book 2, Chapter 1).

Strategy without tactics is imaginary; tactics without strategy is impossible.

I restate here some remarks from 'The Naming of Parts and the 20th Century War' in *The Rules Are No Game* (1987). How strategies and tactics are used – how a particular end is attained by a particular means – is a matter of ethics. The basis of a truly democratic ethic is not the imperial belief that to be good at what we do and proud of who we are, we have to be superior to some other group of people. It is the belief that we are just as good and just as human as everyone else. In the democratic ethic, the Rule of Rules is simple and direct:

The Democratic Rule: Everyone a strategist.

This contrasts with the Colonial Rule:

The Colonial Rule: Teach tactics only, especially kamikaze tactics;

make strategy, and indeed the very idea of strategy, a secret never to be revealed.

The four-level model displays requisite diversity. It warns us that if information appropriate to one order of communication or reality is used to make decisions about another order, the resulting reduction, symmetrization, or confusion of levels can prove disastrous. At every level success depends on reliable information and intelligence and the capacity to tell good information from bad. This in turn depends on a perspective adequate and rich enough to evaluate with accuracy and insight the context one is in.

The hierarchy of levels (or orders) of communication and reality in Figure 6.1 – levels (or orders) of organization, responsibility, decision, goal-seeking, and so on – is a model of a both-and hierarchy between levels within which one makes either/or decisions at the various levels. The levels are distinct from each other but not opposed to each other. Like the dialectic of life and society explained in the last chapter of *The Rules Are No Game* (1987), the logic of this hierarchy is dialectical: *both* both-and *and* either/or. (Analytic logic, which is a subset of dialectical logic, is *either* either/or *or* both-and.)

In war, says Clausewitz in the chapter on 'Criticism',

> as generally in the world, there is a connection between everything which belongs to the whole; and therefore, however small a cause may be in itself, its effects reach to the end of the act of warfare, and modify or influence the final result in some degree, let that degree be ever so small (Book 2, Chapter 5).

The task of critical theory, he says, is 'to throw the requisite light on the interrelations of things, and to distinguish from amongst the endless connections of events those which are really essential'.

> We can therefore trace the effects of a cause as long as events are worth noticing, and in the same way we must not stop at the testing of means for the immediate goal, but test also this goal as a means to a higher one, and thus ascend the series of facts in succession, until we come to one so absolutely necessary in its nature as to require no examination or proof.

This 'succession of facts' is in reality a hierarchy. As Clausewitz explains in Book 2, Chapter 4, to understand method and method of action in war we must look at 'the logical hierarchy through which, as through regularly constituted authorities, the world of action is governed'.

In considering the hierarchy of events, our approach involves 'following the clue up and down' (both 'top-down' and 'bottom-up'):

> It is evident that in thus ascending, at every new station which we reach, a new point of view for the judgment is attained, so that the same means which appeared advisable at one station, when looked at from the next above it, may have to be rejected.

When not restructured by innovation from below, strategy constrains tactics. If one's strategy is wrong, tactical victories cannot prevent strategic defeats. The arrival of Napoleon's Grand Army in Moscow in 1812 was a tactical victory, but since the Russians had abandoned the city, there was no one to negotiate peace or anything else with. By their absence the Russians inflicted a strategic defeat. Tactically that defeat was expressed in the almost complete destruction of the Grand Army of France in its disastrous retreat.

But if one's strategy is right, tactical defeats do not necessarily prevent strategic success. In many of the wars of independence since 1945, the rebels were defeated militarily but the strategic aim of political independence was nevertheless achieved.

Here we are reminded, both as a human population and as a biological species, not to confuse the tactics of short-range survival with the grand strategy of long-range survival.

> Amid the seeming confusion of our mysterious world, individuals are so nicely adjusted to a system, and systems to one another and to a whole, that, by stepping aside for a moment, a man exposes himself to a fearful risk of losing his place forever.
>
> Nathaniel Hawthorne: *Wakefield* (1835)

6.3 Strategic and tactical innovation

In March 1934 an upper-class British agent masquerading as a Nazi sympathizer, Major Frederick W. Winterbotham, was dumbfounded to have the entire plan for the German invasion of Russia outlined to him by General Walther von Reichenau at a luncheon party in Berlin.

As Winterbotham explains in *The Nazi Connection* (1978, pp. 100-20), this was not just a matter of having Hitler's long-term war aims revealed seven years before their time (Germany invaded Russia in May 1941), it was also an announcement that the German Army had developed a radically new offensive strategy, the mechanized warfare of mobility and manoeuvre called *Blitzkrieg*, 'lightning war'.

In World War One the tank had been used by the British and the

French at the tactical level as an addition to other weapons, without any significant change in tactics, organization, methodology, or battle strategy. The war ended before 'Plan 1919', devised by the British prophet of Blitzkrieg war J.F.C. Fuller (1878-1966), could be put into effect. Fuller saw the tank as the best answer to the superiority conferred on the defense by the machine gun. He envisaged the combined use of armor, motorized infantry, and aircraft to break through the German lines and destroy their capacity for organized tactical response by destroying their centers of command and control and their lines of communication.

Although Fuller's concepts were largely neglected by the British and the French – in spite of his influence on Basil Liddell Hart and Charles de Gaulle – both the Russians and the Germans, notably Heinz Guderian, one of the fathers of 'lightning war', were thoroughly familiar with his writings. The German Army integrated with the panzer or tank division motorized infantry and tactical air support (dive bombers used as artillery). The resulting mobile force was capable of advancing at the then unheard-of rate of 200 miles a day. This would require faster communication between front line and rear echelons than any normally used at the time, and Winterbotham realized that the German force would be advancing faster than British intelligence could communicate information about it.

On attempting to explain to the military and the ministries the vital significance of this information, Winterbotham ran into a blank wall:

> The British still thought in terms of battleships and destroyers, of artillery and divisions of soldiers. . . . The idea of divisions of tanks on the German scale backed by massive air support never entered their minds. It was not that the military did not understand the words I used but rather that the ideas I was trying to put across did not fit in with their thinking (p. 155).

This was the first great failure of Allied intelligence in World War Two (the second was Pearl Harbor). Repeated indications that Germany would attack Russia in spite of the non-aggression treaty signed in 1939 were ignored right up to the day of the invasion itself. Stalin (who had also ignored the warnings) was so traumatized by the event that he retreated to his country residence and refused to come out.

Major Winterbotham was faced, not by an ignorance resulting from an absence of information, nor by an ignorance resulting from the presence of false information, both of which involve message (tactical) information, but rather by an ignorance at the level of the code. This is strategic ignorance, a perspective that actively distorts or otherwise renders unintelligible any attempt to turn it into useful knowledge.

(As the Swedish sociologist Gunnar Myrdal brightly observed: 'Ignorance, like knowledge, is purposefully directed.')

Tactical and strategic ignorance

Tactical ignorance means ignorance we are aware of, ignorance that can be reduced or eliminated by the use of familiar strategies. Strategic ignorance, in contrast, is an ignorance we are not aware of. When strategically ignorant, we do not recognize what we lack, or indeed that we lack any kind of perception, experience, or understanding at all. This is a learned disability that one can come to recognize only by a radical change in perspective at the level of the code – by the very change in outlook that strategic ignorance normally prevents. In ordinary circumstances, then, the required change cannot be brought about alone – and yet it can only be accomplished by the person actually involved. In the absence of suitable experience, another person with suitable insight but without the same disability is needed to mediate the transformation.

Between unrecognized strategic ignorance and the development of a new perspective there may appear to be an abyss of lost or confused identity that cannot at first be crossed.

In communications a strategic innovation is not necessarily expressed in tactics. The electric telegraph, invented in 1800, was being used at the administrative and strategic levels in the American Civil War (1861-65), but it was not until the end of the century that it was used for tactical communications on the battlefield. The Japanese were the first to use radio telegraphy (at sea) in defeating the Russians in the war of 1904-5, and the first to use the telephone in war.

The Nazi *Blitzkrieg* was a strategic innovation that fundamentally altered tactics at the lower level and at the higher level made the grand strategy of French and British warfare as obsolete as the Maginot Line or the capital ship unprotected by fighters – as the Royal Navy tragically discovered when Japanese bombers off the coast of Malaya sent to the bottom in quick succession the battleship *Prince of Wales* and the battle cruiser *Repulse*, just three days after the attack on Pearl Harbor in December 1941.

At the tactical level, the organization and communications of the panzer division were far superior to those of its British and French counterparts. Of the Battle of France in 1940 the German commander F.W. von Mellenthin reports in *Panzer Battles* (1958):

Our panzer corps and divisions not only had the advantage of excellent training and communications, but the commander at every level fully appreciated that panzer troops must be commanded from the front. Thus they were able to take immediate advantage of the rapid changes and opportunities which armored warfare brings. Perhaps I should stress that although we attached the greatest importance to armor, we realized that tanks cannot operate without the close support of motorized infantry and artillery. Our panzer division was a balanced force of all arms – a lesson the British did not learn until well into 1942 (quoted in Welchman, 1982, p. 223).

In contrast the French forces were commanded from the rear – and it took forty-eight hours for an order from French headquarters to be executed at the front.

In North Africa the British had the advantage of high-level and highly accurate information about the strength and order of battle of Rommel's Afrika Corps. This information came from the decoding of German Ultra traffic following the breaking of the Enigma coding system. But if the British had a great asset in intelligence, the Germans had a big advantage in communications. Although the British had pioneered the use of radio in tanks in 1931, their tank radios of the 1940s could not survive the desert environment, whereas the Afrika Corps was well co-ordinated by good radios, and commanded from the front.

With the Italians the British had fought tank on tank; not so with Rommel's forces, however. On November 23, 1941, a British tank force with numerical superiority, but unsupported by infantry and without properly organized tactical communications or even a co-ordinated chain of tactical command, tried to get at the German armor in a series of tank cavalry charges. They found the Germans supported by motorized infantry, anti-tank weapons, and artillery (ibid., pp. 226-7). The result was disaster. The German anti-tank gunners shot the British to a standstill. Out of 450 cruiser tanks committed to the action that day the British Eighth Army lost over 300. The British learned (once again) that without radical innovation you can't beat strategy with tactics.

Culloden

The tactical innovation devised by the 29-year-old Duke of Cumberland to neutralize the power of the Highland charge and turn its energy against itself on that tragic April day at Culloden in 1746 was a tactical innovation with strategic implications.

In his *History of the Rebellion of 1745* (1827, revised editions in 1840 and 1869) Robert Chambers explains the Highland tactics as follows (p. 125):

The mode of fighting practised by the Highlanders, though as simple as can be well conceived, was well calculated to set at nought and defeat the tactics of a regular soldiery. . . . They advanced with the utmost rapidity towards the enemy, gave fire when within a musket-length of the object, and then throwing down their pieces, drew their swords, and holding a dirk in their left hand along with the target [shield], darted with fury on the enemy through the smoke of their fire.

When within reach of the enemy's bayonets,

bending their left knee, they contrived to receive the thrust of that weapon on their targets; then raising their arm, and with it the enemy's point, they rushed in upon the soldier, now defenceless, killed him at one blow, and were in a moment within the lines, pushing right and left with sword and dagger, often bringing down two men at once. The battle was thus decided in a moment, and all that followed was carnage (pp. 125-6).

The superiority of the broadsword or claymore over the bayonet at Prestonpans and Falkirk had given rise to much discussion in the public journals as to how the weapons of regular troops could be put on a par with those of the insurgents (p. 287).

The first and simplest change was to draw up the Hanoverian and other troops in three ranks instead of two, providing more depth in the line to counteract the shock of the assault.

The second was more subtle, as Chambers explains (p. 287):

The duke conceived that if each man, on coming within the proper distance of the enemy, should direct his [bayonet] thrust, not at the man directly opposite to him, but against the one who fronted his right-hand comrade, the target would be rendered useless, and the Highlander would be wounded in the right side, under the sword-arm, ere he could ward off the thrust. Accordingly, he had instructed the men during the spring in this new exercise (p. 287).

James Grant, in *British Battles on Land and Sea* (1886), shocked at the calculating nature of Cumberland's new tactic, called it 'the idea of an assassin'. It worked so well that at some points along the British and Hanoverian line bodies were found piled in layers two and three deep. No Highlander succeeded in penetrating the third line.

Cumberland's innovation thus took effect at both the tactical and the strategic levels. It killed men with great efficiency – stopped the charge – and destroyed the Highland battle strategy as effectively as the brutal and vengeful repression in the months after the battle destroyed the Highland lifeways and the Highland clans.

Discipline is the soul of an army. It makes small numbers
formidable; procures success to the weak, and esteem to all.
George Washington: Letter of Instructions to the Captains of the
Virginia Regiments (July 29, 1759)

6.4 Discipline

Sun Tzu begins 'Estimates', the first chapter of *The Art of War*
(c. 400-320 BCE), by saying:

War is a matter of vital importance to the State; the province of life
or death; the road to survival or ruin. It is mandatory that it be
thoroughly studied.

In war there are five fundamental factors:

moral influence [*Tao*], weather, terrain, command, and doctrine [*fa*,
law, method].

The moral influence of *Tao*, meaning 'the Way' or 'the Right Way'
refers in this context to the benevolence, justice, and righteousness of
the sovereign in feudal China. Sun Tzu says:

By moral influence I mean what causes the people to be in harmony
with their leaders, so that they will accompany them in life and unto
death without fear of mortal peril.

A later commentator, Chang Yü, adds:

The *Book of Changes* says: In happiness at overcoming difficulties,
people forget the danger of death.

'By command', Sun Tzu declares,

I mean the general's qualities of wisdom, sincerity, humanity,
courage, and strictness (p. 65).

In eloquent testimony to the power and vitality of the Chinese classics,
and the Chinese respect for learning, we find the poet and councillor
of state, Tu Mu (803-52 CE), remarking on this passage twelve
centuries later:

If wise, a commander is able to recognize changing circumstances and to act expediently. If sincere, his men will have no doubt of the certainty of rewards and punishments. If humane, he loves mankind, sympathizes with others, and appreciates their industry and toil. If courageous, he gains victory by seizing opportunity without hesitation. If strict, his troops are disciplined because they are in awe of him and are afraid of punishment (p. 65).

Not all discipline is based on fear. Writing in 1957, in *One Hundred Hours to Suez*, an account of Israel's pre-emptive strike at Gamal Abdel Nasser's Egypt in the Suez War of 1956 (in which Britain and France also joined), Robert Henriques, a retired British Army officer who describes himself as a Jew but not a Zionist, sought to explain the origin of the distinctive spirit of the Israeli Army:

Although Israeli units can be extremely smart on a ceremonial parade, there is very little discipline in the ordinary sense. Officers are often called by their first name amongst their men, as amongst their colleagues; there is very little saluting: there are a lot of unshaven chins; there are no outward signs of respect for superiors; there is no word in Hebrew for 'sir'.

He continues:

A soldier genuinely feels himself to be the equal of his officer – indeed of any officer – yet in battle he accepts military authority without question.

Henriques exaggerates. Like Americans, Israeli soldiers are more likely than most to question orders, but this is not the point. The point is that provided one has been brought up with the necessary self-esteem in the first place, equality of the person can be maintained even in an authoritarian system based on a strictly defined division of labor and a hierarchy of power.

T.E. Lawrence made a similar observation about the Bedouin of the desert during the Arab Revolt against the Turks in the First World War, saying of an Indian Army unit that the manner of the British officers to the rank and file horrified his Bedouin bodyguard, 'who had never seen personal inequality [between men] before'. The remark, which there seems no reason to disbelieve, is reported by Liddell Hart in *Colonel Lawrence* (1935, p. 289).

Liddell Hart added on the subject of official or 'smartening discipline' that its price in war is a 'loss in individual intelligence and initiative':

The straitly disciplined soldier is apt to feel uneasy, if not helpless, unless in a herd. War . . . brings frequent shocks that . . . throw the individual on his own resources. If these have atrophied under restraint he is unable to cope with the emergency. Lawrence once remarked that 'lack of *independent* courage' is the root fault of the military system (p. 292).

Following his comment on the sense of personal equality in the Israeli Army, Henriques says that experience in the British and American armies had taught him that 'first-class discipline in battle depends on good discipline in barracks' (pp. 23-4). The Israeli Army seemed to refute that traditional lesson. 'I cannot explain', he says, 'I cannot begin to understand, how or why it works.'

He later asked General Moshe Dayan, the Israeli Chief of Staff, what accounted for the highly developed integration of individuals of varying national origins, including Jews of Oriental stock, in this citizen army, in whose formal and informal reserves every able-bodied Israeli man and woman is enrolled. Dayan replied, 'The Bible' – not in the religious sense, but in the historical, philosophical, and cultural sense of an ancient text known to all, a source of spoken and written style continually recalled in everyday metaphor and popular wisdom – the Bible as the source of a shared epistemology, mythology, and ideology mediating all relations between Jews, and between Jews and their environments, including the Arab states.

Consider now the views of Major-General J.F.C. Fuller (1878-1966), the British strategist and exponent of lightning war already mentioned, on the British soldier in the first half of this century. As quoted by Douglas G. Browne in *Private Thomas Atkins* (1940, p. 280), in *The Army in My Time* Fuller wrote:

> As a stubborn and tenacious fighter I doubt whether the English soldier has an equal; yet as an attacker and an exploiter in all probability he has many, because he is not a quick thinker. . . . He is seldom good at shifting for himself. He has, in all probability, never been in an independent position, as have his brothers from the Dominions or the Colonies.

(Similar distinctions between British and Commonwealth troops, and between British and American troops, were noted in both world wars. It was said at the turn of the century that individuality was not encouraged in the British soldier, with the result that 'the man's mind does not grow with his body'.)

Fuller continued:

> He will follow to heel without question, not because he fears to lead – far from it – but because he has never been encouraged or

taught to do so. He expects everything to be done for him, and normally he has an unwavering faith in his officers. To obey is natural to him, to give an order is not. . . .

What is being exposed here is of course the sense of inferiority and helplessness instilled in the private soldier by the combination of the Army system and the British class structure. The Cinderella Complex is not confined to women.

The first English commander to detect and put to use the intimate connection between discipline, strength of character, and ideological commitment was Oliver Cromwell, one of the great English generals – and a dictator whose attempt to exterminate the Irish was as vicious and inhuman as the Irish wars of any English king. The occasion was his training of the first units of what later became the New Model Army during the three phases of the English Civil War (1642-46, 1648, 1649-51), in the midst of the English Revolution of 1642-88.

At Marston Moor in 1644, the biggest battle ever fought on English soil, about 18,000 Royalists faced about 22,000 Parliamentary and Scottish troops. Cromwell, in command of his New Model Cavalry on the Parliamentary left wing – they were nicknamed that day by the Royalist Prince Rupert 'Old Ironsides' and called that ever afterwards – had taken especial care to recruit only men of religious devotion into the cavalry. These were men whose commitment to their beliefs meant that they understood the importance of the rebellion against Charles I and his claim to dictatorial powers based on the 'divine right of kings', each viewing the struggle in a personally significant light. These he trained in discipline as men had not been trained in England before.

As Edwin Paxton Hood put it in 1852, in his *Cromwell*:

[Cromwell] tells us how he saw that the Parliamentarians must have been beaten, unless a better race of men could be raised – men who would match the high notions of chivalry and loyalty, and overreach them with a nobler and worthier feeling. Cromwell plainly saw that, even in battles, it is not brute force that masters, but invincible honour and integrity, and faith in the purity and truth of the cause (p. 72).

According to Lady Antonia Fraser's account of the battle in *Cromwell The Lord Protector* (1973, pp. 125-32), the attack began sometime after 7 o'clock in the evening, when

the Parliamentary left wing, Cromwell's well-tried men of the Eastern Association with Leslie's Scots behind them, began one of their new type charges, rapid, controlled, riding short-reined and short-stirruped, close in together, probably at something like a fast trot rather than the modern gallop.

The Ironside charge routed the Royalist cavalry led by Lord Byron to meet them. Prince Rupert's horse then counter-charged Cromwell's force in the front and flank and sent them flying. However, the Scots horse in the second line attacked Rupert's cavalry in the flank and gave the Ironsides time and space to recover. Cromwell then led a second great assault and scattered Rupert's cavalry, who fled the field.

It was at this point that Cromwell's training showed its worth, for instead of letting his troopers abandon the field to pursue and plunder Rupert's men, as would have been expected, Cromwell pulled them up short, an extraordinary feat at the time, says Lady Fraser, and keeping them 'close and firm together in a body', returned to aid the Parliamentary right wing, which was on the verge of defeat. Charging the Royalists from the rear, for the Ironsides were now where the Royalist left wing had been, Cromwell's force caught the Royalist cavalry completely by surprise and drove them from the field. Some two hours after it began, the Battle of Marston Moor was all but won.

It was generally agreed at the time that at least 3000 Royalists were killed at Marston Moor (some said 7000); 1500 were made prisoner. Although there were numerous Parliamentary and Scottish wounded, they lost no more than 300 dead. Aided at a critical point by Leslie's Scottish cavalry, Cromwell and the Ironsides, and their novel training, tactics, and discipline, had been cruelly vindicated.

Do not think dishonestly.
The Way is in training.
Become acquainted with every art.
Know the Ways of all professions.
Distinguish between gain and loss in wordly matters.
Develop intuitive judgment and understanding for everything.
Perceive those things which cannot be seen.
Pay attention even to trifles.
Do nothing which is of no use.
    Miyamoto Musashi (1584-1645): *A Book of Five Rings* (1645)

6.5 Character

Sun Tzu defined the five virtues of the general as wisdom, sincerity, humanity, courage, and strictness. Clausewitz defined fourteen qualities or types of qualities required of the military commander. Let us continue to take war as a metaphor, and apply both Sun Tzu's and Clausewitz's definitions of character not to the general but to the citizen, on the democratic principle of 'Everyone a strategist'.

But first a comparison between these two radically different strategists so that we can understand each in the light of the other.

Sun Tzu's theory of war is poetic, holistic, organicist, existentially realistic, moderate, dominated by common sense, oriented to persuasion rather than killing, and primarily concerned not with the destruction or subjugation of armies or states in conflict but with the resolution of conflict by any means other than war wherever possible. As he says: 'Weapons are ominous tools to be used only when there is no other alternative.'

Although often subtle and always logically and philosophically interesting, Clausewitz's theory of war is atomistic, mechanistic, logically extreme, absolutist, dominated by rationalism, oriented to killing rather than persuasion, and primarily concerned with violence and destruction as the inevitable means of resolving conflict. As he said, and his disciples repeated after him: 'To introduce into the philosophy of war a principle of moderation would be an absurdity – war is an act of violence pushed to its utmost bounds.'

Sun Tzu's view would be called today a non-zero-sum or 'win-win' contest, always and everywhere negotiable. Clausewitz's view is a zero-sum or 'win-lose' contest, closer to the policy of unconditional surrender.

Sun Tzu's view is dominated by the limitless combinations, interpenetrations, and interchanges of the direct and the indirect approaches (*cheng* and *ch'i*, the 'ordinary' and the 'extraordinary' forces), and evoked by phrases such as 'swift as the wind', 'as calmly majestic as the forest', 'plundering like fire', 'flowing like water', 'steady as the mountains'.

Clausewitz's view is dominated by metaphors of mechanical assemblies, well-oiled cogs and gears, inertia, friction, mechanical forces, equilibrium, and Newtonian rest and motion.

Sun Tzu's theory of war is dominated by metaphors of subtlety, intimacy, relationships, ebb and flow (yin and yang), continuity, topology, shaping, imagination, and creation.

Clausewitz's view is dominated by metaphors of collision, separation, entities, action and reaction, discontinuity, geometry, forcing, rationality, and destruction.

Sun Tzu remains the philosopher of the traditional Chinese golden mean; Clausewitz remains the disciple of Napoleon and the philosopher of 'total war', foreshadowing by some thirty years the huge increase in killing and destruction in the first great war of industrial capitalism, the American Civil War (1861-65).

Liddell Hart says of the two men in his introduction to Samuel B. Griffith's translation of Sun Tzu:

Sun Tzu's essays on 'The Art of War' form the earliest of known treatises on the subject, but have never been surpassed in comprehensiveness and depth of understanding. They might well be termed the concentrated essence of wisdom on the conduct of war. Among all the military thinkers of the past, only Clausewitz is comparable, and even he is more 'dated' than Sun Tzu, and in part antiquated, although he was writing more than two thousand years later. Sun Tzu has clearer vision, more profound insight, and eternal freshness.

He goes on to say:

Civilization might have been spared much of the damage suffered in the world wars of this century if the influence of Clausewitz's monumental tomes *On War*, which moulded European military thought in the era preceding the First World War, had been blended with and balanced by a knowledge of Sun Tzu's exposition on 'The Art of War'.

In Chapter 3 of *Vom Kriege*, Clausewitz sets out to define 'the genius for war'. This consists of the 'tendencies of the mind and soul' co-ordinated in a 'harmonious combination of powers, in which one or another may predominate, but none must be in opposition'. He lists fourteen qualities or types of qualities. Consider them in the light of daily life, rather than war, and as qualities required of the citizen-strategist – as part of the basis of liberty and equality – rather than simply of the general.

1 *Courage* War is the province of danger. Courage is of two kinds, first, courage in the face of danger to the person, and second, courage in the face of moral responsibility, 'whether it be before the judgment seat of external authority, or of the inner power, the conscience'. Physical courage may arise, first, from indifference to danger, or secondly, from positive motives such as personal pride, patriotism, or enthusiasm of any kind.

2 *Strength of body and soul (body and mind)* War is the province of physical exertion and suffering. Under the guidance of a sound understanding the strength of body and soul, which may be either 'natural or acquired', fits a person for war.

3 *A fine and penetrating mind* [a matter for lifelong education, training, and practice] War is the province of uncertainty: three-quarters of what one needs to know lies hidden from us. This

quality of mind enables one 'to search out the truth by the tact of its judgment'.

4 *Coup d'oeil* War is the province of chance. *Coup d'oeil* (meaning 'the capacity to take in a situation at a glance' or 'pick out the essentials of a pattern') is a quality that along with *resolution* is necessary for one to get safely through the perpetual conflict with the unexpected in war. Battle requires rapid and correct decisions about matters in time and space. All able decisions made 'in the moment of action' come under the heading of *coup d'oeil*. The expression includes not only the physical act of seeing but also the 'mental eye'. It means the rapid discovery of a truth – a connection, a relationship, a pattern – which to others is either not visible at all or only becomes so after long examination and reflection.

5 *Resolution* This quality is an act of moral courage in the face of responsibility. It has often been called *courage d'esprit* ('courage of the mind or spirit'), but it is not an act of the understanding, as this suggests, it is rather an act of feeling. We often see the most apparently intelligent people devoid of resolution. (Wu Ch'i (c. 430-381 BCE), whose work is always associated with Sun Tzu, says: 'To unite resolution with resilience is the business of war.') The task of resolution is to remove the 'torments of doubt and the dangers of delay, when there are no sufficient motives for guidance'.

6 *Presence of mind* This is a kindred quality with *coup d'oeil* and resolution. It is a conquest of the unexpected. We admire presence of mind in a pithy answer to some unexpected remark. Whether this quality depends on a peculiarity of mind or an equanimity of the feelings depends on circumstances. It is evident in a telling repartee that bespeaks a ready wit, or when a ready expedient is found in sudden danger.

7 *Force of mind and understanding, force of the soul, force of the will, energy of purpose, energy in action* These qualities are all associated. They refer to the great efforts necessary to continue through with one's convictions in war and the even greater strength required to restore morale when an army is demoralized, dissatisfied, or defeated.

8 *The soul's thirst for honor and renown* These 'proud aspirations', which are among the 'noblest feelings' which belong to 'human nature', are indispensable. 'They are the vivifying principle which gives the enormous body [of war] a spirit.'

9 *Firmness* This denotes the 'resistance of the will in relation to the force of a single blow, *staunchness* in relation to a continuance of blows'.

10 *Strength of mind or soul* This is the power to listen to reason in the midst of the most intense excitement. It involves the power of *self-command*, which has its roots in the heart. 'This counterpoise is

nothing but a sense of the dignity of man, the noblest price, that deeply-seated desire of the soul always to act as a being endued with understanding and reason.'

11 *Strength of character* This, or *character* alone, denotes tenacity of conviction. 'Between the particular case and the principle [in war] there is often a wide space which cannot always be traversed on a visible chain of conclusions, and where a certain faith in self is necessary and a certain amount of scepticism is serviceable.' When in doubt, adhere to the first opinion without giving it up unless a conviction forces one to do so. Force of character may lead to a spurious variety of it, *obstinacy.*

12 *Sense of locality (Ortsinn)* This concerns the relation between war and country or ground. 'It is the power of quickly forming a correct geometrical idea of any portion of the country, and consequently of being able to find one's place in it exactly at any time.' It is a faculty of the imagination. One would now extend the notion to mean 'facility in using the topology of the terrain', of grasping in an instant ground and situation and the relation between the two, and of relating the local to the general (Liddell Hart).

13 *A good memory* [another matter for education, training, and practice; and one that goes without saying]

14 *Statesmanship* 'What is here required from the higher powers of the mind is a sense of unity, and a judgment raised to such a compass as to give the mind an extraordinary faculty of vision which in its range allays and sets aside a thousand dim notions.' This, says Clausewitz, is 'the glance of genius'.

(It is worth noting that *coup d'oeil*, resolution, presence of mind, and the sense of locality are mainly right-brain functions.)

Missing here, and indeed throughout Clausewitz's work, is any profound understanding of the role of psychology in war or the role of psychological factors in the general's character – in what Sun Tzu, one of the great masters of psychological warfare, would call the general's 'shape' as perceived by the opponent.

John Churchill, Duke of Marlborough (1650-1722), ancestor of Winston Churchill, provides an example. As commander of William III's British and Dutch forces he opposed on the Continent the expansionism of Louis XIV of France, who had designs on the vacant Spanish throne and the Spanish Empire. Marlborough's opportunistic political views, his role as a courtier, his condemnation by the House of Commons for embezzlement, and his general character as a man do not recommend him highly to the modern student, but his ten successive campaigns in Europe and his four brilliant victories at Blenheim in 1704, Ramillies in 1706, Oudenaarde in 1708, and Malplaquet in 1709 mark him as one of the great British generals.

THE HEFFALUMP TRAP

Piglet and Pooh have fallen into a Hole in the Floor of the Forest. They have Agreed that it is Really a Heffalump Trap, which makes Piglet Nervous. He imagines that a Heffalump has Landed Close By:

HEFFALUMP (*gloatingly*): "Ho-*ho!*"
PIGLET (*carelessly*): "Tra-la-la, tra-la-la."
HEFFALUMP (*surprised, and not quite so sure of himself*): "Ho-ho!"
PIGLET (*more carelessly still*): "Tiddle-um-tum, tiddle-um-tum."
HEFFALUMP (*beginning to say Ho-ho and turning it awkwardly into a cough*): "H'r'm! What's all this?"
  PIGLET (*surprised*): "Hullo! This is a trap I've made, and I'm waiting for a Heffalump to fall into it."
  HEFFALUMP (*greatly disappointed*): "Oh!" (*after a long silence*): "Are you sure?"
  PIGLET: "Yes."
  HEFFALUMP: "Oh!" (*nervously*): "I – I thought it was a trap I'd made to catch Piglets."
  PIGLET (*surprised*): "Oh, no!"
  HEFFALUMP: "Oh!" (*apologetically*): "I – I must have got it wrong, then."
  PIGLET: "I'm afraid so." (*politely*): "I'm sorry." (*he goes on humming*).
  HEFFALUMP: "Well – well – I – well. I suppose I'd better be getting back?"
  PIGLET (*looking up carelessly*): "Must you? Well, if you see Christopher Robin anywhere, you might tell him I want him."
  HEFFALUMP (*eager to please*): "Certainly! Certainly!" (*he hurries off.*)
  POOH (*who wasn't going to be there, but we find we can't do without him*): "Oh, Piglet, how brave and clever you are!"
  PIGLET (*modestly*): "Not at all, Pooh." (*And then, when Christopher Robin comes, Pooh can tell him all about it.*)

– A.A. Milne: *The House at Pooh Corner* (1928). Decorations by Ernest H. Shepard.

As W.H. Davenport Adams records in *Battle Stories from British and European History* (1889), Marlborough's motto was patience. 'Patience', he said, 'will overcome all things.'

Davenport continues:

> When Marlborough had once laid down the plan of a battle or campaign, and fixed the goal at which he wished to arrive, he was above all discouragement, all uncertainty. He moved forward with a steady and persistent motion which seemed to crush every obstacle; if one road failed him, he calmly took another. His fertility of resource was so great, that the failure of a portion of his scheme never irritated him, because it never gave him any trouble; he at once set to work to replace it by some new and better idea. No general ever conceived more audacious enterprises; none ever studied more deliberately the means of realizing them. His daring seemed to the bystanders absolute rashness, until his signal success demonstrated that it was based on the most frigid prudence (p. 163).

Moreover,

> As success did not elate, so danger did not depress him. He was always his own master: self-possessed, self-reliant, self-controlled (p. 164).

But above all, Marlborough was a past master of attacking the minds and morale of his opponents, from generals to front line troops, and thereby inducing in them the canker of defeatism by which he began to win his battles, strategically, before a single shot had been fired.

William Makepeace Thackeray (1811-63), who called Marlborough 'the very Genius of Victory', gave an account of his psychological strategy in Chapter 12 of *Henry Esmond* (1852), which Davenport quotes (pp. 186-7):

> I think it was more from conviction than policy, though that policy was surely the most prudent in the world, that the great duke always spoke of his victories with extraordinary modesty, and as if it was not so much his own admirable genius and courage which achieved those amazing successes; but as if he was a special and fatal instrument in the hands of Providence, that willed irresistibly the enemy's overthrow. . . . All the letters which he wrote after his battles show awe rather than exultation; and he attributes the glory of these achievements . . . to the superintending protection of heaven, which he ever seemed to think was an especial ally. And our

army got to believe so, and the enemy learned to think so too; for we never entered into a battle without a perfect confidence that it was to end in victory; nor did the French, after the issue of Blenheim, and that astonishing triumph of Ramillies, ever meet us without feeling that the game was lost before it was begun to be played, and that our general's fortune was irresistible.

Invincibility depends on one's self; the enemy's vulnerability on him.

Sun Tzu: *The Art of War* (*c.* 400-320 BCE)

6.6   Fortune favors the brave

Dan Pitzer of the Green Berets was a prisoner of the Viet Cong in the U Minh Forest from October 1963 to November 1967. As he recounts in Al Santoli's *To Bear Any Burden* (1986, pp. 89-97):

> They kept me in a bamboo cage all those years, four feet wide, six feet long, just big enough to sit up in. I never gave up hope unless I was extremely ill or mad within myself . . .

Disease aside, survival was a matter of mental attitude:

> When I think about all the guys that died in captivity and the guys that lived, it was a difference of just two words: 'if' and 'when'. A guy saying, 'If I go home' or 'If I'm released' – he's buried. But those who said, 'When I go home' or 'When I escape' or 'When the war is over' – we survived.

The Viet Cong techniques were both physical and psychological:

> The levers the VC used on us were food deprivation, sleep deprivation, and illness. Physical torture was to heighten the psychological pressure, intimidate. This would create a pain reflex, so whenever they would threaten you, your mind would create the previous physical trauma.

They used the term 'correctional period' for torture:

> They used these twisted semantics because 'torture' is against their 'humane and lenient policy'. They would say, 'We are not torturing

you. You are being corrected because you erred and have done this to yourself.'

There was always a fate worse than death:

> The first thing that hit me and stuck with me the whole time in captivity was what the first interrogator who spoke English said: 'You can stay here forever. This war can end tomorrow, but you can be here for the rest of your life.'

Not to yield was a matter of honor:

> Nick and I made an agreement that no matter what the VC did to us, even if we had to die, we were not going to disclose any information.

Rank was a special factor:

> The VC realized Rocky was a captain, Nick a lieutenant, and I a sergeant, so they singled him out as ranking man. Rocky stood toe to toe with them. He told them to go to hell in Vietnamese, French, and English. He got a lot of pressure and torture, but he held his path. As a West Point grad, it was Duty, Honor, Country. There was no other way. He was brutally murdered because of it.

But even in death there could be strategic victory:

> Up until the time I was released in 1967, the main interrogator, Mafia, asked me what made Rocky work. The VC could understand somebody dying for a political cause or a political god, but they couldn't understand Rocky dying for something they didn't understand. That in itself was a triumph for Rocky. He flat beat them on their own ground.

'I did get strung up once', Dan said:

> I had the great pleasure of decking a guard, whose name was Shithead. I didn't know that Nick Rowe had decked him the week before. When I hit this guy I felt that I broke his jaw. The guards came in and strung me up in the rafters outside my cage. They stripped me naked and tied ropes around my wrists and ankles. They let me hang all night. The next morning, my eyes were swollen shut from mosquito bites. They stayed shut for a whole week.

There was a psychology of survival:

You learn to live day to day. When I got up in the morning, 'If I can just make it until noon . . . Okay, now I've made it to noon. Now if I can just make it till the evening meal and then go to bed. Then it's all over with.' Sleep was an escape.

But Pitzer almost didn't make it:

When I was extremely ill, I got into a very dangerous thing – astral projection. I could separate my mind from my body. Go any place I wanted with physical sensation. I could set my mind up on top of the cage I was being held in with leg irons. I'd look down at my body and say, 'That physical wreck of skin and bone, eaten up with ringworm, doesn't belong to me.' But then my mind would say, 'But that is my main mode of transportation, so I have to get back to the filth.' At that point I really had one foot in the grave.

To conclude on the topic of both discipline and character, I repeat here a passage from the first page of the British *Field Service Regulations* for 1912:

Success in war depends more on moral than physical qualities. Skill cannot compensate for want of courage, energy, and determination; but even high moral qualities may not avail without careful preparation and skilled direction. The development of the necessary moral qualities is therefore the first of the objects to be attained; the next are organization and discipline, which enable those qualities to be controlled and used when required.

If we replace 'success in war' by 'success in life' or 'success in peace', every word of this can be read in terms of the democratic ethic and human creativity, without reference to war.

FRONTISPIECE: Advertising Guess? Inc.: Sexism: The indirect approach. Reprinted from the *New York Times*, July 13, 1986. Ad by Paul Marciano, photo by Wayne Maser. The original is in sepiatone, with black borders.

CHAPTER 7

The strategic envelopment

Strategy is the study of communication.

Wilhelm von Willisen

7.1 Thinking strategy

'Strategy is the study of communication': I know nothing about the author of that insight beyond his name. The quotation occurs in *The Seven Pillars of Wisdom* (1935) and other writings by T.E. Lawrence (1888-1935), the English archeology student who played a leading if still disputed role in the Arab Revolt against the Turks of the Ottoman Empire in 1916-18.

Led by Sherif Feisal (later King of Iraq) under his father Sherif Hussein (later King of the Hejaz), the Arab forces ranged over the desert of the Hejaz along the Red Sea coast from some hundreds of miles south of Mecca northward to Aqaba, the southern seaport of modern Jordan, then inland east of the railway in a right hook into Damascus in Syria, controlling an area about 75-100 miles wide and 1100 miles long (Map 7.1) (Barraclough, 1982, p. 125; Orgill, 1973).

Besides their successes in their own theater of war, the Arabs' hit-and-run guerrilla warfare assisted the advance from Cairo to Jerusalem and Damascus (which the Arabs reached first) of the British force of over a quarter of a million men led by General Allenby. Lawrence's force never numbered more than 3000, with a fighting core of about 600, but by 1918 it was helping to tie down some 40,000 Turks.

Lawrence had learned conversational Arabic and become familiar with the terrain of the Middle East in 1909, during a walking tour without guides through Syria and Palestine studying Crusader castles for his BA thesis at Magdalen College, Oxford. He had gained further experience of the language and people in 1910-14, when he directed

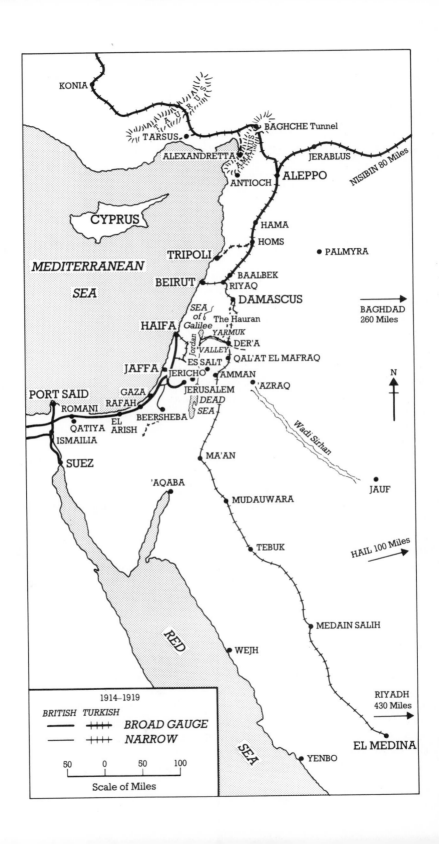

KONIA

BAGHCHE Tunnel

TARSUS

ALEXANDRETTA

JERABLUS

ANTIOCH ALEPPO

NISIBIN 80 Miles

CYPRUS

HAMA

HOMS

PALMYRA

MEDITERRANEAN
SEA

TRIPOLI

BAALBEK

BEIRUT RIYAQ

DAMASCUS

BAGHDAD
260 Miles

SEA
of
Galilee   The Hauran

HAIFA   YARMUK

DER'A

Jordan VALLEY

ES SALT   QAL'AT EL MAFRAQ

JAFFA   JERICHO

AMMAN

N

GAZA   JERUSALEM   'AZRAQ

PORT SAID

RAFAH   DEAD
ROMANI   SEA

EL   BEERSHEBA
QATIYA   ARISH

Wadi Sirhan

ISMAILIA

SUEZ   MA'AN

'AQABA   JAUF

MUDAUWARA

HAIL 100 Miles

TEBUK

MEDAIN SALIH

RED   WEJH

1914–1919

BRITISH   TURKISH

RIYADH
430 Miles

━━━   ┼┼┼┼   BROAD GAUGE

───   ┼┼┼┼   NARROW

EL MEDINA

SEA   YENBO

50   0   50   100

Scale of Miles

part of a British archeological dig at Carcemish in Mesopotamia, supervising with unusual success its 200 Arab and Kurdish laborers.

He was made world-famous after the war as Lawrence of Arabia by the films and lectures of the American war correspondent Lowell Thomas, who had met him while covering the Middle Eastern war, and who wrote a romantic book about him, *With Lawrence in Arabia*, in 1924. He owed his reputation as a strategist largely to Basil Liddell Hart, who called him 'one of the great captains' and compared him with Napoleon in a reverent biography, *Colonel Lawrence*, first published in 1934. We owe our knowledge of the impostures, exaggerations, and untruths in the words and writings of this many-sided, manipulative genius to Richard Aldington, who published a violent but well-argued, and well-documented attack on him, *Lawrence of Arabia*, in 1955. One published Arab verdict on Lawrence is *T.E. Lawrence: An Arab View* (1962) by Suleiman Mousa, who attacks his veracity and denies the importance of his role in the Revolt.

The following outline of Lawrence's strategy of guerrilla warfare is taken from his article on the lessons of Arabia published in the 14th edition of the *Encyclopedia Britannica* in 1929. Similar accounts appear in *The Seven Pillars of Wisdom* and in Liddell Hart's biography. The only doubts raised about Lawrence on this score suggest that he made the theory up after the war as part of the creation of his own legend, having arrived at the results by intuition at the time. This of course does not invalidate the theory itself.

It is not known precisely who – Arab or English – actually made the key decision on which the novelty of the new strategy hinged – the decision not to attack Medina – at the time.

Lawrence begins by distinguishing between the abilities of regular and irregular troops and their relative significance in current military theory. In keeping with the Clausewitzian theory of 'absolute' war espoused by the French General Ferdinand Foch (1851-1929):

MAP 7.1   Map to illustrate the guerrilla strategy of the Arab Revolt (1916-1918) against the Ottoman Empire in World War One. The Hejaz Railway was 'Turkey's lifeline' says Liddell Hart in *Colonel Lawrence: The Man Behind the Legend* (1934, 1935), from which the illustration is taken. Linked to Istanbul, Aleppo, Mosul, and Baghdad in the north, the railway ended at Medina, some 200 miles north of Mecca. Control by the Arab guerrillas eventually extended in a 100-mile-wide strip from several hundred miles south of Mecca along the Red Sea Coast north to the port of Aqaba, and then to the east of the railway and Jerusalem (captured by General Allenby's troops in December 1917) and on to Damascus (captured by the Arab force in September 1918). This area is now part of Saudi Arabia, Jordan, Israel, and Syria, touching on Lebanon.

military opinion was obsessed by the dictum of Foch that the ethic of modern war is to seek for the enemy's army, his center of power, and destroy it in battle. Irregulars would not attack positions and so they were regarded as incapable of forcing a decision (in Laqueur, ed., 1977, p. 127).

By blockade the Arabs had forced the Turks to abandon Mecca in 1916, only to be faced by a Turkish army corps despatched down the Hejaz railroad to its southern terminus, Medina, some 200 miles north of Mecca. When the Turkish regulars advanced from end-of-track down the main road to Mecca, the Arab forces were unable to stop them, from which Lawrence concluded that irregulars are as incapable of defending a definite point or line as they are of attacking one.

In the emergency it occurred to the author that perhaps the virtue of irregulars lay in depth, not in face, and that it had been the threat of attack by them upon the Turkish northern flank that had made the enemy hesitate so long.

The actual Turkish flank, he noted, ran some 50 miles from their front line north to Medina. But if the Arab forces moved against the Hejaz railway, they might stretch their threat to the Turks – and accordingly, stretch the Turkish flank – all the way up the line to Damascus, 800 miles to the north. Such a move would put the Turks on the defensive and allow the Arabs to regain the initiative.

As a result, in January 1917, Feisal's tribesmen simply left the Turks where they were and left for Wejh on the Red Sea coast, some 200 miles away. 'The eccentric movement acted like a charm', says Lawrence. The Turks abandoned the defense of the road to Mecca and retreated back to end-of-track at Medina, where half of the force settled down in entrenchments to guard the city and the other half began patrolling the railroad line to the north (p. 128).

The problem, Lawrence saw, was that irregulars could not endure heavy casualties. There could therefore be no Arab attack on the Turkish 'center of power', as demanded by Foch's strategy of concentrated force. But the Arabs were in fact winning the war. They were in occupation of practically every square mile of the Hejaz, while the Turks were clustered in Medina and along their line of communication, the railroad. Lawrence had arrived at the question whose answer would define the new Arab strategy, the strategy of the 'indirect approach' or 'strategic envelopment' (7.5), by which the irregular force would not simply outflank the Turks, but outflank the Turkish strategy: 'So why bother about attacking Medina?'

The Arab aim was to occupy all Arabic-speaking lands in Asia. Turks might be killed, but killing Turks was incidental to the Arabs' political goals. If the Turks would leave the Arab lands quietly, then the war would end. If they would not, then they would have to be driven out – but still with the least possible Arab losses, 'since the Arabs were fighting for freedom, a pleasure only to be tasted by a man alive' (p. 129).

Lawrence divided the problem into three factors:

> the mathematical or algebraical: space and time, inorganic things like hills, climates, and railways, and the mechanical aids of technology: the non-human factors;
> the biological: life and death, wear and tear, the human element;
> the psychological: the minds of the Arabs, the Turkish troops, the Turks at home, the Germans advising the Turks (General Liman von Sanders tried in vain to get the Turks to withdraw from Medina), and the neutrals looking on (7.5).

In the Arab case the algebraic factor was the area to be conquered – some 140,000 square miles. There follows one of the passages most often cited from Lawrence:

> How would the Turks defend all that – no doubt by a trench line across the bottom, if the Arabs were advancing with banners displayed . . . but suppose they were an influence, a thing invulnerable, intangible, without front or back, drifting about like a gas? Armies are like plants, immobile as a whole, firm-rooted, nourished through long stems to the head. The Arabs might be a vapor, blowing where they listed. It seemed that a regular soldier might be helpless without a target.

The Turk would believe that the rebellion was absolute, like Napoleonic warfare, and make the mistake of treating it so (p. 130).

(In 1967 a US Congressman interrogating a high-ranking military officer about the seemingly endless war in Vietnam was assured that the US had enough equipment, enough planes, enough guns and ammunition. 'So why can't you whip that little country of North Vietnam?' 'Targets-targets', came the reply.)

The vapor metaphor in the passage just quoted is an extended echo of Clausewitz on the strategy of people's war – here he drops his insistence on the 'absolute' nature of war – in Book 6, Chapter 26 of *On War*, 'Arming the Nation':

> According to our idea of a people's war, [the people's army] should, like a kind of nebulous vapory essence, nowhere condense into a solid body; otherwise the enemy sends an adequate force against this core, crushes it and takes a great many prisoners; then courage

sinks; everyone thinks the main question is decided, any further effort is useless and the weapons fall from the people's hands.

However, he adds,

> on the other hand it is necessary that this mist should gather at some points into denser masses and form threatening clouds from which now and again a formidable flash of lightning may burst forth. These points are chiefly on the flanks of the enemy's theater of war . . .

The second factor, the biological, says Lawrence, is 'humanity in battle, an art touching every side of our corporal being'. This is the human variable, sensitive and illogical, prone to accident, against which generals guarded themselves by the device of a reserve, 'the significant medium of their art'.

But to limit the art to humanity seemed too narrow. Why not materials as well? In the Turkish Army men were plentiful but materials were scarce: 'The death of a Turkish bridge or rail, machine or gun, or high explosive was more profitable than the death of a Turk' (p. 131). In contrast, in the Arab forces material was plentiful – they were supplied by air, land, and sea by the British in Cairo – but men were scarce. Foch had laid down the maxim, applying it to men, of being superior at the critical point and moment of attack. The Arabs might apply it to materials and be superior in equipment in one dominant moment or respect.

> For both men and things [one] might try to give Foch's doctrine a negative, twisted side, for cheapness' sake, and be weaker than the enemy except in one point or matter.

Moreover:

> Most wars are wars of contact, both forces striving to keep in touch to avoid tactical surprise. The Arab war should be a war of detachment: to contain the enemy by the silent threat of a vast unknown desert, not disclosing themselves till the moment of attack.

The attack would not be against the enemy's main strength or weakness, but against his most accessible material, the Hejaz railway. This would ensure tactical success.

> From this theory came to be developed ultimately an unconscious habit of never engaging the enemy at all.

(Along with train and railway wrecking there were of course many Arab engagements with the Turks, some of which turned into no-quarter beserker blood lust – Arab massacres of Turkish prisoners. Apart from killing and raping Arab civilians, the usual Turkish policy with Arab prisoners was to torture them to death.)

Many Turks on the Arab front never had the chance to fire a shot – no targets – and thus the Arabs were never on the defensive, except by accident. This required them 'to obtain perfect intelligence', so that plans could be made in complete certainty, for there was no room for chance. 'The headquarters of the Arab army probably took more pains in this service than any other staff' (pp. 131-2).

The third factor was the psychological:

It concerns the crowd, the adjustment of spirit to the point where it becomes fit to exploit in action. . . . The command of the Arab army had to arrange their men's minds in order of battle, just as carefully and formally as other officers arranged their bodies: and not only their own men's minds, though them first; the minds of the enemy, so far as it could reach them; and thirdly, the mind of the nation supporting it behind the firing line, and the mind of the hostile nation [Germany] waiting the verdict, and the neutrals looking on.

It was the ethical in war and the process on which the command mainly depended for victory on the Arab front (p. 132).

Let the enemy stay in Medina, therefore, and in every other harmless place, in the largest numbers. If they tried to withdraw then the Arabs should restore their confidence by feigning defeat. The ideal was to keep the railway just working, only just, with a maximum of loss and discomfort to Turkish officers and rank and file (p. 133).

The Turkish army was an accident, not a target. Our true strategic aim was to seek its weakest link, and bear only on that till time made the mass of it fall. The Arab army must impose the longest possible passive defense on the Turks (this being the most materially expensive form of war) by extending its own front to a maximum. Tactically it must develop a highly mobile, highly equipped type of force, of the smallest size, and use it successively at distributed points of the Turkish line, to make the Turks reinforce their occupying posts beyond the economic minimum of twenty men.

The power of this Arab striking force was not therefore to be reckoned merely by its strength. It was the ratio between the number of troops available and the area to be covered or occupied that mainly constrained the character of the war. But because they had five times the mobility of the Turks, the Arabs could meet them on equal terms with only one-fifth the number of men.

The contest was not physical, but moral, and so battles were a mistake. . . . The Arabs had nothing material to lose, so they were to defend nothing and to shoot nothing. Their cards were speed and time, not hitting power, and this gave them strategical rather than tactical strength. Range is more to strategy than force (pp.-133-4).

The tactics were thus to be hit and run, 'not pushes but strokes'. The necessary speed and range were secured by the frugality of the desert men and their efficiency on camels, which even in the heat of summer could cover as much as two hundred and fifty miles, or three days march, between drinks. Technically, apart from explosives, the major requirement for the raiding force would be light machine guns used as automatic rifles. In the process the orthodox principle of the concentration of force would be replaced by the irregular principle of the distribution of force, keeping the greatest number of raids on hand at once, and adding fluidity to speed by using men from one district on Monday, from another on Tuesday, from a third on Wednesday, and so on (pp. 135-6).

The Arab army had no discipline in the ordinary sense of barracks-discipline, which sacrifices individual capacity and efficiency to the lowest common denominator, making men into mere types, so as to reduce the uncertainty of the human element.

The Arab fighter was self-contained. 'The moral strain of isolated action makes this simple form of war very hard on the individual soldier, and exacts from him special initiative, endurance, and enthusiasm.' One depends on quality, not quantity: 'Guerrilla war is far more intellectual than a bayonet charge' (p. 137).

(Here Lawrence illustrates the sense and need of the democratic principle of 'Everyone a strategist'. Since one may often find oneself facing an emergency alone, one must be as capable as possible of making any decision at any level of abstraction or action.)

Here is the thesis, Lawrence writes:

> Rebellion must have an unassailable base, something guarded not merely from attack, but from the fear of it: such a base as the Arab revolt had in the Red Sea ports, the desert, or *in the minds of men converted to its creed*. It must have a sophisticated alien enemy in the form of a [negatively] disciplined army of occupation too small to fulfill the doctrine of acreage: too few to adjust number to space, in order to dominate the whole area effectively from fortified posts (p. 138, emphasis added).

It must have at least a passively friendly population that will not betray rebel movements to the enemy: Rebellions can be 2 per cent active in the striking force and 98 per cent passively sympathetic.

The few active rebels must have the qualities of speed and
endurance, ubiquity and independence of arteries of supply. They
must have the technical equipment to destroy or paralyze the
enemy's organized communications, for irregular war is fairly
Wilhelm von Willisen's definition of strategy, 'the study of communication', in its extreme degree, of attack where the enemy is not.

And finally:

In fifty words: Granted mobility, security (in the form of denying
targets to the enemy), time and doctrine (the idea to convert every
subject to friendliness), victory will rest with the insurgents, for the
algebraical factors are in the end decisive, and against them
[Turkish] perfections of means and spirit struggle quite in vain.

Or in other words, granted the guerrilla strategy and mobility and the
support of the population, as in Vietnam, in the 10,000 day war
(1945-75), the inability of the enemy to control territory and people
with the troops available is ultimately decisive.

War admittedly has its own grammar, but not its own logic.
Carl von Clausewitz: *On War* (1832)

7.2 The seven classic manoeuvres

Imagine once again that in spite of the terminology we are not dealing
with warfare but with the strategy of everyday life. As the quotation
from Clausewitz tells us, the logic of strategy is not confined to the
grammar of war.

War is not a language, but it is a system of communication. Seen in
terms of pattern, topology, and structure, the basic manoeuvres are
not confined to warfare, nor are their objectives confined to military
attacks on those whose conduct has defined them as enemies.

Any of the seven classic manoeuvres may be employed alone or in
combination with others, and each of them may be strategical or
tactical depending on the context. In the following outline, taken from
David Chandler's lucid account in *The Art of Warfare on Land*
(1974), each is treated as a tactical manoeuvre in a particular
situation. I have retained his use of the masculine pronoun.

In what follows the singular embraces the collective.

1 *Penetration of the centre* This is probably the oldest tactical
manoeuvre, originally consisting of an advance to contact followed by

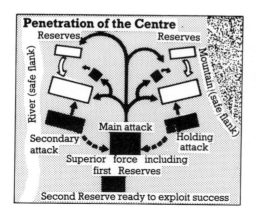

FIGURE 7.1

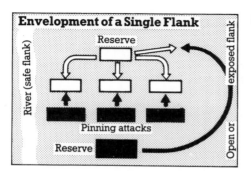

FIGURE 7.2

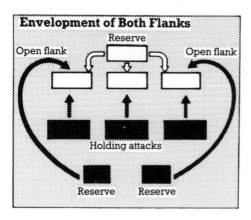

FIGURE 7.3

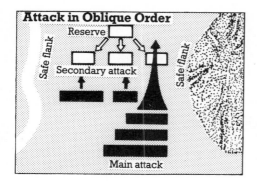

FIGURE 7.4

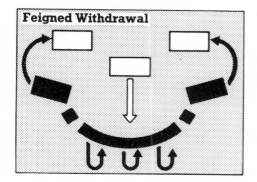

FIGURE 7.5

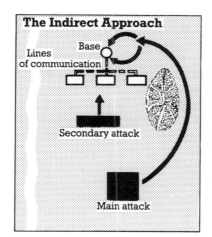

FIGURE 7.6

Reprinted from David Chandler: *The Art of Warfare on Land* (1974).

a mass of individual fights. Eventually some commander must have realized the importance of a reserve, using it to smash through the center of the opponent's tiring battle line, destroying its cohesion and thus its power to continue fighting (Figure 7.1). Marlborough was a past-master at the use of this gambit, e.g. at Blenheim (1704) and Ramillies (1706).

The shock of an attack of this kind is both matter-energy and information, as Lynn Montross (1974) points out:

> Shock effect [in battle] is rarely the product of an actual physical impact. The shock is communicated to the soldier's mind rather than his body. . . . [The defeated troops] are beaten because of their conviction that further resistance is hopeless, and it is the business of the tactician to convince rather than crush his opponents.

The advantage of this manoeuvre is that a successful penetration may make it possible to encircle large parts of the broken army or to continue onwards and attack its bases (see 7.7 below). The disadvantages are a possibly excessive weakening of the flanks or a break-*in* that does not lead to a break-*through*, making it possible for the defenders to cut off the salient or bulge formed by the attackers and surround them instead.

2 *Envelopment of a single flank* Here the skillful general would pin the enemy's attention by frontal attacks with infantry and then suddenly unleash his mounted forces in a mad dash to turn one or the other extremity of the enemy's line and if possible to threaten his rear as well (Figure 7.2). When successful this manoeuvre may enable the attack to roll up the hostile battle line from one end towards the center, creating a growing chaos in the process.

The advantage of this manoeuvre is that it may totally disrupt the opponent as the flank attack threatens his line of retreat, and permit the attacker to envelop a part of the opponent's army. Its danger is the possibly excessive weakening of the center to build up sufficient strength on the flank. At Austerlitz in 1805, as a result of weakening their center in an attempt to strike a decisive blow at Napoleon's right flank, the Russians and Austrians laid themselves open to a fatal counter-blow and were decisively defeated.

3 *Envelopment of both flanks* If successful, this double tactical envelopment can lead to the annihilation of the trapped opponent (Figure 7.3). At Cannae in 216 BCE Hannibal used this method to defeat with 50,000 troops a Roman army of 80,000, of whom only 10,000 lived to tell the tale. This manoeuvre was the major tactical innovation of the impis of the Zulu Empire in Africa in the nineteenth century, the two flanking forces being viewed as the horns of a bull.

To be feasible the double envelopment requires either great

superiority of numbers or quite exceptional skill in the general. The danger of this gambit is the over-extension of the attacker's resources in trying to complete the encircling ring, which may allow the foe to smash their way out and perhaps turn the tables on the attacker.

4 *Attack in oblique order* Here the commander masses steadily increasing strength against one wing of the other battle line until it breaks, using smaller forces in other sectors to attract the defender's attention and conceal the build-up, while hindering the defender's transfer of reserves to the threatened flank (Figure 7.4). Properly employed this gambit can shatter the opponent's line. The attackers run the danger of unbalancing their own forces, however, thus inviting a strong counter against their weaker sectors.

5 *The feigned withdrawal* This manoeuvre is often associated with the double envelopment. Its aim is to induce the opponent to abandon a strong position, or blunder forward into an ambush, by tempting him with the prospect of plunder and easy victory (Figure 7.5). The Normans won at Hastings with this manoeuvre. The Iranians used it to bait the trap for the strategic envelopment of the Reagan Administraion in the arms-for-hostages swaps in 1985-6.

The dangers of this gambit are considerable. Once troops begin to retreat only exceptional discipline and high morale can prevent the possibility of the withdrawal turning into a headlong and genuine flight. As Sun Tzu says:

> Apparent confusion is a product of good order; apparent cowardice, of courage; apparent weakness, of strength.

If employed by a cool general with a superb sense of timing, this manoeuvre is well-designed to surprise an opponent and throw him off balance, for its psychological effect is powerful.

6 *Attack from a defensive position* (not illustrated) Napoleon once wrote: 'The whole art of war consists in a well-reasoned and extremely circumspect defensive, followed by a rapid and audacious attack.' In adopting this method an army prepares a strong defensive position, lures the enemy into exhaustion by useless attacks against the perimeter, and then the garrison sallies forth to bring about his defeat. The English used this gambit successfully at Agincourt in 1415. The French attempted it at Dien Bien Phu in Indochina in 1954 but were defeated by General Vo Nguyen Giap and the Viet Minh and lost the war. The Americans tried the same gambit at Khe Sanh in Vietnam in 1967-8, but after testing the ground Giap did not take the bait.

This manoeuvre is often associated with the feigned withdrawal, but there are many variations. Properly employed it can lead to decisive results. But it can also lead to dangerous defensive thinking, as with the French belief in the sanctity of the fortresses of the Maginot Line, which the Germans simply outflanked in the Blitzkrieg of 1940. For this to work, the opponent must of course be induced to accept the challenge, which he may not do, or the attack may come from an unexpected direction, as when the Japanese overran the seaward-oriented fortress of Singapore from the landward side in February 1942.

7 *The indirect approach* This manoeuvre is based on absorbing the opponent's attention by means of secondary operations while the main body, or at least a major force, marches to envelop his flank and rear *strategically* (Figure 7.6). The effect is to interrupt the opponent's lines of communication and supply, cut him off from reinforcements, shake his composure, and force him to about-turn and fight a reversed front battle (where each force fights facing its own base), which if lost can lead only to disaster, as the defender has no line of retreat open to him. Speed and surprise are vital to success.

This method, with many variations, was probably the supreme example of offensive warfare down to 1945. Between 1796 and 1812 it underlay thirty of Napoleon's major manoeuvres. This gambit can be combined with others. The Germans converted their penetration of the Allied center at Sedan in 1940 into a strategic envelopment as the Panzers raced for the coast far to the rear of the front line and bottled up 330,000 British troops at Dunkirk, who escaped because Hitler did not wish to press the attack, but lost all their equipment.

The advantage of this manoeuvre is the promise of decisive results. It also forces action on an opponent unwilling to accept battle because it is too dangerous to be ignored. To be successful, however, it requires considerable superiority of force and a well-developed sense of timing. Indulged in rashly, or repetitively, it can lead to failure and catastrophe if the opponent counters the threat by taking steps to meet and thwart each outflanking attempt in turn, or maintains concealed avenues of retreat – as Colonel von Lettow-Vorbeck never failed to do in his successful guerrilla war against the British in East Africa in 1914-18 (Hoyt, 1981). Of all the manoeuvres it is the most intellectual, the most apt to application by intelligence (information) rather than force – as Iran showed the world in the American arms affair of 1986.

The conduct of war is very largely a matter of communicating true and false information, and of recognizing which is which.
Gordon Welchman: *The Hut Six Story: Breaking the Enigma Codes* (1981)

As Sun Tzu says (p. 102):

Nothing is more difficult than the art of manoeuvre. What is difficult about manoeuvre is to make the devious route the most direct and to turn misfortune to advantage . . .

'One able to do this,' he says, 'understands the strategy of the direct and the indirect'.

I knew my ground, my material and my allies. If I met fifty checks I could yet see a fifty-first way to my object.

T.E. Lawrence (1888-1935)

7.3 The indirect approach

In his Foreword to Bryan Perrett's *Lightning War* (1983, pp. 11-13), General Sir John Hackett explains the connection of *Blitzkrieg* with the indirect approach:

Lightning strikes swiftly, in unexpected places and with enormous violence. Even when the probability of a lightning strike is known to be high, its target cannot be predicted with confidence and the blow, when it falls, comes with complete and often devastating surprise.

But a lightning strike is a single instantaneous event. Consideration of the nature of *Blitzkrieg* operations suggests that this label is inappropriate:

For although these operations may be conducted with speed, violence and initial surprise, it is not through instantaneous, but in sustained action that they succeed. The duration of the operation may be relatively short . . . but it is in the unremitting maintenance or pressure during the whole of it that success lies. This is not at all the single, flashing, violent sword-stroke that the name implies.

The strategic essence of *Blitzkrieg* warfare, says Hackett, is the indirect approach. Liddell Hart's book on that subject is probably the most authoritative examination of the topic. He examines twelve wars which decisively affected European history from ancient times onwards, starting with the first 'Great War' in European history, that between the Greeks and Persians (modern Iran) in the fifth century BCE. Counting the Napoleonic Wars as one, Liddell Hart considers eighteen other major wars, up to 1914:

In these 30 conflicts there were more than 280 campaigns. In only six of these campaigns, Liddell Hart points out 'did a decisive result follow a plan of direct strategic approach to the main army of the enemy'. 'With the exception of Alexander', Liddell Hart claims, 'the most consistently successful commanders when faced by an enemy in a position that was strong naturally or materially, have hardly ever tackled it in a direct way. And when, under pressure of circumstances, they have risked a direct attack, the result has commonly been to blot their record with a failure'.

His enquiry leads him to two final conclusions:

'The first is that, in face of the overwhelming evidence of history, no general is justified in launching his troops to a direct attack upon an enemy firmly in position. The second, that instead of seeking to upset the enemy's equilibrium by one's attack, it must be upset before a real attack is, or can be, successfully launched'.

In *Blitzkrieg*, says Hackett, meaning

the application of the principles of the indirect approach through . . . the most appropriate tactical methods, the destruction of the enemy's equilibrium, both physically and psychologically, forms the essential basis of success. The attack itself, launched swiftly, violently, with maximum surprise and sustained with great speed and destructive force, is built upon it.

Hackett concludes:

Tactically the *Blitz* method demands the swift exploitation of successes achieved in deep penetration between, or round, main centres of resistance, which are left for later reduction by follow-up forces. This is just the reverse of the practice to which so much of the appalling slaughter on the Western Front in World War I was due – the committing in the attack of the strongest forces against the enemy's strongest defensive positions.

The basic principle of *Blitzkrieg*

is to seek out for attack the points where the enemy is weakest and least expecting to be attacked; then, having broken in to secure a foothold, to pour in whatever can be found to develop, out of the break-in, a break-through. Liddell Hart, in analysing the theory after World War I, used to apply the descriptive term 'expanding torrent' to indicate the nature of the follow-through.

The metaphor of the 'expanding torrent' might have been taken directly from Sun Tzu.

7.4 Principles of action

Underlying the successful use of strategy and tactics and manoeuvre are the following principles of action. One seeks to seize the initiative so as to place the opponents, as soon as possible, in a situation as unfavorable as possible; to define the context so as to oblige them to respond to one's own initiatives rather than initiate their own; to employ strategic manoeuvre – such as the rapid movement of forces from one sector or front to another – so as to be as nearly as possible ensured of a favorable outcome before the contest begins; to employ tactical manoeuvre where its mobility is necessary to offset the greater numbers or other advantages of the opponent; to avail oneself of surprise and everything associated with it – surprise is perhaps the most effective of all the moral factors in war, says Colonel T.N. Dupuy, US Army, Ret., in *The Evolution of Weapons and Warfare* (1980, pp. 161-5), and the 'greatest multiplier' of all (the other is skill: both Wellington and Blücher said of Napoleon that his presence on the battlefield was worth 40,000 men); to try to imagine every possible manoeuvre or response of the opponents by reconnaissance, intelligence, and putting oneself in their shoes; to remain mobile and capable of improvisation; to remain cool, calm, and collected, patiently restraining any tendencies to gamble or indulge in recklessness; to keep the opponents guessing, worried, off-balance, and feeling hoodwinked or strategically inferior; to project an image of invulnerability; and not to repeat oneself or betray one's strategies by revealing or repeating a fixed pattern. One would also add: to seek and obtain the best from friends and allies, remembering that one does not have to love one's allies to enjoy the benefits of mutual aid.

Sun Tzu's 2300-year-old outline of the principles of action in warfare is characteristically succinct. The following direct quotation summarizes the hierarchy of the principles of offensive strategy given in Chapter 3 of *The Art of War* (pp. 77-84), along with the more significant remarks of Sun Tzu's commentators:

1 Generally in war the best policy is to take a state intact; to ruin it is inferior to this.
Li Ch'üan: Do not put a premium on killing.
2 To capture the enemy's army is better than to destroy it; to take intact a battalion, a company or a five-man squad is better than to destroy them.
3 For to win one hundred victories in one hundred battles is not the

acme of skill. To subdue the enemy without fighting is the acme of
skill.

4 Thus, what is of supreme importance in war is to attack the
enemy's strategy.

Tu Mu: The Grand Duke said: 'He who excels at resolving
difficulties does so before they arise' . . .

5 Next best is to disrupt his alliances.

Tu Yu: Do not allow your enemies to get together . . .

6 The next best is to attack his army . . .

7 The worst policy is to attack cities. Attack cities [i.e. fortified
places] only when there is no alternative . . .

9 If the general is unable to control his impatience and orders his
troops to swarm up the wall like ants, one-third of them will be
killed without taking the city. Such is the calamity of these
attacks . . .

10 Thus, those skilled in war subdue the enemy's army without
battle. They capture his cities without assaulting them and
overthrow his state without protracted operations.

Li Ch'üan: They conquer by strategy . . . [During the siege of the
'Yao' rebels at Yüan Wu] the King of Tung Hai spoke to Tsang
Kung, saying 'Now you have massed troops and encircled the
enemy, who is determined to fight to the death. This is no strategy!
You should lift the siege. Let them know that an escape route is
open and they will flee and disperse. Then any village constable will
be able to capture them!' Tsang Kung followed his advice and took
Yüan Wu.

In the chapter on manoeuvre Sun Tzu makes his meaning more
precise (pp. 109-10):

28 Do not attack his elite troops.

29 Do not gobble profferred baits . . .

30 Do not thwart an enemy returning homewards.

31 To a surrounded enemy you must leave a way of escape.

Tu Mu: Show him the way to safety, and so create an alternative to
death. Then strike . . .

32 Do not press an enemy at bay.

Tu Mu: Prince Ch'ai said: 'Wild beasts, when at bay, fight
desperately. How much more is this true of men! If they know there
is no alternative they will fight to the death' . . .

Returning to offensive strategy, Sun Tzu says (p. 79):

Your aim must be to take All-under-Heaven intact. Thus your

troops are not worn out and your gains will be complete. This is the art of offensive strategy . . .

Therefore I say: 'Know your enemy and know yourself and you can fight a hundred battles without disaster' (p. 84).

Again:

Know the enemy, know yourself; your victory will never be endangered. Know the ground, know the weather; your victory will then be total (p. 129).

Everyone educated as a strategist and serving their own best interest will follow the humanistic precepts of Sun Tzu. Strategists brought up on Sun Tzu meeting in conflict will never go to war. They will adopt win-win strategies and negotiate, both demonstrating their mastery of the art of strategy by winning without fighting at all.

Subtle and insubstantial, the expert leaves no trace; divinely mysterious, he is inaudible. Thus he is master of his enemy's fate.
                              Sun Tzu: *The Art of War* (400-320 BCE)

7.5   The strategic envelopment

Among the classical manoeuvres the seventh, the indirect approach or strategic envelopment, developed to near perfection by Napoleon, is not of the same logical type, or level of communication and reality, as the others. In classical warfare the indirect approach forces on the opponent a radical shift in battle strategy. In modern war, where the indirect approach has become the basis of revolutionary and guerrilla war waged offensively, it forces on the opponent a radical shift in grand strategy, for offensive guerrilla warfare is not simply a new strategy but a new kind of war entirely (Chandler, 1974).

Napoleon called guerrilla warfare 'A war without a front', like Mao's well-worn definition of the guerrilla fighter as 'a fish in the sea', and Che Guevara's remark that the freedom fighter aims to be 'everywhere but nowhere' at the same time. Or as Sun Tzu puts it: 'The ultimate in disposing one's troops is to be without discernable shape' (p. 100).

Before 1945, with the exception of the Arab Revolt, most if not all guerrilla warfare was employed defensively as a last resort in a regular war, as the Spanish did against the French in the Peninsular War

(1808-14), as the Boers did against the British in South Africa (1900-02), and as Russian, Yugoslav, and other partisans did against the Germans and their collaborators in World War Two.

Offensive guerrilla war is another matter, says Chandler:

> Part of its originality lies in the relative unimportance of conventional military success. The revolutionary cause, indeed, may even be able to absorb conventional military defeat and still emerge as the ultimate political winner.

The political aim is twofold:

> to persuade the uninvolved part of the population to support the guerrilla programme; and to convince the third-world nations and the liberal elements within the power whose influence is under attack, that right and justice, as well as convenience, lie in recognition of the new regime.

The principal target of the guerrillas is not the colonizer's military forces, but their morale and the morale and staying power of their home population and government. What Chandler calls 'the Third World War' is being fought 'on the psychological and political planes', not simply on the military one. 'The French army won the war in Algeria [1954-62], but French power collapsed soon afterwards. The British defeated the Mau Mau in Kenya [1948-60], but victory served only to hasten the granting of independence' (p. 20). The successful anti-colonial wars in Indochina, Indonesia, Tunisia, Vietnam, Angola, Mozambique, Aden, and Zimbabwe are other examples.

Successful guerrilla war – and guerrillas are not to be confused with bandits, mercenaries, dirty tricksters, *agents provocateurs*, or special service units operating in disguise – is the prime example of the power of ideological commitment, strict discipline, and strategic flexibility over superior technology, industrial might, machine mobility, massive firepower, tactical air support, and strategic command of the air.

Chandler concludes:

> An eighth manoeuvre of war – one that favours the physically weak (but strongly motivated) group over the physically stronger but less inspired conventional power – may therefore be justly recognized.

That at least was his view in 1974. In his later *Atlas of Military Strategy* (1980), Chandler summarizes the seven classical manoeuvres but makes no mention of the eighth.

The indirect approach of the eighth manoeuvre is much more than a mere physical act. As Brigadier General Samuel B. Griffith remarks in the introduction to his translation of Sun Tzu (p. 39): 'Sun Tzu believed that the moral strength and intellectual faculty of man [are] decisive in war.'

> His primary target is the mind of the opposing commander; the victorious situation, a product of his creative imagination. Sun Tzu realized that an indispensable preliminary to battle was to attack the mind of the enemy (pp. 41-2).

'Shape him', says Sun Tzu.

In 'shaping' the opposition one seizes the initiative, attacks the opponent's strategy, and obliges him to manoeuvre within the unfavorable strategic context thus created. But that is not all, says Sun Tzu, for there is a still greater subtlety to be sought after (p. 139): shaping him while letting him think he is shaping you:

> The crux of military operations lies in the pretence of accommodating one's self to the designs of the enemy.

This was the essence of Iran's startlingly successful strategic envelopment of the Reagan Administration's strategy in the arms affair of 1985-86.

When there is no alternative to war, says Sun Tzu, the following principles apply:

FIGURE 7.7 Sun Tzu, author of the Chinese classic, *The Art of War* (4th century BCE), depicted on a cigarette card from the series 'China's Famous Warriors', first issued in Wills' Pirate Cigarettes (overseas markets) in 1911 (actual size). The flag in his hand bears the character for 'command'.

All warfare is based on deception [of the opponent].
Therefore, when capable, feign incapacity; when active, in-
activity.
When near, make it appear that you are far away; when far
away, that you are near.
Offer the enemy a bait to lure him; feign disorder and strike
him . . .
When he concentrates, prepare against him; where he is strong,
avoid him.
Anger his general and confuse him . . .
Pretend inferiority and encourage his arrogance . . .
Keep him under strain and wear him down . . .
When he is united, divide him . . .
Attack where he is unprepared; sally out when he does not
expect you . . .
These are the strategist's keys to victory.

Thus although attacking the minds of one's opponents may not
necessarily involve the strategic envelopment of their forces, it always
involves the strategic envelopment of their strategy.

The power that makes the trigger-finger hesitate, or obey, is more
        powerful than armed force.
It controls it.
The power is the Power of the Word.
The Word of Persuasion – the Word of Command.
Words are weapons.
We must not despise words and the use of words.
Words win wars.

John Hargrave: *Words Win Wars* (1940)

7.6   Guerrilla strategy

The system we live in is at war with itself. Its dominant parts divide
and rule the rest by means of every kind of war, using every kind of
weapon, including the stuff of life itself. People are pitted against
people, religion against religion, class against class, race against race,
family against family, adult against child, man against woman. We are
at war with nature too, and any society that competes with nature is
doomed to complete and devastating defeat.

   Like revolutions in ideas, revolutions in society do not come about
until they are called for, until conditions make them necessary.

Revolutions are radical changes in the basic structure and grand strategy – the basic aims and values – of a dominant science, philosophy of life, society, or economic system. They are successful solutions to insoluble conflicts generated by the system they overthrow.

Whether measured in moments ($E = mc^2$), or spread over centuries (the capitalist revolution beginning with the sixteenth-century Age of Discovery), revolutions are the processes by which solutions impossible in one system are discovered by transforming it into another one. The system survives, not by staying the same, but by a radical transformation, a radical change in structure.

If a way of thinking and being does not in fact subvert the grand strategy – the real goals – of the dominant ways of thinking and being it is in conflict with, then by the same definition it is not a revolution, but a rearrangement.

A revolution is a strategic envelopment of the system in which it arises. In a tactical envelopment, as we have seen, one outflanks and surrounds parts of the system, but not the whole. In a strategic envelopment, your normal or *cheng* forces hold the opponents' attention, while your special or *ch'i* forces cut between the opponents and their base. You cut into the very roots of the dominating system, you break through its established lines of communication and supply, you capture its base.

By capturing the base of the dominating system, I mean gaining command of its basic imagery and ideas, and recognizing what they stand for, when it is a question of imagery and ideas, and gaining political and economic control over our own resources – our own defenses – when it is a question of society.

Here, as elsewhere, honesty is the best policy; quality, the best argument; diversity, the best method; example, the best teacher; and reality, the best proof.

In 1931, in *The European Revolutions*, the historian Eugene Rosenstock-Huessy (1888-1973), using the masculine gender, put it this way (he is discussing the Russian Revolution, the French Revolution, and the Reformation):

> Revolution . . . implies the speaking of a previously unheard of language. . . . the emergence of another kind of logic, operations with other proofs . . . Each major revolution has used another style of argument, a way of thinking which pre-revolutionary men simply could not conceive nor understand. Men might hear with their ears, but there could be no meeting of minds between [French President] Poincaré and Lenin, Burke and Robespierre, Henry V and Luther. Once men begin to talk according to the new syntax of a major revolution, a rupture of meaning has occurred; and the old and the

new type of man appear insane to each other.

That is why, in such epochs, times are truly out of joint. Brothers, friends, colleagues, who shared a common education, suddenly rise up against each other and understand each other no more. They can no longer deal as man to man: the old are for the new corpses, ripe to rot; and to the old, the new appear as madmen. Both are indignant. The old Adam is inwardly beside himself with rage about this new madness. The revolutionist lifts his sword because he lives outside this dead world and considers it good riddance.

. . . The result is a revaluation of all values. The men who have not been revolutionized, and those who have, live in opposite [i.e. contradictory] universes of values, and, therefore, do not seem human to each other. . . .

No epoch of revolution ends with the complete erasure of the old type of man, but rather with a new reunion . . . a symbiosis of the old natural ethnic traditions with the spiritualized carriers of the revolution. Instead of the mutual war of annihilation there follows . . . the labor of education . . . the test of everyday life.

The passage is quoted by Karl W. Deutsch in *Nationalism and Social Communication* (1953, 1966, pp. 290-1).

In *The War of the Flea* (1965), Richard Taber calls guerrilla warfare 'the strategy of contradictions' (p. 16). It is the manipulation of the contradictions of colonization, no longer in the interests of the colonizer, but in the interests of the colonized – who must liberate themselves from the mental and physical acting out in their daily tactics of the strategy of domination and destruction imposed on them by the power of the colonizer to manipulate and undermine their self-esteem, their pride in their heritage, their respect for their peers, their trust in each other, and their belief in the real possibility of change.

One begins to think about the unthinkable, and this is critically important. As Saul Alinsky (1909-72) said in *Rules for Radicals* in 1971 (p. 105):

The issue that is not clear to organizers, missionaries, educators, or any outsider, is simply that if people feel they don't have the power to change a bad situation, *then they do not think about it.*

The *will to revolt*, says Taber, seems to express

a newly awakened consciousness, not of [political] 'causes' but of *potentiality*. It is a spreading awareness of the possibilities of human existence, coupled with the growing sense of the *causal* nature of the universe, that together inspire, first in individuals, then in communities and entire nations, *an entirely new attitude to life* (pp. 18-19).

The will to revolt, says Taber, is allied with the conviction that radical change is actually possible, that individuals (including oneself) can actually make a difference, from which there arises the *will to act*. This describes the state of mind of the modern insurgent, 'whatever his slogans or his cause':

> his secret weapon, above and beyond any question of strategy or tactics or techniques of irregular warfare, is nothing more than *the ability to inspire this state of mind in others* (p. 19).

The primary effort of the guerrilla, therefore, 'is to militate the population, without whose consent no government can stand for a day'.
Moreover:

> The guerrilla fighter is primarily a propagandist, an agitator, a disseminator of the revolutionary idea, who uses the struggle itself – the actual physical conflict – as an instrument [or medium] of agitation (p. 23).

As a result the guerrilla's mere survival is already a political victory.

> The object of the guerrilla is not to win battles, but to avoid defeat, not to end the war, but to prolong it, until political victory, more important than any battlefield victory has been won (p. 130).

Success must invariably depend on constant and careful reconnaissance, the best sources of the best information, and the ability to tell good information from bad. It depends also on the way one uses what one has, for above all:

> Revolutionary propaganda must be essentially *true* in order to be believed. . . . A high degree of selfless dedication and high purpose is required. . . . Insurgency is thus not a matter of manipulation but of inspiration (p. 138).

And finally:

> To be successful, the guerrilla must be loved and admired.

– and be armed with an unfailing sense of humor.
As it happens the punch line of a joke is not unlike a strategic

envelopment of the text leading up to it, for both strategy and jokes are dialectical operations. Just as a strategic envelopment creates a new context that changes the meaning of our original dispositions, making us act, so also does a punch line create a new context that changes the meaning of the original text, making us laugh:

> For twenty years Mr Sokoloff had been eating at the same restaurant on Second Avenue. On this night, as on every other, Mr Sokoloff ordered chicken soup. The waiter set it down and started off. Mr Sokoloff called 'Waiter!'
> 'Yeah?'
> 'Please taste this soup.'
> The waiter said, '*Hanh*?' Twenty years you've been eating the chicken soup here, no? Have you ever had a bad plate – '
> 'Waiter', said Sokoloff firmly, 'taste the soup.'
> 'Sokoloff, what's the *matter* with you?'
> 'Taste the *soup!*'
> 'All right, all right', grimaced the waiter.
> 'I'll taste – where's the spoon?'
> 'Aha!' cried Sokoloff.

The story is from Leo Rosten's *Joys of Yiddish* (1968). Like the dialectic, the joke is discontinuous and irreversible (Wilden, 1987, pp. 246-50, 271-8) (for a catastrophe theory model of the joke process, see Paulos, 1980).

> In my opinion the partisan is of all leaders in war the most justified in tempting fate and, by trusting to his own eye and talent for making snap decisions, in thumbing his nose at the sacred rules constructed on mathematical principles. . . . Let him develop his military gifts to the highest degree and, above all, let him acquire that *attentiveness* which allows us to exploit the present moment to the full and enables us to learn more from practical life than from books.
>
> Georg Wilhelm Freiherr von Valentini:
> *A Treatise on the Small War and the Employment of Light Troops*
> (Berlin, 1799)

7.7   Respect, love, zeal, and vigilance

'Partisan' is the early term for 'guerrilla' (from the Spanish for 'small war'). As quoted by Walter Laqueur in his indispensable *Guerrilla Reader* (1977, pp. 86-7), the Polish strategist Karol Stolzman wrote in 1844:

[Guerrilla] war gives rise to countless reasons for solidarity between one province and another, one district and another, and one man and another. It leaves room for personal talent, arouses the nation from its lethargy, and both cultivates and channels a feeling of independence, . . . It helps . . . to bring out the most talented among the masses, those who desire to throw off as soon as possible their shameful shackles . . . Guerrilla warfare causes minds to adapt themselves to independence and to an active and heroic life . . .

The center of guerrilla warfare is everywhere, says Stolzman, its range of activity is unlimited.

In 1759 a book appeared in Holland on 'the art of waging little wars', written by a certain De Jeney, a man about whom little is known beyond the fact that he served in the French Army of the Rhine. *Le partisan ou l'art de faire la petite guerre* (excerpted in Laqueur, 1977, pp. 19-20) is the first systematic treatise on guerrilla war. De Jeney lists the qualities required of the guerrilla:

A good partisan should possess:
1 An imagination fertile in schemes, ruses, and resource.
2 A shrewd intelligence, to orchestrate every incident in an action.
3 A fearless heart in the face of all apparent danger.
4 A steady countenance, always unmoved by any token of anxiety.
5 An apt memory, to speak to all by name.
6 An alert, sturdy, and tireless constitution, to endure all and inspire all.
7 A rapid and accurate glance, to grasp immediately the defects and advantages, obstacles and risks presented by a terrain, or by anything it scans.
8 Sentiments that will engage the respect, confidence, and affection of the whole corps. . . .

Besides this, the partisan must know Latin, German, and French so as to make his meaning clear when he may meet men of all nations. He should have a perfect knowledge of military practice, chiefly that of light troops, and not forget that of the enemy. He should possess the most exact map of the theater of war, examine it well, and master it thoroughly. It will be highly advantageous to him to keep some able geographers under his orders who can draw up correct plans of the armies' routes, their camps, and all places to be reconnoitered. . . .

Nor should he be at all parsimonious, if he can thereby obtain from able spies sure information of the enemy's line of march, his forces, his intentions, and his position. All such disclosures will enable him to serve his general to great advantage; they will be of incalculable benefit to the army's security and to his own corps' standing, good fortune, and glory.

His own interest and honor also require that he should retain a secretary to draw up the diary of his campaign. In it, he will cause to be set down all orders received and given, as in general all his troop's actions and marches; so that he may always be in a position to account for his conduct and justify himself when attacked by criticism, which never spares partisans.

As a leader, he owes to his troop the example of blameless conduct, entirely commensurate with the care and affection of a father for his children. He will thereby inspire them all with respect, love, zeal, and vigilance, and will win all hearts to his service.

I leave the final word to General Chu Teh (b. 1886) and the Fifteen Rules of Discipline he drew up in 1928, when his peasant guerrillas were fighting the Nationalist troops of General Chiang Kai-shek and the warlords, in the uprising whose failure led to the formation of the famous 4th Red Army and a 22-year-long partnership between Chu Teh and Mao Tse-tung. I quote these rules with due allowance for the military nature of the first rule, while drawing your attention to the tenth (implicitly observed by the victors in Vietnam), for, other than Guiseppe Mazzini's rule, it is the only one of its kind I have seen:

Rules of Discipline

1 Obey orders in all your actions.
2 Do not take a single needle or piece of thread from the people.
3 Turn in everything captured.
4 Speak politely.
5 Pay fairly for what you buy.
6 Return everything you borrow.
7 Pay for anything you damage.
8 Do not hit people or swear at them.
9 Do not damage crops.
10 Do not take liberties with women.
11 Do not ill-treat prisoners.
12 Keep your eyes and ears open.
13 Know the enemy within.
14 Always guide and protect the children.
15 Always be the servant of the people.

Envoi

I have probably talked too much politics in my letters but it
should be remembered by the reader that politics is the science
which teaches the people of a country to care for each other.
William Lyon Mackenzie: *The Colonial Advocate*,
June 27, 1933

Win/Win negotiators

The following is taken from Tessa Albert Warshaw's *Winning by
Negotiation* (1980, pp. 61-8).

They move into your life with fluid ease, then stand, centered and
secure, their faces smooth, unlined by destructive emotions. . . . No
translations of their statements are necessary, no allowances
required for guile; they speak, like music, directly to the spirit. They
are authentic; what you hear, see, feel, and experience is real.

. . . They do get angry, rattled, impatient. But they know and you
know it will pass. They have fought the conventional professional
and social battles, seen the flow of blood, tossed through sleepless
nights, and decided that no prize can be worth the cost of relentless
tension and minimal joy. Survival, they have learned, depends on
other people.

But mere survival is not their objective. They want a balanced life,
the kind achieved only in community with other people, who believe
as they do that caring and nurturing are reciprocal.

. . . If they are committed to mutuality, it's not primarily because
they are charitable but because they're emphatically pragmatic.

What makes Win-Win Negotiators important, both socially and
historically, is that, in modifying their perception of what they need
to win, they have redefined what winning means. They consider not
just their own goal, but the other person's goal and the common
goal. They know that negotiating is not solely a question of how
much they will win, but *how much the loss will affect the other
person*. They have no desire to live in an unstable environment of a
few winners and a multitude of embittered losers. In short, they
don't have to have it all; what's there can be shared.

Postscript: the fourth wave

> What worse thing, after all, can you say about a system built on the cult of *success* than that it *fails*?
>
> Garry Wills: *Nixon Agonistes* (1969)

The long waves of economic life

We saw in the paradoxes of Chapter 4 the periodic oscillations of expansion and contraction in the surface structure of the ordinary short-term business cycle – the cybernetic oscillations by means of which the economic system regulates itself in relation to certain of its diverse environments (including the imaginary environment made up of what the inhabitants of the system expect the economy to do). The key relationship in this, the surface structure, the short-term survival system, is that between the rate of profit and the costs of production.

We saw also a second pattern: an exponentially increasing J-curve of growth in the capacity to produce at the level of the deep structure of the system – the system of long-range survival. This very long-term curve of positive feedback is limited only by the carrying capacity of the economic system's human and natural environments. It displays as yet no negative feedback that would bring it under control (Figure 4.1). The key relationship here is economic growth for the sake of (temporary, competitive, and irregular) stability.

There is a third pattern also – a pattern which suggests that warfare – just another kind of business – is an essential part of the business cycle under state and private capitalism. Figure P1, 'Inflation in history', provides a rapid overview of three hundred years of rising and falling prosperity and the timing of major wars from a British perspective; the American Civil War (1861-1865) and the Franco-Prussian War (1870) are not mentioned. The more detailed information in Figure P2, which is based on American data, shows the third oscillation called the Kondratieff Wave. The key relationships here are war and prosperity and war and depression.

Source for historical data: Statistics Canada (*Vancouver Sun*, June 5, 1982).

FIGURE P1   War, inflation, and prosperity: a general view. Some dates: The American War of Independence (1775-83); the Revolutionary and Napoleonic Wars (1789-1815); the Crimean War (1854-56); the Boer War (the Second South African War) (1899-1902); the First World War (1914-18); the Second World War (1939-45); the Korean War (1950-53); and the American war in Vietnam (the Second Indochina War) (1955-73). Missing from the graph are the following major wars: the American Civil War (1861-65); the Franco-Prussian War (1870); the Sino-Japanese War (1894-5); the Spanish-American War (1898); the Philippine-American War (called the 'Philippine Insurrection') (1898-1906); the six-nation punitive expedition against the Boxer Rebellion (1899-1901); the Russo-Japanese War (1904-5); the Sino-Japanese War (1932-45); the Spanish Civil War (1936-39); the First Indochina War (1946-54); and the Algerian War of Independence (1954-62).

Beginning in 1919 the Russian economist Nikolai Kondratieff (later purged by Stalin) studied and then defined a pattern of 'long waves' in economic life lasting on the average 54 years from peak to peak. His pioneering theory of the long waves was introduced to the West by the celebrated student of business-cycle theory, Joseph Schumpeter (1883-1950).

In 'The Long Waves in Economic Life' (1926), which was translated into English in *The Review of Economic Statistics* in November 1935, Kondratieff used Western wholesale and securities prices to identify two-and-a-half long waves in British, American, and French economic history. Later writers, using price data from two or more of these three countries, identified three long waves more precisely (1789-1974):

Wave 1	Wave 2	Wave 3
US and UK	UK and France	US, UK, and France
1789-1849	1849-1896	1896-1941
(60 years)	(47 years)	(45 years)

and added a fourth: 1941-2000 (59 years) (Storey and Boeckh, 1974).

Each long wave consists of a period of rising prosperity and prices followed by a period of declining prosperity and prices:

rising prosperity	declining prosperity
1 1789-1814	1814-49 (the 'hungry forties')
2 1849-73	1873-96 (the 'great depression')
3 1896-1929 (the 'gay nineties' and the 'roaring twenties')	1929-41 (the 'dirty thirties')
4 1941-1974	1974-2000 (the future)

The last period of generally rising prosperity, 1941-74, was the longest general economic boom in American history.

As the chart of US wholesale prices in Figure P2 suggests, the rising wave includes the 3- to 10-year recessions and recoveries of the short-term business cycle, but with prosperity more common than recession (Chapter 4). Similarly with the falling wave, except that here recession is more common than recovery.

FIGURE P2   The Kondratieff Wave, as manifest in the economic history of the United States. An idealized K-wave is superimposed over actual US wholesale prices since the 1780s (*The Media General Financial Weekly*, August 1972; reprinted in *The Bank Credit Analyst*, October 1974). The pattern of the K-wave is as follows: a 20- to 30-year period of rising prosperity and prices ending in a major war (1843-64, for example); a period of about 10 years consisting of a brief 'primary recession', a short recovery, and a slowly declining 'plateau'; and finally a long decline in prosperity and prices ending in another war (the Spanish-American War of 1898, for instance, continuing to 1906 in the Philippines). The 'peak' wars, bigger and more violent than the 'trough' wars, are the result of a boom with no further place to go. The trough wars, smaller and cheaper, help the system to recover from the long decline. The three longest and worst depressions in the US all came 8 to 10 years after the peak, in 1825-29, 1874-79, and 1929-33, each followed by a further period of deflation. In US economic history the *peak wars* are the Revolutionary and Napoleonic Wars (including the war of 1812-14) (1789-1815); the Civil War (1861-65); World War One (1914-18); and the escalated Vietnam War (1965-74). The *trough wars* are the Mexican War (1846); the Spanish-American and Philippine Wars (1898-1906); and World War Two (1941-45) – the latter coming rather earlier than the pattern strictly suggests.

THE KONDRATIEFF WAVE

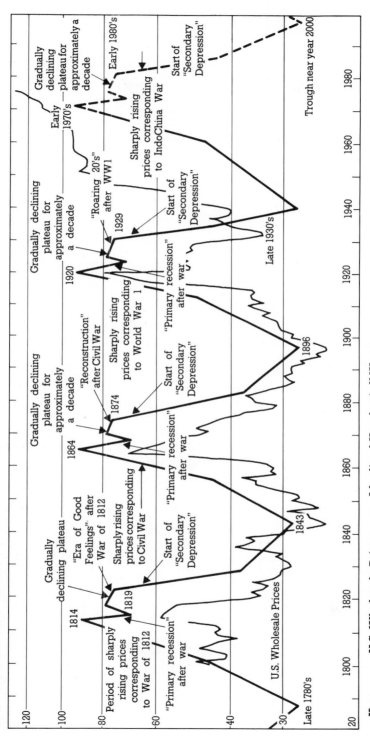

Key —— U.S. Wholesale Prices ▬▬ Idealized Kondratieff Wave

Except for the special role of war, it appears that the predominantly economic factors responsible for the K-wave are not fundamentally different from those involved in the short-term business cycle (Chapter 4).

Writing in the *Bank Credit Analyst* for October 1974, Donald Storey and Anthony Boeckh assert that the reason we have heard so little about the Kondratieff Wave stems from the ascendancy of the economics of Keynes's followers between the 1930s and the 1960s:

> The followers of Keynes considered only the short-term business or trade cycle and devoted their time and study to finding ways of eliminating this cycle in order to eliminate cyclical unemployment.

For Keynesians to acknowledge the existence of long waves in the business cycle is in complete contradiction with their theory and practice, say Storey and Boeckh,

> since it implies that government short-run stabilization is successful only at the expense of long-run destabilization since the postponement of short-term cyclical corrections should be expected to magnify the amplitude of the long-term cycles through the cumulation of uncorrected distortions.

Or in other words, economic policies that are adaptive in the short term may have counter-adaptive effects over the long term (Chapter 4).

(Manipulated almost beyond recognition, the K-wave resurfaced in the weekly newsmagazine *US News and World Report* in 1984 (August 20) and in the *Wall Street Journal* in 1986 (December 1). (It had first appeared in the *Wall Street Journal*, in the version given here, in 1974.) *US News* retains some aspects of the general shape of the wave; but set the fourth wave trough in 1983; predicted a fifth wave boom beginning in 1985; and omitted all reference to war. The *Journal* further reduced the wave to what looks like a slightly irregular sine wave; placed the fourth wave trough in the year 2000; and also omitted any reference to the arms trade or to war.)

According to Kondratieff's article of 1926, the long waves display the following general characteristics:

1 The long waves, whether rising or falling, include the ups and downs of the short-term business cycle.
2 The long waves, whether rising or falling, include the irregularities resulting from uneven performances by different economic units, industries, or regions.
3 During the period of rising prosperity, prosperous years are more

numerous, whereas years of recession or depression predominate during the period of decline.

4 During the period of decline, an especially large number of important discoveries and inventions in the technique of production and communication are made, but these are usually applied on a large scale only after the beginning of the new period of rising prosperity.

5 Prosperity produces the need for further expansion. It makes necessary and possible the exploitation of new countries, new markets, and new sources of raw materials, thus accelerating the pace of economic development.

6 It is during the period of rising prosperity and economic expansion that, as a rule, the most disastrous and extensive wars and revolutions occur.

7 Wars and revolutions are symptoms of the interplay of the political, social, and (predominantly) economic factors behind the long waves, not their causes. Once they have occurred, however, wars and revolutions exert a potent influence on the pace and direction of the economy and the shape of its future dynamics.

Storey and Boeckh explain the distinction between the two major kinds of war as follows:

Since the trough wars, unlike the peak wars, land on an economy with unused resources, low prices, low debt levels and low interest rates, they can be handled relatively easily and serve to assist in the recovery phase of the long cycle. Peak wars, on the other hand, occur in just the opposite conditions – high prices, high debt levels, high interest rates and a fully employed economy. The peak wars sharply accentuate the distortions arising from the expansion phase and set the stage for the inevitable deflation which follows.

Does the K-wave chart give us reliable information about the future? Perhaps. The future behavior of a goal-seeking, time-dependent, adaptive system like state and private capitalism cannot be predicted with any detail or accuracy. General patterns and trends can be singled out. The K-wave represents a pattern of economic behavior which cannot at present be shown to be true, but which can always be proved by becoming true.

The interest of the K-wave chart, in my view, is that although it was drawn up in 1972, over 15 years ago and before the oil price hike in October 1973, the shape of the curve still fits the general pattern of behavior of the world economy.

The question to be decided of course is whether or not we are in the middle of a fourth K-wave. Is the world economy presently recovering

EArth, this is God!
I waNt all you people
to clear out before
the end of the month.
I have A cLient
who's interested
in the property.

from what may have been the 'primary recession' after the US withdrew from Indochina and about to embark on the long decline of the 'secondary depression', with a cataclysmic war at the end of it, near the turn of the century?

Acknowledgments

If I had to put into a list the names of at least some of the people who have helped me work this out over many years – and I do have to – I would thank Sushil Anand, Nancy Armstrong, Godwin Assogba, Yves Barel, Gregory Bateson, Michel Benamou, Len Berggren, Janet Blanchet, Robert C. Brown, Paul Bouissac, Diana Burfield, Amoy Chan, Victoria Chen, Michael Cherniavsky, Jimmy Cliff, Linda Clarke, Rick Coe, Bill Cooper, Jeff Couser, Larry Crawford, Creedence Clearwater, Dorothy Cruikshank, Gill Davies, Ioan Davies, Nathan Edelman, Tom Edens, Robert Elliott, Anne Fleming, René Girard, Jack Goellner, Lucien Goldmann, Lionel Gossman, Kate Guiton, Patrick Guiton, Takao Hagikawa, Elizabeth Hall, Rhonda Hammer, Michael Harding, Clarke Harmeson, Newton Harrison, John Harvard-Watts, Harry Hickman, Peter Holland, Ray Holland, Peter Hopkins, Hidetaka Ishida, Glyn Jones, Dennis Judd, Maxine Judd, Georges Khal, Kirby, Hermann Koenig, Alistair Lachlan, Ned Larsen, Nigel Lawson, Keith Lowe, Edith E. Lucas, Alan Luke, Carmen Luke, Dean MacCannell, Juliet MacCannell, Jane-Anne Manson, Brian Markham, Glen Markham, Michael Marland, Lucie Menkveld, William Miller, Edgar Morin, Ray Morris, Nikkohouye Panahi Hassan, Joseph Needham, Nyree, Taku Oikawa, Steve Osborne, Pamela Parford, Jean Petitot, Massimo Piatelli-Palmarini, Gary Pitcher, J.-B. Pontalis, Kathleen Porter, The President's Research Grant Committee at Simon Fraser University, G. van Praagh, Terry Quigley, Roy A. Rappaport, Joan Rayfield, Anthony Read, Otis Redding, Klaus Rieckhoff, Klaus Riegel, Philip T. Rogers, David Roberts, Judy Rosenthal, Norbert Ruebsaat, Bob Scholte, Thomas Sebeok, Bob Seeds, Harley Shands, Nina Simone, Marie-Hélène Simonis, Yvan Simonis, Peter Smith, Jim Sturgeon, Mark Thomas, Ron Tippe, Mathilde Vilas, Thanh H. Vuong, An Wang, Julia Warner, Mrs Watson, Chester Wickwire,

Patricia Wilden, Tim Wilson, Kathleen Woodward, Mr Yardley, Sylvia Yip, and many students at the University of California at San Diego and Simon Fraser University. The errors are of course my own. My thanks to Ann Hall for compiling the indexes.

Bibliography

Abbott, Edwin A. 1884 *Flatland: A Romance of Many Dimensions*. Oxford: Blackwell, 1978.

Adams, W.H. Davenport 1889 *Battle Stories from British and European History*. London: Swann Sonnenschein & Co. 4th edition.

Aldington, Richard 1955 *Lawrence of Arabia: A Biographical Inquiry*. Harmondsworth, Middlesex: Penguin, 1969.

Alinsky, Saul 1971 *Rules for Radicals*. New York: Vintage, 1972.

Amin, Samir 1973 *Unequal Development. An Essay on the Social Formations of Peripheral Capitalism*. Tr. by Brian Pearce. New York: Monthly Review, 1976.

Anon, 1916 *Women on War Work*. London and Montreal: Carreras Black Cat Cigarettes. Set of 50 cards in color.

1985 *Clandestine Operations Manual for Central America*. English translation of *Psychological Operations in Guerrilla Warfare*. Cornville, Arizona: Desert Publications.

Aristotle n.d. *Politics* [c. 335 BCE]. Tr. by H. Rackham. Cambridge, Mass.: Harvard University Press; London: William Heinemann, 1968. The Loeb Classical Library.

Associated Press 1982 Mounting oil debts, trade deficits threaten to collapse world economy. *Vancouver Sun*, May 31, 1982.

Attneave, Fred 1971 Multistability in perception. *Scientific American*, 225/6, pp. 62-71.

Axelrod, Robert 1984 *The Evolution of Cooperation*. New York: Basic.

Baker, Mark 1981 *Nam: The Vietnam War in the Words of the Men and Women Who Fought There*. New York: Wm. Murrow.

Barel, Yves 1979 *Le Paradoxe et le système: Essai sur le fantastique sociale*. Grenoble: Presses Universitaires de Grenoble.

Baritz, Leon 1985 *Backfire: A History of How American Culture Led Us into Vietnam and Made Us Fight the Way We Did*. New York: Ballantine.

Barraclough, Geoffrey (ed.) 1982 *The Times Concise Atlas of World History*. London: Times Books; Maplewood, NJ: Hammond, 1985.

Bateson, Gregory 1972 *Steps to an Ecology of Mind: Collected Essays in Anthropology, Psychiatry, Evolution, and Epistemology*. New York: Ballantine.

1979 *Mind and Nature: A Necessary Unity*. New York: Bantam.

Bateson, Gregory, Don D. Jackson, Jay Haley, and John Weakland 1956 Toward a theory of schizophrenia. *Behavioral Science*, 1, pp. 251-64. Reprinted in Bateson 1972, pp. 201-27.

Baunoch, Joseph W., and Betty E. Chmaj n.d. Film stereotypes of American women: An outline of star roles from the thirties to the present. Source not known.

Beckwith, Col. Charlie A., and Donald Knox 1983 *Delta Force: The U.S. Counter-Terrorist Unit and the Iran Hostage Rescue Mission*. New York and London: Harcourt Brace Jovanovich.

Bergman, Arlene Eisen 1975 *Women of Vietnam*. Illustrated by Jane Norling. San Francisco: People's Press [2680 21st Street, San Francisco, Ca., 94110]. With Susan Adelman, Diana Block, Penny Johnson, and Peggy Tucker. Complete revision of the 1974 edition.

Bernard, Claude 1865 *An Introduction to the Study of Experimental Medicine*. Tr. by Henry Copley Greene. New York: Collier, 1961.

Bjerg, Kresten 1980 The hollow men and the public speech-act. Source not known.

Blairne, Hon. James G., Secretary of State, et al. 1892 *Columbus and Columbia. A Pictorial History of the Man and the Nation*. Richmond, Va.: B.F. Johnson & Co.

Brand, Stewart 1974 *II Cybernetic Frontiers*. Conversations with Gregory Bateson. New York: Random House.

Brenner, Harvey 1980 *The Reckoning*. The World in Action. London: Granada International Television, 30 minutes.

Browne, Douglas G. 1940 *Private Thomas Atkins 1840-1940*. London: Hutchinson.

Browne, Sir Thomas 1967 *The Prose of Sir Thomas Browne*. Ed. by Norman J. Endicott. New York: Norton, 1972.

Brownmiller, Susan 1975 *Against Our Will: Men, Women and Rape*. New York: Simon & Schuster. Bantam edition 1976.

Bunker, Stephen G. 1985 *Underdeveloping the Amazon. Extraction, Unequal Exchange, and the Failure of the Modern State*. Chicago: University of Illinois Press.

Burke, Kenneth 1941 *The Philosophy of Literary Form: Studies in Symbolic Action*. New York: Vintage. Revised edition 1957, abridged by the author.

Burns, Arthur F. 1968 Business cycles. *International Encyclopedia of the Social Sciences*. Ed. by David Sills. New York: Macmillan; London: Collier-Macmillan, vol. 2, pp. 323-54.

Campbell, Jeremy 1982 *Grammatical Man: Information, Entropy, Language and Life*. New York: Simon & Schuster.

Carson, Rachel 1962 *Silent Spring*. Introduction by Paul R. Ehrlich. Greenwich, Conn.: Fawcett, 1970.

Camus, Albert 1942 *Le Mythe de Sisyphe: Essai sur l'absurde*. Paris: Gallimard.

Césaire, Aimé 1955 *Discourse on Colonialism*. Tr. by Joan Pinkham. New York: Monthly Review Press, 1972.

Chagnon, Napoleon A. 1968 *Yanomamö The Fierce People*. New York: Holt, Rinehart & Winston.

Chambers, R., editor 1869 *The Book of Days: A Miscellany of Popular Antiquities*. London and Edinburgh: W. & R. Chambers. Two vols.

Chambers, Robert 1869 *History of the Rebellion of 1745-6*. Edinburgh and London: W. & R. Chambers 7th edition.

Chandler, David G. 1974 *The Art of Warfare on Land*. London and New York: Hamlyn.

1980 *Atlas of Military Strategy*. New York: Macmillan.

Chesler, Phyllis 1974 *Women and Madness*. New York: Avon.

Chevalier, Jean, and Alain Gheerbrant, eds 1969 *Dictionnaire des symboles: Mythes, rêves, coutûmes, gestes, formes, figures, couleurs, nombres*. Paris: Seghers, 1973. Four vols.

Chou, Hung-hsiang 1979 Chinese oracle bones. *Scientific American*, 240/4, pp. 134-49.

Church, R.A. 1975 *The Great Victorian Boom 1850-1873*. London: Macmillan.

Cirlot, J.E. 1962 *A Dictionary of Symbols*. Foreword by Herbert Read. Tr. by Jack Sage. London: Routledge & Kegan Paul; New York: Philosophical Library.

Clarke, Donald, 1978 *The How It Works Encyclopedia of Great Inventors & Discoveries*. London: Marshall Cavendish, 1982.

Clausewitz, Carl von 1832a *Vom Kriege: Auswahl*. Ed. by Ulrich Marwedel. Stuttgart: Philip Reclam Jun., 1981.

1832b *On War*. Trans. by O.J. Matthijs Jolles. New York: The Modern Library, 1943.

Coe, Richard M., and Anthony Wilden 1978 Errore. *Enciclopedia Einaudi*. Torino: Einaudi Editore, vol. 5, pp. 682-711.

Cohen, John 1966 *Africa Addio*. New York: Ballantine.

Commoner, Barry 1971 *The Closing Circle: Nature, Man, and Technology*. New York: Bantam, 1973.

Cooper, Charles F. 1961 The ecology of fire. *Scientific American*, 204/4, pp. 150-60.

Cronen, Vernon E., Kenneth M. Johnson, and John W. Lannaman 1982 Paradoxes, double binds, and reflexive loops, *Family Process*, vol. 21, pp. 91-112.

Daly, Mary 1978 *Gyn/Ecology: The Metaethics of Radical Feminism*. Boston: Beacon; London: The Women's Press, 1981.

Dean, Loral 1984 Getting away with murder: The victims are children; the murderers are their parents or guardians. *Quest* (March).

de la Haye, Yves, editor 1979 *Marx and Engels on the Means of Communication: The movement of commodities, people, information and capital.* New York: International General.

Delgaty, Kie 1984 Beating domestic violence. *Quest* (May).

de Lorris, Guillaume, and Jean de Meung 1962 *The Romance of the Rose.* Tr. into verse by Harry W. Robbins, Ed. by Charles W. Dunn. New York: Dutton. [De Lorris began the poem about 1237, leaving it incomplete at line 4058. Beginning in about 1277, de Meung ended the poem at line 21,780.]

de Pisan, Christine 1405 *The Book of the City of Ladies.* Tr. by Earl Jeffrey Richards. New York: Persea Books, 1982.

Deregowski, J.B. 1984 *Distortion in Art: The Eye and the Mind.* London and Boston: Routledge & Kegan Paul.

Deutsch, Karl W. 1953 *Nationalism and Social Communication: An Inquiry into the Foundations of Nationality.* Cambridge, Mass.: MIT Press. 2nd edition, 1966.

Dostoevsky, Fyodor 1960a *Three Short Novels of Dostoevsky: The Double, Notes from Underground, and The Eternal Husband.* Tr. by Constance Garnett. Rev. and ed. by Avrahm Yarmolinsky. Garden City, N.Y.: Anchor.

1960b *Notes from Underground and The Grand Inquisitor.* Ed. and tr. by Ralph E. Matlaw. With extracts from Chernyshevsky, Schedrin, and Dostoevsky's other works. New York: Dutton.

Dowling, Colette 1981 *The Cinderella Complex: Women's Hidden Fear of Independence.* New York: Pocket Books; Glasgow: Fontana 1982.

Dranoff, Linda Silver 1977 *Women in Canadian Life: Law.* Toronto: Fitzhenry & Whiteside.

Dunnigan, James F. 1982 *How To Make War. A Comprehensive Guide to Modern Warfare.* New York: William Morrow.

Dupuy, Col. T.N. 1980 *The Evolution of Weapons and Warfare.* Indianapolis and New York: Bobbs-Merrill.

Dyer, Gwynne 1985 *War.* New York: Stoddart. From Dyer's National Film Board Television Series.

Eckhart, Meister 1941 *Meister Echkart.* Tr. by Raymond Bernard Blakney. New York: Harper Torchbooks, n.d.

Edwards, Richard C., Michael Reich, and Thomas E. Weisskopf, editors 1978 *The Capitalist System: A Radical Analysis of American Society.* Englewood Cliffs, N.J.: Prentice-Hall. 2nd edition.

Ehrenreich, Barbara, and Deirdre English 1973a *Witches, Midwives, and Nurses: A History of Women Healers.* Old Westerbury, N.Y.: The Feminist Press.

1973b *Complaints and Disorders: The Sexual Politics of Sickness.* Old Westerbury, N.Y.: The Feminist Press.

1978 *For Her Own Good: 150 Years of the Experts' Advice to Women.* New York: Anchor.

Einsenstein, Sergei 1947 *The Film Sense*. Ed. and tr. by Jay Leyda. New York: Harvest Books.

1949 *Film Form*. Ed. and tr. by Jay Leyda. New York: Harvest Books.

Engels, Frederick 1872-82 *Dialectics of Nature*. Tr. and ed. by Clemens Dutt. Preface and notes by J.B.S. Haldane. New York: International Publishers, 1940. Reprinted 1963. [*Marx Engels Werke*. Berlin: Dietz Verlag, 1972, vol. 20, pp. 305-568.]

Escher, Maurits C. 1960 *The Graphic Work of M.C. Escher*. Tr. from the Dutch by John E. Brigham. New York: Hawthorne Books, n.d. New and revised edition.

Ettlinger, Harold 1943 *The Axis on the Air*. Indianapolis and New York: Bobbs-Merrill.

Fanon, Frantz 1952 *Black Skin, White Masks: The Experiences of a Black Man in a White World*. Tr. by C.L. Markmann. New York: Grove Press, 1967.

1963 *The Wretched of the Earth*. Tr. by Constance Farrington. New York: Grove Press, 1968.

Farrington, Benjamin 1964 *The Philosophy of Francis Bacon*. Chicago: Phoenix.

Fekete, John 1977 *The Critical Twilight: Explorations in the ideology of Anglo-American literary theory from Eliot to McLuhan*. London and Boston: Routledge & Kegan Paul.

Fisher, David, and Anthony Read 1984 *Colonel Z. The Secret Life of a Master of Spies*. New York: Viking 1985.

Fisher, Peter 1972 *The Gay Mystique*. New York: Stein & Day.

Fortune, R.F. 1932 *Sorcerers of Dobu*. New York: Dutton.

Fraser, Antonia 1973 *Cromwell: The Lord Protector*. New York: Knopf.

Fraser, Mrs Hugh 1910 *A Diplomatist's Wife in Many Lands*. New York: Dodd, Mead and Co., 1913. Two vols.

Freedman, Daniel Z., and Peter Van Nieuwenhuizen 1978 Supergravity and the unification of the laws of physics. *Scientific American*, 238/2, pp. 126-43.

Frege, Gottlob 1919 Negation. *Philosophical Writings*, 1952, pp. 117-35.

1952 *Philosophical Writings*. Ed. by Peter Geach and Max Black. Oxford: Blackwell, 1966.

Freire, Paulo 1968 *The Pedagogy of the Oppressed*. Tr. by M.B. Ramos. Sommers, Ct.: Seabury Press, 1971.

Fuller, Major-General J.F.C. 1932 *Armored Warfare*. Military Classics IV. Harrisburg, Pa: Telegraph Press, 1943. First American edition.

1961 *The Conduct of War 1789-1961*. London: Methuen University Paperbacks, 1979.

Gardner, Howard 1983 *Frames of Mind: The Theory of Multiple Intelligences*. New York: Basic Books.

Gardner, Martin 1960 *The Annotated Alice*. New York: Bramhall House.

1968 The world of the Möbius strip: endless, edgeless and one-sided. *Scientific American* (December), pp. 112-15.

1974 The combinatorial basis of the *I Ching*. *Scientific American* (January), pp. 108-113.

1980 Monkey business. *New York Review of Books*, March 20.

1981 *Aha! Gotcha: Paradoxes to Puzzle and Delight*. San Francisco: W.H. Freeman.

George, Susan 1977 *How the Other Half Dies: The Real Reasons for World Hunger*. New York: Universe Books.

Goldstein, Kurt 1939 Methodological approach to the study of schizophrenic thought disorder. Kasanin, ed., 1944, pp. 17-40.

Gossman, Lionel 1964 The comic hero and his idols. *Molière*. Ed. by Jacques Guicharnaud. Englewood Cliffs, N.J.: Prentice-Hall, 1964, pp. 69-78.

Gosz, James R., et al. 1978 The flow of energy in a forest ecosystem. *Scientific American*, 238/3, pp. 92-102.

Gould, Stephen Jay 1981 *The Mismeasure of Man*. New York and London: Norton.

Grant, James n.d. *British Battles on Land and Sea*. London, Paris, and New York: Cassell, Petter, Galpin & Co., c. 1885. Four vols.

Greenburg, Dan 1964 *How to be a Jewish Mother*. Los Angeles: Price, Stern, Sloan, Inc.

Hammer, Rhonda 1981 'The Pattern Which Connects; The Communicational Approach.' Burnaby, B.C.: Simon Fraser University. Unpublished MA thesis.

Hammer, Rhonda, and Anthony Wilden 1981 *METROPOLIS in 30 Minutes*. Burnaby, B.C.: Simon Fraser University/Instructional Media Centre. Videotape montage. Broadcast December 14.

1982 *Women in Production: The Chorus Line 1932-1980*. 55-minute videotape montage. 5th edition.

1984a Report on *The Chorus Line* for 1984. Reprinted in Wilden 1987.

1984b *Busby Berkeley and The Mechanical Bride: From Flying Down to Rio to The Lullaby of Broadway: 1932-1935*. Video montage, 35 minutes.

Hammerton, J.A., editor n.d. *Mr Punch's Cavalcade: A Review of Thirty Years*. London: The Educational Book Co., c. 1934.

Hargrave, John 1940 *Words Win Wars: Propaganda the Mightiest Weapon of All*. London: Wells Gardner, Darton & Co.

Harris, John 1704 *Lexicon Technicum Or An Universal Dictionary of Arts and Sciences*. London. Volume I. New York and London: Johnson Reprint Corporation, 1966. Facsimile edition.

Harris, Marvin 1968 *The Rise of Anthropological Theory: A History of Theories of Culture*. New York: Crowell.

1971 *Culture, Man and Nature*. New York: Crowell.

1974 *Cows, Pigs, Wars and Witches*. New York: Vintage, 1975.

1977 *Cannibals and Kings*. New York: Vintage, 1978.

Hart, Liddell 1935 *Colonel Lawrence: The Man Behind the Legend*. New York: Halcyon House, 1937. New and enlarged version of the 1935 edition.

Haskell, Molly 1973 *From Reverence to Rape: The Treatment of Women in the Movies*. New York: Holt, Rinehart & Winston.

Heilbroner, Robert, and Lester Thurow 1982 *Economics Explained*. Englewood Cliffs, N.J.: Prentice-Hall.

Heller, Joseph 1955 *Catch-22*. New York: Dell, 1965.

Henderson, Harry 1982 'TV and Behavior': A look at the report. *The Press* (December), pp. 16-17.

Henriques, Robert 1957 *One Hundred Hours to Suez: An Account of Israel's Campaign in the Sinai Peninsula*. London: Collins.

Herr, Michael 1968 *Despatches*. New York: Avon, 1978.

Hofstadter, Douglas 1979 *Gödel, Escher, Bach: An Eternal Golden Braid*. New York: Vintage.

Hofstadter, Richard 1947 *Social Darwinism in American Thought*. Boston: Beacon.

Holland, Ray 1977 *Self and Social Context*. London: Macmillan.

Hollander, Nicole 1981 *'That Woman Must Be On Drugs': A Collection of Sylvia*. New York: St Martin's.

Hood, Edwin Paxton 1852 *Cromwell: His Times and Contemporaries*. London: Partridge & Oakey.

Horowitz, David, editor 1968 *Marx and Modern Economics*, New York: Monthly Review Press.

Hughes, Patrick 1983 *More on Oxymoron: Foolish Wisdom in Words and Pictures*. Harmondsworth, Middlesex: Penguin.

Hughes, Patrick, and George Brecht 1975 *Vicious Circles and Infinity*. New York: Doubleday; Harmondsworth, Middlesex: Penguin, 1978.

Huizinga Johan 1921 The political and military significance of chivalric ideas in the late middle ages. In: Huizinga: *Men and Ideas*. Tr. by James S. Holmes and Hans van Marle. New York: Meridian Books, 1959, pp. 196-206.

Hutchinson, Lucy 1846 *Memoirs of the Life of Colonel Hutchinson*. London: Henry G. Bohn. 5th edition.

Idris-Soven, Ahmed, Elizabeth Idris-Soven, and Mary K. Vaughan, eds 1978 *The World as a Company Town: Multinational Corporations and Social Change*. The Hague: Mouton; Chicago: Aldine.

Jacobsen, Thorkild, and Robert M. Adams 1958 Sand and silt in ancient Mesopotamian agriculture. *Science*, 128, pp. 1251-8.

Jakobson, Roman 1956 Two aspects of language and two types of aphasic disturbances. In Jakobson and Halle, 1966, pp. 67-96.

Jakobson, Roman, and Morris Halle 1966 *Fundamentals of Language*. The Hague: Mouton, 1971. Revision of 1956 edition.

James, C.L.R. 1938 *The Black Jacobins. Toussaint L'Ouverture and the San Domingo Revolution*. London: Allison & Busby, 1980. New edition, revised, with a new introduction.

Jameson, Anna 1894 Zenobia, Queen of Palmyra. *Great Men and Famous Women*. Ed. by Charles F. Horne. New York: Selmar Hess. Vol. 5, *Workmen and Heroes*, pp. 26-30.

Jantsch, Erich 1980 *The Self-Organizing Universe*. Oxford and New York: Pergamon Press.

Jomini Antoine Henri *Précis de l'art de la guerre* Paris: Champ Libre, 1977.

Jones, William 1880 *Credulities Past and Present*. London: Chatto & Windus.

Jordan, Z.A. 1967 *The Evolution of Dialectical Materialism: A Philosophical and Sociological Analysis*. London: Macmillan; New York: St Martin's.

Kafka, Franz 1919 In the penal colony. *Franz Kafka: The Complete Stories*. Ed. by Nahum N. Glatzer. New York: Schocken Books, 1976, pp. 140-67.

Kahl, Joachim 1968 *The Misery of Christianity*. Tr. by N.D. Smith. Harmondsworth, Middlesex: Penguin, 1971.

Kaplan, E. Ann, editor 1978 *Women in Film Noir*. London: British Film Institute, 1980.

Kasanin, J.S., 1944 *Language and Thought in Schizophrenia*. New York: Norton, 1964.

Keay, Carolyn 1975 *American Posters of the Turn of the Century*. London: Academy Editions; New York: St Martin's.

Keynes, John Maynard 1936 *The General Theory of Employment Interest and Money*. London, Melbourne, and Toronto: Macmillan, 1967.

Kidron, Michael, and Ronald Segal 1981 *The State of the World Atlas*. London and Sydney: Pan.

Kliban, B. 1971 *Tiny Footprints*. New York: Workman Publishing.

Koestler, Arthur 1971 *The Case of the Midwife Toad*. London: Pan, 1975.

Kondratieff, Nicolai 1926 The long waves in economic life. Tr. in *The Review of Economic Statistics*, 1935 (November).

Kracauer, Siegfried 1927 The mass ornament. Tr. by Barbara Correll and Jack Zipes. *New German Critique*, no. 5, Spring 1975, pp. 67-76.

Kramer, Heinrich, and James Sprenger 1486 *Malleus Maleficarum: The Hammer of the Witches*. Tr. with introduction, bibliography, and notes by the Rev. Montague Summers (1928). New York: Dover Books, 1971. With a new introduction (1948).

Kreuger, Miles, 1975 *The Movie Musical: From Vitaphone to 42nd Street*. As reported in *Photoplay*. London and New York: Hamlyn.

Lacan, Jacques, and Anthony Wilden 1968 *Speech and Language in Psychoanalysis*. Baltimore: Johns Hopkins Paperbacks, 1981. Original title: *The Language of the Self*.

Laing, R.D. 1960 *The Divided Self*. Harmondsworth, Middlesex: Penguin.

1970 *Knots*. London: Tavistock; New York: Vintage.

1971 *Politics of the Family and Other Essays*. London: Tavistock.

Lakoff, George, and Mark Johnson 1980 *Metaphors We Live By*. Chicago and London: University of Chicago Pbks.

Laqueur, Walter, ed. 1977 *The Guerrilla Reader: A Historical Anthology*. Philadelphia: Temple University Press.

Lawrence, Hal 1979 *A Bloody War*. Scarborough, Ont.: Signet.

Lawrence, T.E. 1929 The lessons of Arabia. In Laqueur, ed., 1977, pp. 126-38. Reprinted from the *Encyclopaedia Britannica*, 14th edition.

1935 *The Seven Pillars of Wisdom: A Triumph*. London: World Books, 1939. Two vols.

Leakey, Richard 1981 *The Making of Mankind*. London: Book Club Associates.

Lee, Richard B., Irven DeVore, and Jill Nash, eds 1968 *Man The Hunter*. Chicago: Aldine.

Lenin, V.I. 1961 *Collected Works: Philosophical Notebooks*. Moscow: Progress Publishers, vol. 38.

Leulliette, Pierre 1961 *St. Michael and the Dragon: Memoirs of a Paratrooper*. Foreword by Max Lerner. Tr. by John Edmonds. Boston: Houghton Mifflin; Cambridge: Riverside Press, 1964.

Lewontin, R.C., Steven Rose, and Leon J. Kamin 1984 *Not in our Genes, Biology, Ideology, and Human Nature*. New York: Pantheon.

Logan, Ian, and Henry Nield 1977 *Classy Chassy: American Aircraft 'Girl Art' 1942-1953: A book of paintings the art historians have missed*. London: Mathews, Miller & Dunbar; New York: A & W Visual Library.

Lopez, Barry 1976 Wolves. *Vancouver Sun*, November 12.

Lopez, Laura 1984 Torture: A worldwide epidemic. *Time*, April 16, p. 41.

McNeill, William H. 1982 *The Pursuit of Power: Technology, Armed Force, and Society since A.D. 1000*. Chicago: University of Chicago Press.

McWhiney, Grady, and Perry D. Jamieson 1982 *Attack and Die: Civil War Military Tactics and the Southern Heritage*. University, Ala.: University of Alabama Press.

Malinowski, Bronislaw 1922 *Argonauts of the Western Pacific*. New York: Dutton.

Mallin, Jay, and Robert K. Brown 1979 *Merc: American Soldiers of Fortune*. New York and London: Macmillan/Collier Macmillan.

Mandel, Ernest 1962 *Marxist Economic Theory*. Tr. by Brian Pearce. London: Merlin, 1971.

Mao Tse-Tung 1937 On Contradiction. *Four Essays on Philosophy*. Peking: Foreign Languages Press, 1966, pp. 23-78. Revised 1952.

Margalef, Ramon 1968 *Perspectives in Ecological Theory*. Chicago: University of Chicago Press.

Margulis, Lynn 1971 Symbiosis and evolution. *Scientific American*, 225/2. pp. 48-57.

1982 Symbiosis and the evolution of the cell. *Encyclopaedia Britannica 1982 Yearbook of Science and the Future*, 1981, pp. 104-21.

Margulis, Lynn, and Karlene V. Schwartz 1982 *Five Kingdoms: An Illustrated Guide to the Phyla of Life on Earth*. San Francisco: W.H. Freeman.

Marney, Milton C., and Nicholas M. Smith 1964 The domain of adaptive systems: A rudimentary taxonomy. *General Systems Yearbook*, vol. 9, pp. 107-33.

Marx, Karl 1849 *Wage Labor and Capital*. Ed. by F. Engels (1891). *Marx-Engels Selected Works*, 1968, pp. 64-94.

1857-8 *Grundrisse: Foundations of the Critique of Political Economy (Rough*

Draft). Tr. with a foreword by Martin Nicolaus. Notes by Ben Fowkes. London: Allen Lane/New Left Review, 1973. [*Grundrisse*. Frankfurt: Europäische Verlagsanstalt; Wien: Europa Verlag, 1939.]

1861-3 *Theories of Surplus Value*. London: Lawrence & Wishart, 1963-72. Three parts.

1867 *Capital I: A Critical Analysis of Capitalist Production*. London: Lawrence and Wishart, 1961.

Marx, Karl, and Frederick Engels 1968 *Selected Works*. New York: New World Pbks.

Mason, Robert 1983 *Chickenhawk*. New York: Viking.

Maspero, Henri 1971 *Le Taoïsme et les religions chinoises*. Paris: Gallimard.

Maynard, Rona 1983 Let's Stop Blaming Mum *Homemaker's Magazine*, vol. 18, May 1983, pp. 8-26.

Mayr, Otto 1969 *The Origins of Feedback Control*. Cambridge Mass.: MIT Press, 1970.

Memmi, Albert 1957 *The Colonized and the Colonizer*. Tr. by Howard Greenfeld. Boston: Beacon, 1969.

Merchant, Carolyn 1980 *The Death of Nature: Women, Ecology and the Scientific Revolution*. San Francisco: Harper & Row.

Miller, Kelly 1919 *The World War for Human Rights . . . and the Important Part Taken by the Negro*. Washington, D.C.: Austin Jenkins.

Milne, A.A. 1928 *The House at Pooh Corner*. Decorations by Ernest H. Shepard. New York: Dutton.

Montross, L. Tactics, *Encyclopedia Britannica*, 15th edition, vol. 19, pp. 572-83.

Moore, Omar Khayyam 1965 Divination – A new perspective. Vayda, ed., 1969, pp. 121-9.

Moore, Jr., Barrington 1966 *Social Origins of Dictatorship and Democracy*. Boston: Beacon Paperbacks; Harmondsworth, Middlesex: Penguin.

Morin, Edgar, and Anthony Wilden 1972 Rumor in Orléans. *Psychology Today* (October).

Myers, Henry F. 1986 The growth in services may moderate cycles. *Wall Street Journal*, September 22.

Needham, Joseph 1956 *Science and Civilisation in China*. Cambridge: Cambridge University Press. Vol. 2: *History of Scientific Thought*.

1965 *Science and Civilisation in China*. Cambridge: Cambridge University Press. Vol. 4, part 2: *Mechanical Engineering*.

Nelson, Joyce 1983 As the brain tunes out, the TV admen tune in. *Common Ground*, Winter 1983-84, issue 5, pp. 38-9. Originally in the *Toronto Globe & Mail*, April 16, 1983.

The New Internationalist 1984 *Economics in seven days: A short-cut through the books*. By Peter Stalker. Oxford: New Internationalist Publications, no. 134 (April).

Newnes, Geo., 1894 Muzzles for ladies. *The Strand Magazine: An Illustrated Monthly*, vol. 8 (July-December), pp. 485-9.

Nonini, Donald M. 1985 Varieties of materialism. *Dialectical Anthropology*. 9/1-4, pp. 7-63. [Critique of Marvin Harris's 'cultural materialism'.]

Nova 1980 *The Pinks and the Blues* (WGBH Boston). Public Broadcasting System: 60-minutes.

Odum, Eugene P. 1974 Ecosystem. *Encyclopaedia Britannica*. 15th edition, vol. 6, pp. 281-5.

Ogden, C.K. 1932 *Opposition*. With a new introduction by I.A. Richards. Bloomington, Ind.: Indiana University Press, 1967.

Orgill, Douglas 1973 *Lawrence*. New York: Ballantine's Illustrated History of the Violent Century.

Pagels, Elaine 1979 *The Gnostic Gospels*. New York: Vintage, 1980.

Pattee, H.H., editor 1973 *Hierarchy Theory: The Challenge of Complex Systems*. New York: Braziller [Includes important articles by Clifford Grobstein and Herbert A. Simon.]

Paulos, John Allen 1980 *Mathematics and Humor*. Chicago and London: University of Chicago Press, 1980.

Pearl, David, Lorraine Bouthilet, and Joyce Lazar, eds 1982 *Television and Behavior: Ten Years of Scientific Progress and Implications for the Eighties*. Rockville, Md.: National Institute of Mental Health. Two vols.

Perrett, Bryan 1983 *Lightning War: A History of Blitzkrieg*. Foreword by General Sir John Hackett. London: Panther, 1985.

Phinney, Richard 1987 South Pacific a third world minus tyranny. *Toronto Globe and Mail*, January 1.

Polyani, Karl 1944 *The Great Transformation*. New York and Toronto: Farrar & Rhinehart.

Prigogine, Ilya 1980 *From Being to Becoming: Time and Complexity in the Physical Sciences*. San Francisco: W.H. Freeman.

Prigogine, Ilya, and Isabelle Stengers 1979 *La Nouvelle alliance: Métamorphose de la science*. Paris: Gallimard.

Rappaport, Roy A. 1969 *Pigs for the Ancestors*. New Haven, Conn.: Yale Paperbacks.

1971a The flow of energy in an agricultural society. *Scientific American*, 225/3, pp. 116-32. Also in *Energy and Power*. San Francisco: W.H. Freeman, 1971.

1971b Nature, culture, and ecological anthropology. *Man, Culture and Society*. Ed. by Harry L. Shapiro. Oxford: Oxford University Press. Only in the 2nd edition.

1971c Ritual, sanctity, and cybernetics. *American Anthropologist*, 73/1, pp. 59-76.

Reichardt, Jasia 1978 *Robots: Fact, Fiction and Prediction*. London: Thames and Hudson.

Richards, Paul W. 1973 The tropical rainforest. *Scientific American*, 229/6, pp. 58-67.

Rifkin, Jeremy, with Ted Howard 1980 *Entropy: A New World View*. Afterword by Nicholas Georgescu-Roegen. New York: Bantam, 1981.

Robinson, Joan 1948 Marx and Keynes. Horowitz, ed., 1968, pp. 103-16.

Rosten, Leo 1968 *The Joys of Yiddish.* New York: Pocket Books.

Russell, Mary 1983 Where credit is due: Banking guarantees for women. *New Internationalist* (November), p. 5.

Sahlins, Marshall 1972 *Stone Age Economics.* Chicago: Aldine.

Sartre, Jean-Paul 1946 *Anti-Semite and Jew (Réflexions sur la question juive).* Tr. by George J. Becker. New York: Schocken Books, 1948, 1968.

Schatzman, Morton 1971 Paranoia or Persecution: The Case of Schreber. *Family Process,* vol. 10, pp. 177-212.

1973 *Soul Murder: Persecution in the Family.* New York: Signet.

Scientific American 1970 *The Biosphere.* San Francisco: W.H. Freeman.

1971 *Energy and Power.* San Francisco: W.H. Freeman.

1972 *Communication.* San Francisco: W.H. Freeman.

Seligmann, Jean, Janet Huck, et al. 1984 The date who rapes. *Newsweek,* April 9, pp. 91-2.

Selsam, Howard, and Harry Martel, eds. 1963 *Reader in Marxist Philosophy* New York: International Publishers, 1968.

Shapiro, Evelyn, and Barry Shapiro, eds 1973 *PsychoSources: A Psychology Resource Catalog.* New York and Toronto: Bantam.

1979 *The Women Say/The Men Say: Women's Liberation and Men's Consciousness: Issues in Politics, Work, Family, Sexuality, and Power.* New York: Delta.

Shepard, Paul, and Daniel McKinley, eds 1969 *The Subversive Science: Essays toward an Ecology of Man.* Boston: Houghton Mifflin.

Sladek, John 1975 Machine Screw. *Men Only* (October).

Sluzki, Carlos E., and Donald C. Ransom, eds 1976 *Double Bind: The Foundation of the Communicational Approach to the Family.* New York: Grune & Stratton.

Smith, Alfred G., ed. 1966 *Communication and Culture: Readings in the Codes of Human Interaction.* New York, Toronto, and London: Holt, Rinehart & Winston.

Springer, Sally P., and Georg Deutsch 1985 *Left Brain, Right Brain.* San Francisco: W.H. Freeman.

Stanley II, USAF, Col. Roy M. 1982 *Prelude to Pearl Harbor: War in China, 1937-41, Japan's Rehearsal for World War II.* New York: Charles Scribner's Sons.

Stockman, David A. 1986 *The Triumph of Politics: Why the Reagan Revolution Failed.* New York: Harper & Row.

Stone, Lawrence 1977 *The Family, Sex and Marriage in England 1500-1800.* New York and London: Harper & Row.

Storey, Donald R., and J. Anthony Boeckh 1974 Kondratieff and the supercycle: Deflation or runaway inflation? *The Bank Credit Analyst* (October), pp. 12-38.

Summers, Anne 1975 *Damned Whores and God's Police: The Colonization of Women in Australia.* Harmondsworth, Middlesex: Penguin, 1980.

Sun Tzu 1963 *The Art of War* [c. 400-320 BCE]. Tr. and annotated with an introduction by Brigadier General (ret.) Samuel B. Griffith, U.S. Marine Corps. Foreword by B.H. Liddell Hart. London and New York: Oxford Paperbacks, 1981. [The most reliable modern translation.]

Sweezy, Paul M. 1942 *The Theory of Capitalist Development*. New York and London: Modern Reader Paperbacks, 1968.

Taber, Robert 1965 *The War of the Flea: Guerrilla Warfare Theory and Practice*. London: Paladin, 1970. Updated 1969.

Taylor, A.J.P., and J.M. Roberts, 1973 *20th Century*. Milwaukee, Toronto, Melbourne, and London: Purnell Reference Books. Revised edition, 1979. 20 vols.

Teuber, Marianne L. 1974 Sources of ambiguity in the prints of Maurits C. Escher. *Scientific American*, 231/1, pp. 99-104.

Thomas, Lewis 1974 *Lives of a Cell*. New York: Bantam, 1980.

Thomas, Lowell 1924 *With Lawrence in Arabia*. New York and London: The Century Co.

Thomson, George 1941 *Aeschylus and Athens: A Study in the Social Origins of Drama*: London: Lawrence & Wishart, 1966.

Time Magazine 1983 Private violence: Child abuse, wife beating, rape. September 5, pp. 14-22.

Troubetzkoy, N.S. 1939 *Principes de phonologie*. Tr. by J. Cantineau. Paris: Klincksieck, 1970.

Tustin, Arnold 1952 Feedback. *Scientific American*, 187, pp. 48-55.

Van Wagenen Keil, Sally 1979 *Those Wonderful Women in their Flying Machines: The Unknown Heroines of World War II*. New York: Rawson, Wade.

Vayda, Andrew P., 1969 *Environment and Cultural Behavior: Ecological Studies in Cultural Anthropology*. Garden City, N.Y.: The Natural History Press.

Vincent, Benjamin, editor 1889 *Haydn's Dictionary of Dates and Universal Information*, London, New York and Melbourne; Ward, Lock, 19th edition.

Von Foerster, Heinz 1980 Epistemology of communication. In Woodward, ed., 1980, pp. 18-27.

War Office, General Staff 1912 *Field Service Regulations Part I. Operations 1909. Reprinted, with Amendments, 1912*. London: HMSO.

Warshaw, Tessa Albert 1980 *Winning by Negotiation*. New York: Berkley Books, 1981.

Warusfel, André 1969 *Les Mathématiques modernes*. Paris: Le Seuil.

Watzlawick, Paul, Janet Beavin, and Don D. Jackson 1966 *The Pragmatics of Human Communication: A Study of Interactional Patterns, Pathologies, and Paradoxes*. New York: Norton.

Weber, Henry, editor 1812 *Popular Romances: Consisting of Imaginary Voyages and Travels*. Edinburgh and London.

Weiner, Annette B. 1976 *Women of Value, Men of Renown: New*

Perspectives in Trobriand Exchange. Austin: University of Texas Press.

Welchman, Gordon 1982 *The Hut Six Story: Breaking the Enigma Codes.* New York: McGraw-Hill.

Wells, H.G. 1933 *The Shape of Things to Come.* New York: Macmillan.

Whymant, Robert 1983 Prolonged sighs of inner longing: The Japanese obsession with comic books. *Manchester Guardian Weekly*, September 4.

Wiener, Norbert 1948 *Cybernetics: Or Control and Communication in the Animal and the Machine.* Cambridge, Mass.: MIT Press, 1961. Second edition.

1950 *The Human Use of Human Beings: Cybernetics and Society.* Garden City, N.Y.: Anchor, 1954.

Wilden, Anthony 1953 Flea market. *The Outlook*, no. 14, p. 25.

1965 An editorial. *The Stag* (Summer).

1966a Jacques Lacan: A partial bibliography. *Yale French Studies*, vol. 36-7, pp. 263-8. Also in: *Structuralism.* Ed. by Jacques Ehrmann. New York: Anchor, 1970, pp. 253-60.

1966b Freud, Signorelli, and Lacan: The repression of the signifier. *American Imago*, vol. 23, pp. 332-66.

1968 *Par divers moyens on arrive à pareille fin*: A reading of Montaigne. *Modern Language Notes*, vol. 83, pp. 577-97.

1969a Death, desire, and repetition in Svevo's *Coscienza di Zeno. Modern Language Notes*, vol. 84, pp. 98-119.

1969b Marcuse and the Freudian model: Energy, information, and *Phantasie. Salmagundi*, vol. 10-11, pp. 196-245. Also in: *The Legacy of the German Refugee Intellectuals.* Ed. by Robert Boyers. New York: Schocken, 1972.

1970 Montaigne's *Essays* in the context of communication. *Modern Language Notes*, vol. 85, pp. 454-78.

1971a Review of O. Mannoni: *Freud. Psychology Today* (August), pp. 8, 12.

1971b Epistemology and the biosocial crisis: The difference that makes a difference. *Coping with Increasing Complexity.* Ed. by D.E. Washburn and D.R. Smith. New York: Gordon & Breach, 1974, pp. 249-70.

1971c Review of Piaget: *Structuralism. Psychology Today* (October), pp. 10, 13.

1972a L'Ecriture et le bruit dans la morphogénèse du système ouvert. *Communications*, vol. 18, pp 48-71. Special Issue: *L'Evénement*, ed. by Edgar Morin.

1972b Libido as language: The structuralism of Jacques Lacan. *Psychology Today*, vol. 5, no. 12 (May), pp. 40-2, 85-9.

1972c Analog and digital communication: On negation, signification, and the emergence of the discrete element. *Semiotica*, vol. 6, no. 1, pp. 50-82.

1972d Structuralism, communication, and evolution. *Semiotica*, vol. 6, no. 3, pp. 244-56.

1972e On Lacan: Psychoanalysis, language, and communication. *Contemporary Psychoanalysis*, vol. 9, no. 4, pp. 445-70.

1972f Review of Leiss: *The Domination of Nature. Psychology Today*

(October), pp. 28, 30, 32.

1972g *System and Structure: Essays in Communication and Exchange.* London: Tavistock. London & New York: Social Science Paperbacks, 1977.

1973a Ecology and ideology. In Idris-Soven and Vaughan, eds, 1978, pp. 73-98.

1973b Review of Bateson: *Steps to an Ecology of Mind. Psychology Today* (November), pp. 138, 140.

1974 Ecosystems and economic systems. *Cultures of the Future.* Ed. by M. Maruyama and Arthur Harkins (Ninth Congress of Anthropological and Ethnological Sciences) (*World Anthropology Series*) The Hague: Mouton; Chicago: Aldine, 1978, pp. 101-24.

1975a Piaget and the structure as law and order. *Structure and Transformation: Developmental Aspects.* Ed. by Kalus F. Riegel and George L. Rosenwald. (*Origins of Behavior Series*) New York: Wiley, pp. 83-117.

1975b The scientific discourse: Knowledge as a commodity. Illustrated in b&w. *MAYDAY*, vol. 1, no. 1, pp. 69-77.

1975c Ecology, ideology, and political economy. Burnaby, B.C.: Simon Fraser University. Unpublished ms., Xeroxed.

1976a Changing frames of order: Cybernetics and the *machina mundi.* In Woodward, ed., 1979, pp. 219-41.

1976b *Communication in Context: A Systems Perspective.* Burnaby, B.C.: Simon Fraser University. Unpublished ms., Xeroxed.

1978 Communicazione. *Enciclopedia Einaudi*, vol. 3, pp. 601-95.

1979a Informazione. *Enciclopedia Einaudi*, vol. 7, pp. 562-628.

1979b Culture and identity: The Canadian question, *Why? Ciné-Tracts,* vol. 2, no. 2, pp. 1-27.

1980a *The Imaginary Canadian.* Vancouver: Pulp Press.

1980b *System and Structure:* Second Edition. London: Tavistock; New York: Methuen. Social Science Paperbacks. With a new introduction and critical notes.

1980c *Greetings from Canada.* Six broadsheets. Printed for the author by Pulp Press, Vancouver.

1981a Semiotics as praxis: Strategy and tactics. *Recherches sémiotiques/-Semiotic Inquiry*, vol. 1, no. 1, pp. 1-34.

1981b Ideology and the icon: Oscillation, contradiction, and paradox An essay in context theory. *Iconicity: The Nature of Culture. Essays in Honor of Thomas Sebeok.* Ed. by Paul Bouissac, Michael Herzfeld, and Roland Posner. Tübingen: Stauffenberg Verlag, 1986, pp. 251-302.

1982a Postscript to 'Semiotics as Praxis: Strategy and Tactics'. *RSSI* vol. 2, no. 2, pp. 166-70.

1982b *I Want Out: A Pictorial Supplement to The 20th Century War: 1880-1982.* Burnaby, B.C.: Simon Fraser University. Xeroxed.

1983a *Système et structure: Essais sur la communication et l'échange.* Tr. by Georges Khal. Montréal: Boréal Express [5450 ch. de la Côte-des-Neiges,

Montréal, Qué., H3T 1Y6]; Paris: Distique [9, rue Edouard-Jacques, 75014, Paris]. Revised edition of Wilden 1980, with two new chapters.

1983b Teaching Media Literacy. *Symposium on Interdisciplinary Aspects of Academic Disciplines*. Bellingham. Wash.: Western Washington University, pp. 335-48.

1983c La Guerre du 20e siècle et Penser la stratégie. Tr. by Yvan Simonis. *Anthropologie et Sociétés: 'Guerres et Stratégies'*, vol. 7, n° 1, pp. 3-38.

1984a Montage analytic and dialectic: The right brain revolution. *American Journal of Semiotics*. 3/1, pp. 25-47.

1984b In the penal colony: The body as the discourse of the Other. *Semiotica*. 54-1/2 (1985), pp. 33-85. Special issue on violence edited by Nancy Armstrong.

1985 Context theory: The new science. *RSSI*, vol. 5, no. 2, pp. 97-116.

1987 *The Rules Are No Game: The Strategy of Communication*. London and New York: Routledge & Kegan Paul/Methuen.

Wilden, Anthony, and Tim Wilson 1976 The double bind: Logic, magic, and economics. *Double Bind: The Foundation of the Communicational Approach to the Family*. Ed. by C.E. Sluzki and D.C. Ransom. New York: Grune & Stratton, pp, 263-86.

Wilder, C., and John H. Weakland 1981 *Rigor and Imagination: Essays from the Legacy of Gregory Bateson*. New York: Praeger Paperbacks, 1982. [Includes 'The charm of the scout' by Stephen Toulmin.]

Wilhelm, Richard, and Cary F. Baynes, trs 1950 *The I Ching or Book of Changes*. Foreword by C.G. Jung. Preface by Hellmut Wilhelm. New York: Bollingen Foundation; Princeton: Princeton University Press, 1980. 3rd edition, 1967.

Winterbotham, Frederick W. 1978 *The Nazi Connection*. New York: Dell.

Wills, Garry 1969 *Nixon Agonistes*. New York: Signet, 1971.

Witte, Karsten 1975 Introduction to Siegfried Kracauer's 'The mass ornament'. Tr. by Barbara Correll and Jack Zipes. *New German Critique*, no. 5, pp. 59-66.

Woodburn, James 1968 An introduction to Hadza ecology. In Lee, DeVore and Nash, eds, 1968, pp. 49-55.

Woodcock, Alexander, and Monte Davis 1978 *Catastrophe Theory*. New York: Dutton; Harmondsworth, Middlesex: Penguin, 1980.

Woodward, Kathleen, ed. 1979 *The Myths of Information: Technology and Postindustrial Culture*. Madison. Wisc.: Coda Press; London: Routledge & Kegan Paul.

Wynne-Edwards, V.C. 1962 *Animal Dispersion in Relation to Social Behavior*. Edinburgh: Oliver & Boyd, 1972.

Yanker, Gary 1972 *Prop Art: 1000 Contemporary Posters*. New York: Darien House.

Zaretsky, Eli 1976 *Capitalism, the Family and Personal Life*. New York: Harper & Row.

Zeeman, E.C. 1976 Catastrophe theory. *Scientific American*, 234/4, pp. 65-83.

Name index

Subject index